[illegible]

From [illegible]

[illegible]

my Friend

& Great Reader

of Books.

[illegible]

PRAISE FOR *THE 1618 PROJECT*

"Steve Vicchio and I grew up as friends in Baltimore's Yale Heights neighborhood, in the same block of row houses, in the '50s and '60s. The values we learned from our parents and neighbors in this urban, blue-collar community served us well over the years, and are reflected in Steve's writings. Today, however, these values are under often violent attack, an attack really on our country's true foundations. If anyone is looking for the correct way forward, *The 1618 Project* is what they need."

Ambassador John Bolton, former national security advisor and US representative to the United Nations, author of *Surrender Is Not an Option* and *The Room Where It Happened*

"Stephen Vicchio has long been a courageous individual, unflinching and unafraid of independent thought, the truth, and rattling a few cages among progressives, especially in the academic asylum. I admire his bold and clever insights and writing. In this book, smartly taking us before 1619, Vicchio once again shows why he's worth reading."

Paul Kengor, PhD, professor of political science at Grove City College in Pennsylvania and editor of *The American Spectator*

The 1618 Project: Essays on the Threat of America's Progressive New Left

For more information, please contact:
Amplify Publishing, an imprint of Amplify Publishing Group
620 Herndon Parkway, Suite 320
Herndon, VA 20170
info@amplifypublishing.com
www.amplifypublishinggroup.com

Library of Congress Control Number: 2023903617

CPSIA Code: PRV0423A

ISBN-13: 978-1-63755-684-9

Printed in the United States

This book is dedicated to my student turned friend and counselor who helped turn me always to the Right—Tina Gioioso.

THE 1619 1618 PROJECT

Essays on the Threat of
America's Progressive New Left

STEPHEN VICCHIO

CONTENTS

INTRODUCTION

Victory has a hundred fathers, while defeat is an orphan.
—John F. Kennedy, April 21, 1961

My son Jack, who has been a dyed-in-the-wool Conservative since early adolescence—he is now twenty-two years old—began a process of converting me from my forty-five-year membership in the Democratic Party. I had a forty-three-year full-time college teaching career that ended in 2016. By the autumn of 2016, in conversations with my son while driving home together from his high school, he gradually turned me into a Conservative.

As a result, I voted for Donald Trump twice. Because of my new political opinions, I began to have a different view of people I had admired for most of my life. Ideas that I believed were central to the republic in which I live were now being called into question, such as freedom and equality, by the Progressive New Left in America.

I now write the introduction to this study of the views of these Progressive New Left advocates on issues in American culture as of early August 2021. As I write, Representative Cori Bush of Missouri, who has advocated for and supported the Defund the Police movement, spent $70,000 in a three-month span on personal security.[1] She appears to want to defund the police for the public but not for herself.

And Ms. Bush is not alone. Between 2015 and 2020, the mayor of San Francisco, London Breed, spent $12 million on security for her and her family. This is now paid for by money that became available when the city cut the funding of its police department in 2020. The mayor of Baltimore, Brandon Scott, slashed his police budget by $22 million but spent $3.6 million of public money on security for himself, the state's attorney, and the police commissioner. Lori Lightfoot, the mayor of Chicago, cut four hundred police officers from her 2020 budget while spending $3.4 million of public money on her own security.[2]

In a recent American poll on citizens' views of how well the Joe Biden-Kamala Harris administration is doing, the following facts were revealed:[3]

1. President Biden now has a 48 percent approval rating.
2. Fifty-five percent of Americans say they are pessimistic about the direction the country is going, with 45 percent being optimistic.
3. Only 40 percent of Americans are in favor of how the Biden-Harris administration is handling gun-violence issues.
4. Similarly, only 40 percent approve of the current administration's handling of the southern border crisis.
5. Thirty-nine percent of Americans approve of the Biden administration's treatment of immigration.
6. Only 45 percent of Americans approve of the Biden administration's treatment of COVID-19.
7. The Biden administration is vocal about becoming vaccinated against COVID-19.

Yet on July 26, 2021, the White House press secretary, Jen Psaki, refused to reveal the statistics of White House staff in terms of the virus numbers. Instead, Ms. Psaki asked, "Why would you want to know those numbers?" The reporter who asked the question then responded this way: "For transparency in relation to the American people."[4]

It did not occur to Ms. Psaki that the rest of us may begin to see her as hypocritical, in much the same way that Cori Bush and

London Breed, and the other mayors, have been hypocritical in their views of "security for me but not for thee."

And it was out of the many examples enumerated here, and many others over the past few years, that this collection of essays was born. The first essay in this study summarizes what I see as the ten most fundamental beliefs of the Progressive New Left in America. Among those are beliefs, as we shall see, that the United States—or at least White people in the US—is "systemically racist," that there is no such thing as *objective truth*, and that equality and freedom are insignificant values in America compared to one's race and gender.

In the second essay, my main focus is on what has come to be known as the Defund the Police movement or the Reimagining the Police movement. In this essay, we will enumerate some of the towns, counties, and cities that have reduced their police budgets since the summer of 2020 and how it has both effected and affected violent crime in those locations.

In the third essay, I will discuss the issue of abortion in the United States and provide a compromise position on that issue between the pro-life and pro-choice advocates in contemporary America. I first developed this compromise view in my book *Ronald Reagan's Religious Beliefs*, published by CrossLink Publishing in 2020.

The origins of COVID-19 and the Biden-Harris administration's responses to that question will be the central concern of Essay Four. As we shall see, there are two competing theories about the origin of the virus—that it came from another species or was created in a laboratory. I will favor the latter theory in my analysis.

The "crisis" at the US southern border and the Biden administration's views about the matter will be the focus of the fifth essay, including Kamala Harris, who was put in charge of the border and refused to visit it for ninety-two days after her appointment by the president to be the "border czar."

The phenomena of gun control and the Second Amendment will be the central concerns of the sixth essay of this study. In that essay, I will discuss what the Second Amendment and the US Supreme Court have said about guns in American culture as well as what the Progressive New Left has said about guns and gun control.

What the Progressive New Left refers to as *hate crime* and *hate speech* will be the focus of Essay Seven. We will begin with how difficult it is to define *hate speech*, followed by what the Progressive New Left has to say about the matter. Then I will supply a philosophical critique of the Left's views on these matters.

The *New York Times*' 1619 Project and its view that the founding of the United States should be changed from 1776 to 1619 will be the focus of Essay Eight. As we shall see, the writers of the project have made at least nine other similar claims about American history, and I will enumerate and then critique each of them.

The central focus of the ninth essay of this study will be on the role that Marxism now plays in American politics—particularly, as we shall see, in the philosophical foundations of critical race theory and the 1619 Project.

The Green New Deal and President Biden's "climate control" plan will be the main subject matter of Essay Ten. Along the way, we will critically evaluate whether climate control is an "existential threat to us as a species" as Vice President Harris has described the issue.[5]

Finally, the focus of Essay Eleven shall be the role that Big Tech and social media now play in American culture. We will also entertain the question of whether Big Tech has, in the last few years, regularly censored content that comes from those with Conservative opinions on a variety of issues. The Big Tech companies say they do not do it, but as we shall see, the American public believes they do censor Republican and Conservative points of view.

In my more than forty-year academic career, I acquired several skills to develop the essays in this study. I have written full-length books about many of the topics of these essays, including books on slavery, Abraham Lincoln, the moral issue of abortion, and moral theory in police work. I have also written many essays and articles about the other topics of these essays, including Marxism, Big Tech, gun control, the Second Amendment, hate speech, and the idea of censorship, among other topics.

Thus, I have written substantial books and articles on nearly all the topics covered in this study. During the course of the book, I will speak specifically about what tools and skills I have acquired in relation to the content of each of the essays. I hope you enjoy reading them as much as I have enjoyed writing them.

One final issue in this introduction is to make some comments on why I chose the name *The 1618 Project* for this collection. The *New York Times*' 1619 Project is so named because their writers began the project by writing about the slave ship called the *White Lion*. This ship brought the first Black people to Virginia in August 1619. Supposedly, these were the first Black people to be in the United States.[6]

I have chosen the year 1618 because there is substantial evidence that Spain and its ships were conducting the slave trade of Africans in Spanish America as early as the year 1500. In addition, many scholars have analyzed the rents obtained by the Spanish Crown from royal grants or "licenses" that authorized individuals or groups of individuals to acquire and transport slaves to Spanish America.[7]

One Spanish voyager, a man named Rodrigo Baco (1499–1565), received a total of 804 licenses in 1561. This places the date of the first Black Africans to arrive in America as far before the year 1619. Other extant records from Spain also suggest that the Spanish were conducting slavery in the Americas as early as the time of Christopher Columbus, around 1500.

I mention this material here in the hope that you are convinced that the name of the *New York Times*' 1619 Project has very little to do with the first Black slaves in the United States. A second reason for believing that the "twenty-odd negroes" were not slaves is that in the 1620s, Virginia records called these Black men "indentured servants" and not "slaves."

I will say more about the status of the "twenty or so Africans" who arrived on the *White Lion* in August of 1619 when we get to Essay Eight in this study. However, it is good now to note that I have employed the 1618 date to indicate that, from roughly 1500 to 1618, Black slavery was already going on in what would become the United States of America.[8]

We are clearly in the midst of a second civil war in the United States. Like the first Civil War, the current civil war is based on ideology. This can be seen, for example, in the first day of testimony of the House hearings on the events of January 6, 2021. This day of testimony and questioning of officers at the Capitol on January 6 included one Hispanic officer, one Black officer, and two White officers, but no women—not a very good display of the Progressive New Left's idea of "inclusion."

The House Committee had a Black chairman but no Black committee members. The summer disturbances of 2020 were labeled by Democrats as being "peaceful protests" or simply "protests." But the Democratic members of the House Committee, as well as the Republicans, called the participants on January 6 "rioters" (Zoe Lofgren, Dem., CA), a "violent mob" (Adam Kinzinger, Rep., IL), and "a mob with weapons" (Peter Aguilar, Dem., CA).[9]

The two Republican members of the committee, Liz Cheney of Wyoming and Adam Kinzinger of Illinois, asked no critical questions of the officers testifying. In fact, rather than doing so, they joined the Democratic Party members in thrashing Mr. Trump and calling the officers *heroes*. The Metropolitan Police officers and US Capitol Police officers who testified on July 27 called the participants on January 6 "insurrectionists," "rioters," and a "violent mob," and one, in a brief moment, even called them "protestors" but was immediately disgruntled for having done so and immediately corrected himself.

The congressional members on the committee called the officers present *heroes* twelve times. They also told these members of law enforcement that they "saved democracy" and "saved the Constitution" another ten times. The officers were asked prepared questions that they knew beforehand, for they came to the hearing with prepared responses, which they read from notes word for word, often stumbling as if they were not the authors of those words.

There was nothing in the January 6 hearing about the young American woman named Ashli Babbitt, who was shot to death by a Capitol police officer, in the discussion of the events surrounding January 6, 2021.

The Democratic members of the committee and Ms. Cheney specifically asked about President Donald Trump's involvement in the January 6 disturbance, but neither of the Republican members asked any critical questions about what was clearly a Progressive New Left hearing.

Throughout this study, we will say more about other manifestations that we are in the midst of this second civil war, particularly in the appendix. In the meantime, it is good to have made a claim up front in these essays.

After a summary of the sources of this introduction, I will turn our attention to some observations about the Progressive New Left Movement in contemporary America and discuss the ten most fundamental philosophical beliefs of that movement. In the rest of this study, I will repeatedly refer back to these fundamental philosophical beliefs and how they relate to the many contemporary issues in this study.

SJV, Baltimore
August 31, 2021

Addendum to the Introduction

As we write this addendum to the Introduction of this study, a Fox News poll distributed on October 2, 2021, reveals that only 33 percent of Americans polled agreed with the assertion that "the United States is going in the right direction." At the same time, a new collection of thirty thousand to fifty thousand migrants is forming in southern Mexico and moving northward. Another thirty thousand immigrants from Haiti entered the southern border, and many have been released into the country.

There is also evidence that the Colombian government is withholding thirty thousand immigrants from moving north. There is evidence that Panama has also kept up to forty thousand migrants from traveling to North America.

Meanwhile, the homicide numbers in the United States for the year 2021 have increased 35 percent over 2020. Inflation is on the rise. Homelessness and unemployment have greatly increased over the last year. The US government has imposed new mandates for COVID-19 testing for any business with one hundred employees or more. And the fine for those who do not comply is $485,000 for the first offense.

The Democratic Congress is seeking to pass more extensive, often New Left legislation that would cost more trillions, without any indication of how these services, mostly of the pork barrel variety, will be paid for.

ESSAY ONE

Introduction to This Study and the Fundamental Beliefs of the New Left in America

I

In the final semester of my forty-three-year college teaching career, I asked my students (one hundred undergraduates and twenty graduate students) to make several judgments about what is important in American life. Among the questions I asked my students were the following:

1. **What is more important: diversity or freedom?**
   Eighty percent answered *diversity.*
2. **Do you view pornography more than five times a month?**
   Fifty-four percent answered *yes.*
3. **Is there such a thing as objective truth?**
   Eighty-two percent answered *no.*
4. **Are all cultures of equal value?**
   Eighty-two percent answered *yes.*
5. **Is race biological or a societal invention?**
   Sixty-seven percent answered *societal invention.*
6. **Is America systemically racist?**
   Eighty-two percent answered *yes.*
7. **How many genders are there?**

Only 15 percent said *two*.

8. **Is climate an "existential threat" to humanity and the planet?**
   Eighty-two percent said *yes*.
9. **Do you think hate speech should be outlawed?**
   Sixty-eight percent said *yes*.
10. **Do you think the Liberal media censor Conservative content?**
    Fifty-seven percent said *yes*.

The anonymous findings of my survey, in one way, were not surprising, for the students I taught for forty-three years changed drastically over that span. From approximately 1990 until when I retired in 2016, I began to see two major changes in my American students. The first is that their bodies of knowledge were considerably less than those of my students from the 1970s and 1980s.

The second change had to do with the writing abilities of my students. Since 1990 and continuing up to 2016, the ability of my students to write in clear, understandable, and straightforward American English prose had greatly deteriorated. I went from a time when my classes in the '70s and '80s contained several poets and skilled writers to a time in the 1990s and beyond when I had none.

My perspective about the abilities of my students is also born out of the Program for International Student Assessment tests for fifteen-year-old students around the world. In 2018, the United States placed eleventh out of seventy-nine nations in science, while in mathematics, it ranked thirtieth out of the seventy-nine countries.[1]

The year 1967 was the first year of the international comparison, when the United States ranked eleventh in mathematics, behind Germany, England, France, and Japan. By the 2018 comparison, the US had dipped to thirtieth of the seventy-nine nations tested. This data also appears to have been confirmed in my personal experiences of American college students.

In another way, however, it is clear to me that the answers given in my survey were connected to a set of ten fundamental philosophical principles that the overall majority of my students by the year 2010 had come to believe. These ten principles can be summarized in the following way:

1. The rejection of absolute or objective truth.
2. All cultures are of equal value.
3. The individual and his or her race, gender, and other characteristics are more important than the collective.
4. Diversity is more important than freedom.
5. Race and gender are not biological but societal constructs.
6. America is a systemically racist nation.
7. Certain races are discussed with much more reverence and attention than others.
8. Individual narratives or storytelling of struggle are often more enlightening than collective expressions.
9. Hate speech and hate crimes in America should be more regulated.
10. America is in the midst of an "existential crisis" regarding the environment and climate control.

These ten basic principles have become the backbone of American education over the last thirty years. One of the ironies of that fact is that I think that none of these ten philosophical claims is actually true. Let us take each of these ten beliefs one at a time to show why I believe that each claim is a bankrupt idea.

The first of our ten ideas can be seen in Barack Obama's 2006 book, *The Audacity of Hope*. In that work, the former president observed that implicit in the Constitution's structure and the very idea of ordered liberty was a rejection of absolute truth.[2]

On April 18, 2021, Mr. Obama's vice president and now president, Joe Biden, in the context of a discussion of the Second Amendment of the US Constitution, remarked in a speech, "No amendment is absolute."[3]

One might ask, of course, whether the claims of Obama and Biden are absolute truths. If the answer is yes, there is no reason to believe them. If the answer is no, then there are no objective truths, and Presidents Obama and Biden speak nonsense.

These claims of Obama and Biden also fly in the face of the religious traditions of the Ten Commandments and the golden rule, not to mention the Sermon on the Mount and the openings of the US Constitution and the Bill of Rights that both hold the view that there are self-evident truths about rights that are endowed by our Creator. And among these rights are several that appear to be absolute truths. This Obama-Biden view about *absolute* or *objective truth* is part of a philosophical movement that has developed in the last fifty years in the West known as relativism. This theory takes two separate forms—individual moral relativism and cultural relativism. The former claims that there are no objective standards for measuring an individual's moral choices.

The individual moral relativist says that "X is morally good if I think, feel, or believe it is good." In this view, any moral judgment is as good as any other moral judgment, even if Charles Manson is the one making that judgment. The bankruptcy of this view becomes clear when using the individual moral relativism theory. If Charles Manson says what he did is morally good, then that makes it morally good. If you and I, however, say that Charles Manson's behavior was not morally good, then using the relativist's theory, we are morally correct as well. Thus, an action or set of actions may be morally good and not morally good at the same time. This is a flawed theory of ethics, indeed.

The other form of relativism is known as cultural relativism. This theory finds its validity in our aforementioned second foundational principle—that all cultures are of equal value. A few years ago, the novelist Saul Bellow was asked what he thought of the literature and cultural diversity of various places on Earth. His response was instructive. He said, "Who is the Tolstoy of the Zulus? The Proust of the Papuans? I'd be glad to read them."[4]

In the outrage that followed Mr. Bellow's remark, he was accused, not surprisingly, of racism, as well as being part of the union of "dead White males." Mr. Bellow had broken the second of the Left's fundamental principles—that one culture is as valuable as another culture—so Mr. Bellow's comment was not to be taken seriously.

Our third fundamental principle listed previously—that the individual is more important than the collective—as well as its vapidness, is exemplified by a recent interview with Hillary Clinton by *Sunday Morning* correspondent Tony Dokoupil, in which she told her interviewer that her husband's affair with Monica Lewinsky was not an abuse of power because both were "consenting adults."[5] In the interview, however, she said nothing about how Ms. Lewinsky's life had been ruined by the encounter with President Clinton, for which, even to date, she has received no apology for Mr. Clinton's abuse of power—even though his wife did not see it that way.

It would appear that Mrs. Clinton had no realization that one of the reasons she lost the 2016 presidential race was because of how she treated her husband's infidelities. Saying that the sexual relationship between the twenty-two-year-old intern and the president of the United States was a moral matter only between two consenting adults is to ignore his marriage vows and her marriage vows as well as the nation's expectations that we deserve a morally good president in the Oval Office.

Was it not a moral matter for the rest of the Clinton family? How about Ms. Lewinsky's family? Or what about the nation as a whole? They had no interests in the matter? Does the consent of any of these people matter? If the answer to any of these questions is yes, then the absurd response from Mrs. Clinton becomes clear.

That most moral matters may be reduced to the rights of two separate individuals is a claim, once again, that flies in the face of the founding documents of this nation. It also seems to be contradicted by the fact that the Clintons, on November 13, 1998, settled a dispute with accuser Paula Jones in which the former paid the latter $850,000 to settle her sexual-harassment claim against Mr. Clinton.[6] If Paula Jones's claims were not true, why would he agree to pay her a fortune?

None of these questions, of course, are related to the ever-increasing evidence that Mr. Clinton also had a relationship with convicted sex offender Jeffrey Epstein and some reports that the former president's name could be found on the flight logs of twenty-six trips that Epstein's private jet made to his island in the Bahamas.[7] As my dear mother used to say while she was still alive, "Once a hound dog, always a hound dog," and perhaps we should leave the matter there.

President Clinton said several times that he never visited Mr. Epstein's private Caribbean island called Little Saint James. But this is contradicted by a report from Doug Band, a former Clinton aide who indicated that Clinton went there in January of 2003. A young woman named Virginia Giuffre, who publicly accused Mr. Epstein of sex trafficking, said that she once saw Mr. Clinton on the island with "two young girls from New York."[8]

In a deposition in the Epstein case, lawyer Jack Scarola asked Ms. Giuffre, "Do you have any recollection of Mr. Epstein specifically telling you that 'Bill Clinton owes me favors'?"

"Yes, I do," she responded. "It was a laugh, though. He would laugh it off. I remember asking Jeffrey Epstein what Bill Clinton was doing here [on Epstein's island], kind of thing, and he laughed it off and said, 'Well, he owes me favors.'"[9]

The claims that race and gender are not biological concepts but social constructions are belied by the fact that men have a Y chromosome, and women do not, and men possess remarkably different kinds of hormones than women. Despite these facts, some writers now suggest that there are as many as sixty-four genders.

Research also shows that the coronavirus disproportionally affects men. The US Centers for Disease Control and Prevention (CDC) reported that the overall mortality rate of the virus has been about two and a half times higher for men than for women.[10] Heart and kidney diseases present differently in women and men, and women report twice as much anxiety and stress as men do.

Several recent studies have shown the many differences between the brains of men and women, such as the study conducted by Arthur P. Arnold et al. and published in the *Endocrine Reviews*.[11] The study shows that there are significant differences between the brains of men and women. To say that there are only minimal differences between the physiology of men and women does not seem to be true. Nor does there appear to be any reason for accepting sixty-two other genders besides those of male and female.

The sixth basic principle mentioned—that America is systemically racist—is perhaps the most disheartening of the ten basic beliefs of the Progressive New Left. Unfortunately, this claim has become an assertion often made in the last few months by both President Biden and Vice President Harris.

For example, in an early June 2021 speech after the verdict was announced in the Derek Chauvin case, Ms. Harris said to the press, "America has a long history of systemic racism." On the following day, however, in an interview on ABC's *Good Morning America*, she observed, "I don't think that America is a racist country." Then the vice president added, "But we also do have to speak the truth about the history of racism in our country and its existence today."

President Biden has also said some contradictory things about systemic racism. On the one hand, President Joe Biden, in a speech in his first day of office, at a breakfast in Washington, DC, honoring Martin Luther King Jr., said, "White Americans need to acknowledge and admit the fact that systemic racism still exists in America and must be rooted out." Mr. Biden also said that day in Washington:

> The bottom line is we have a lot to root out, but most of all, systemic racism that most of us whites don't like to acknowledge even exists. We don't even consciously acknowledge it. But it is built into every aspect of our system.

Mr. Biden also related, "We have a real chance to root out systemic racism that has plagued America."[12] However, on the *Today* show a few days later, he walked back from that comment in early May of 2021.

Although both the president and vice president made these and other pronouncements of systemic racism in America, they also contradicted that view in other speeches or remarks. In an April 29, 2021, interview on *Good Morning America*, the vice president was asked to respond to Senator Tim Scott's statement: "Hear me clearly: America is not a racist country."

Ms. Harris answered by saying, "I don't think America is a racist country."[13]

In an April 28, 2021, speech in Washington, DC, President Biden said, "I do not think the American people are racists, but the country has a history that must be confronted." On several occasions since his election, Mr. Biden has suggested that systemic racism is only in White people. In April 2021, for example, Mr. Biden related, "Systemic racism is a stain on our nation's soul." On March 21, 2021, he said:

> One of the core values and beliefs that should bring us together as Americans is standing against hate and racism, even as we acknowledge that systemic racism and white supremacy are ugly poisons that have long plagued the United States . . . We must change the laws that enable discrimination in our country, and we must change our hearts.[14]

If White Americans are systemically racist—that is, they are racists by their nature—then how can it be rooted out? Some Biden supporters have even gone so far as saying, "Systemic racism is part of the DNA of America." Again, presumably, this means White Americans. Of course, the country of America has no DNA. But the point again seems to be that it is only in the DNA of White Americans.

Another set of questions might also be raised about systemic racism in America. For example, is Mr. Biden systemically racist? How about his wife? Are other races in America—Asian Americans and Hispanic Americans, for instance—systemically racist? If the answer to that question is no, then what about White Europeans who immigrated to America and became White Americans? Are they now systemically racist? They are now White Americans. Has it now become "part of their DNA"?

If Asians and Hispanics cannot be systemically racist, why not? Can any Black Americans be systemically racist? They are, apparently, free to use the N-word whenever they want. Yet any White person who uses it automatically becomes a racist in the minds of the New Left Progressives.

How would one go about proving a claim like systemic racism? What empirical information should we collect to answer empirically that systemic racism claim is shown to be true?

Later, in Essay Two of this project, we will say a great deal about the evidence against the idea that the United States is a systemically racist nation, particularly in relation to White American police officers. As we shall see in that essay, there is sufficient empirical evidence collected, interestingly enough, by the *Washington Post*.[15] It is enough now, however, to point out that we are categorically against the view expressed by President Joe Biden and Vice President Kamala Harris, among many others, that America is a systemically racist nation.

We also may ask: Is it possible for Black Americans to be

racists? Consider Louis Farrakhan, the leader of the American Black Muslim faith for more than thirty years. He is notorious for countless statements against Jews and other White people in America, such as, "White people are potential human beings ... They have not evolved yet."[16] The New Left in America cannot consider the obvious anti-Semitic and racist remarks of Mr. Farrakhan because Mr. Farrakhan is Black. Under the New Left Progressive definition of *racism*, Mr. Farrakhan's remarks may only be considered expressions of racial prejudice but not racism because he is Black. Therefore, he supposedly cannot be a racist.

Or consider the words of New York City psychiatrist Dr. Aruna Khilanani in a speech given at the Yale University School of Medicine on June 4, 2021, when she revealed that she has "fantasies of killing White people" with a revolver.[17] Dr. Khilanani is an Indian American, and thus a woman "of color." Could we not also give her the name *racist*? Consider what we would say of her if she had related that she had fantasies of killing Black people.

In some circles, Mr. Farrakhan's many remarks about Jews and other White people, as well as Dr. Khilanani's remarks, are now considered to be what is called "reverse discrimination." But the proponents of the New Left's definition of *racism* simply deny the existence of reverse discrimination. So all White Americans are inherently and systemically racist, while Americans like Mr. Farrakhan and the New York City psychiatrist are not. This is a bizarre application of reason and logic, indeed.

Dr. Khilanani is one of those scholars who is also related to our seventh belief listed earlier, in that she has written several papers on "White Rage" and "Whiteness" in general, suggesting it is an inferior race psychologically speaking. It is now out of fashion to be White. When asked in a recent interview if White people are psychopathic, her response was chilling. She observed:

> I think so. Yeah . . . the level of lying that White people do that has started from colonialism—we are just used to it. Every time that you steal a country, you loot, you say you have discovered something. I mean, this level of lies [is] actually part of history.[18]

Dr. Aruna Khilanani is not alone. She is part of a contemporary American movement that elevates races other than White people while at the same time denigrating the status and accomplishments of White people. The phenomenon known as *cancel culture* may be directly related to this phenomenon.

Another aspect of this seventh fundamental belief of the New Progressive Left is what is referred to as *toxic masculinity*, a condition apparently from which only White American men appear to suffer—particularly if they are Conservatives.

One of the many ironies that follow from these first seven foundational beliefs of the New American Left is that the Progressives find themselves in bed with the Muslim jihadists of the world, assailing Western colonialism, imperialism, and racism as its defining characteristics. But the vitriol from the Left and from Conservative Islamic thinkers do not wish to eschew the basic human rights that are guaranteed by the founding documents of America, as well as in the Koran, the Muslim holy book. That is that all people are endowed by God with certain inalienable rights such as life, liberty, and property, among many others, as well as similar remarks in Koran 94:4–6, among other places.*

Rather than assenting to these rights, the New American Left wishes to replace them. So we replace the idea of equality with the notion of equity, about which we will say more in a later essay.

In my own discipline of philosophy in the English-speaking world, we have abandoned the traditional emphasis that the foundations of Western philosophy are to be found in the Greeks

* The translations from the Koran are my own.

and Romans, dead White men. The philosophy department from which I retired a few years ago now advertises on its website that they specialize in critical race theory, "feminist philosophy," and the "philosophy of disability." Three of my former colleagues were advocates of the Progressive New Left movement, as witnessed by the courses they taught.

Many of the courses I used to teach at my former university are no longer offered, such as Ancient Philosophy, Medieval Philosophy, Modern Philosophy, and Contemporary Philosophy. In fact, these four courses are now taught as two courses, with ancient and medieval together and modern and contemporary philosophy paired. But how one can teach four courses in the space of two is beyond my understanding.

All three female colleagues in the department from which I retired are now gone from the university. But they have been replaced by a chairperson who claims to be an "intuitive" and a "mystic," but she does not have a PhD in philosophy. Of the other two members of my former department hired since I left, one has a PhD in philosophy and education, and the other, a third woman, is the only of the three with a straight-up doctorate in philosophy. All three are assistant professors, meaning they are just starting out in their careers.

The current chair of my former department published a few books, but the other two members have not. When I retired in the fall of 2016, I had published three dozen books, more than the other three members combined and many more books than the rest of the one-hundred-plus faculty members in the other departments of the entire university.

Gone from the curriculum of my former school are Socrates, Plato, and his student, Aristotle. They have been replaced by ten overarching principles to which nearly every member of the American Academy now must assent. Dissent is discouraged. God is no longer mentioned by members of the Progressive New

Left. In American academia these days, those who complain that beliefs about transgender people are a direct contradiction with their biblical faith are suspended, fired, or forced to change jobs. Or, even worse, they are banned from social media platforms.

For a long time before my retirement from full-time teaching in the fall of 2016, I had been accused of being a racist. This is not surprising given the fact that I am a White, old, straight male who may well suffer from systemic racism and what the aforementioned New York psychiatrist refers to as "White rage." I might add, the semester in which I retired, I gave an African American student of mine, whose husband had recently suffered a stroke, the money to purchase a bicycle for her young daughter for Christmas.

Instead, before I left my former department, I was accused of being a racist by one of my Black students after I told her at 11:00 a.m., an hour into a fifty-minute exam, that her time was up and I needed to take her exam because I had an eleven o'clock class. But rather than hearing my side of the story, the student complained that I was a racist, and that was the end of it.

In the eighth foundational principle, as we shall see in this study, many of the Progressive New Left in contemporary America have pointed out that individual stories or "narratives" of oppression and struggle are often far more important than the expression of collective struggle. The New Left often puts a premium on individuals who are said to have their own "truth" about their narratives, as opposed to anyone else's truth. We will see this claim about individual narratives in our essay on the 1619 Project as well.

In this sense, this eighth foundational principle is ultimately related to the first—that there is no objective truth. That there are only individual truths, apparently one for each person. This brings us to a short discussion of some of the many societal repercussions of these foundational beliefs of the Progressive New Left, the topic of the second section of this first essay.

Regarding our ninth core belief of the Progressive New Left, since the 1990s, the Democratic Party has included hate speech and hate crimes on its party platform. In addition, the FBI now collects data on both of these phenomena. We will say more about these issues in Essay Seven. Based on the poll I conducted, 68 percent of my students believed that hate speech and hate crimes should be outlawed.

At the same time, 57 percent of my students polled agreed that the national Liberal media tends to censure Conservative opinions on their outlets or platforms. Certainly, this is a sign that college students believe it. We will speak more generally about the views of American citizens on this matter in Essay Eleven of this study.

Finally, we have seen in the 2000s several proposals about the environment and climate change. There has been extensive rhetoric about these issues that the Progressive New Left now calls *climate change*, "an existential crisis, that if it is not solved, it will endanger the existence of the human species, as well as the planet Earth." Eighty-two percent of my students in my poll conducted in the spring of 2016 believed that climate change is now at the stage of an "existential crisis," in the words of Vice President Kamala Harris.[19*]

This "existential crisis" will be the subject matter of Essay Ten of this study. All ten of these fundamental claims of the contemporary Progressive New Left will be referred to and discussed throughout these essays, as well as the repercussions of these ideas in twenty-first-century American culture.

* The poll of my students—one hundred undergraduate and twelve graduate students—was conducted in the 2016 spring semester. I have employed the Program for International Student Assessment tests from 1967 until 2018.

II

Several American societal repercussions have followed from our ten foundational principles of the New American Left. One of the most important of these is that, in the United States, we now have two separate understandings of the Constitution and how it works. We call these the Conservative view and the Progressive view. The former view assents to the Constitution as written and amended. This point of view is grounded in the natural rights as outlined in the Declaration of Independence of 1776 and the US Constitution, written in 1787 and ratified a year later.

The other view of the Constitution is the one preferred by the Progressives in America. The view of this group might be called the Living Constitution. In this camp, the adherents say that the US Constitution must be infused with new, ever-changing American rights and duties—particularly in relation to the issue of identity politics.

What follows, of course, is that homosexuals may now marry, abortion becomes allowable at any stage of fetal development, and what counts as a *person* and a *citizen* radically begins to change in America. The Progressive movement now sees the nature of the self and the citizen to be related to the individual's race, gender, sexual orientation, and ethnicity.

The MeToo movement, as we have seen in the Justice Kavanaugh confirmation battle, adopted the credo, "Believe every woman." This chant was tied to many on CNN who said, "We must listen to her truth," referring to one of the justice's accusers. This credo, of course, is directly tied to our first foundational principle. In place of objective or absolute truth, we now have individual, subjective truths, presumably different truths for different persons.

One irony, of course, to this view is that "dead White males"—the race and gender of many scholars for centuries in America—

are no longer relevant. In fact, some Progressives on MSNBC and CNN tell us that American men suffer from what they call *toxic masculinity*, while also maintaining that this is only a Y chromosome condition, and thus only a White male malady, particularly if you are a Conservative.

For the New Left in America, the ideas of rights and duties are grounded in the individual's membership in various groups—racial, ethnic, gender, and class based. From a continual reorientation and consciousness-raising process, the Progressives wish to change the traditional understanding of empowerment. All races, genders—all sixty-four of them—ethnicities, and sexual orientations must be equally empowered.

The Progressives also speak of a "new distribution of wealth" in America, a redistribution that appears to be based on Socialist principles. The wealthy and large corporations must pay more in America. Of course, anyone who does not conform to these views of the New Left and does not believe in these ten fundamental beliefs is instantly labeled a racist, a homophobe, or anti-transgender.

Another repercussion of this new American political correctness is an America that tells us what we can and cannot say and write. Representative Ted Lieu of California told CNN recently that he "would love to regulate the content of speech."[20] Perhaps the greatest repercussion of these ten foundational beliefs of the Progressive New Left is that in the United States in the twenty-first century, the New Left has replaced the First Amendment of the US Constitution with the Fourteenth Amendment—the one that gave Black Americans citizenship and the right to vote.

Traditionally, for the government to regulate speech, it had to show some compelling interest in the regulation of words. This is what John Stuart Mill called the *principle of harm*. I will say more about the regulation of speech and the principle of harm in Essay Seven of this study.

One other repercussion of the New Left Progressives is that they have managed to move the former "centrist" Joe Biden further and further to the Left as his new policies usually verify. He said in his inaugural address that he wanted to "unify America." Instead, as evidenced by what he has done so far to President Trump's policies on the subjects of this book—the wall, the southern border, guns and the Second Amendment, the abortion policy, critical race theory, the 1619 Project, Afghanistan, and many other contemporary issues—there is little sign from the president or his administration of the "unity" about which he spoke of in his inaugural address, nor the Centrist perspective he claimed to have in his January inauguration.

In the meantime, on the horizon, of course, is the specter that the First Amendment, given the "Living Constitution theory," might be eliminated completely and the Second Amendment as well, as we shall see later in Essay Six. For the American Conservative, these are scary thoughts, indeed!

One possible reason for the lack of unity and the impossibility of it in America is the fact, perhaps, that we are in the middle of a second American civil war, just as much mired in ideology in the United States as the first Civil War. But the one in 1860 could not have celebrated, nor envisioned, the first transgender president, as someday soon we may.

III

In the third section of this first chapter, I will sketch out some of my qualifications and background for what will allow me to discuss the issues I shall speak about in the remaining parts of this book. I have a BA in philosophy from the University of Maryland and two master's degrees, one from Yale University and the other from Oxford University in England. My degree from Yale was in the philosophy of religion and the study of wisdom literature of the Hebrew Bible, particularly the book of Job.

My degree at Hereford College, Oxford, an MPhil, was in the PPE Program, which stands for "Politics, Philosophy, and Economics." My MPhil thesis was on the book of Job and the moral implications that the book entails.

My PhD was granted from Saint Mary's College, the Divinity School at the University of St Andrews in Fife, Scotland. My PhD thesis was on the problem of evil. If God is all good, all-knowing, and all-powerful, then why is there so much evil and suffering in the world?

Along the way in my teaching career, I taught for forty-three years, from first-year undergraduates to PhD students. Twenty-five of my former students have also received PhDs from places like Harvard, Yale, Princeton, Oxford, St Andrews, Johns Hopkins, the University of Chicago, Cambridge University in England, and many other universities.

In the past fifteen years, I have also begun to study classical Arabic, the language of the Muslim holy book, the Koran. In fact, I have earned two certificates from the British Association for Koronic Studies, a basic certificate and an advanced certificate. I am now a certified Arabic translator in both Britain and the United States.

For twenty-five years, I also taught hundreds of American police officers in the Johns Hopkins program in public safety. I also did extensive consulting with the FBI, the CIA, the Florida Department of Law Enforcement, and the California Police Officers Standards and Training Commission.

I have conducted three major studies of police first-line supervision with the Baltimore Police Department, the State of Florida, and the Arizona Department of Corrections. Along the way, I have published thirty-six books. One was about Muslim slaves in the Chesapeake Bay region. Several others were about the book of

Job, and many were about moral theories and their applications.

For ten years, I was also the head of the Institute for Public Philosophy, where I mostly consulted with police departments, businesses, organizations, and American, Irish, and English government agencies.

Along the way in my career, I was invited by US Attorney General Janet Reno to give the keynote address at a conference she sponsored in Baltimore in the early 1990s on police integrity. Through my institute, I conducted another study on how schoolchildren, undergraduates, and police officers solve moral dilemmas.

In the past decade, I completed books on George Washington, Thomas Jefferson, Abraham Lincoln, and Ronald Reagan, all regarding their religious views, and I have contracts for books on the religious views of Alexander Hamilton, Benjamin Franklin, and James Madison to be published soon by Calumet Editions in Minnesota.

During my academic career, I have also used several languages in the material I have written and the books I have published and continue to publish. These languages include classical Hebrew, Greek, Latin, German, French, Danish, and several other languages, such as Syriac and Arabic and Aramaic.

For my PhD, I was required to show general reading knowledge of six of these languages. Those were the first six languages mentioned in the previous paragraph. I began studying classical Hebrew, Aramaic, and Syriac with Professor William F. Albright of Johns Hopkins University when I was in high school in Baltimore. I continued to study these Semitic tongues at Yale, then at Oxford, and then at St Andrews in Fife, Scotland.

Along the way, in this study of the views of the Progressive New Left, I will point to other aspects of my personal history that are of some relevance to the content of the essays to follow. It is enough now, however, to point out that this list of my skills is incomplete. All these skills and abilities I have acquired in my academic life will become very important, as we shall see, in the remainder of this study, in which we will apply those skills and abilities to particular problems in contemporary American life, such as the 1619 Project, slavery in America, the state of the American family, the Defund the Police movement, the origin of COVID-19, the redefining of language in America, and many other issues and questions.

The final point we have mentioned here can be seen in many ways. We will point to only two of them: the redefinition of *infrastructure* and the replacement of the idea of *equality* with the notion of *equity*.

In late March 2021, the Biden administration sought to pass a more than $2 trillion infrastructure bill. Traditionally, the term *infrastructure* referred to roads, bridges, waterways, ports, and airports. The Biden administration, however, believes infrastructure also includes $400 billion for "care for the elderly," $300 billion for broadband access, and $58 billion for American manufacturing, research, and development.[21]

In one stroke of the pen, Mr. Biden wishes to change the definition of *infrastructure*. This has caused the Republican National Committee to issue a press release that in part said, "Joe Biden's 'infrastructure' plan is not really about infrastructure, it is a multi-trillion dollar far left wish list. Just take a look at the actual bill. Only 7 percent of the bill's spending is for what Americans have traditionally think of as infrastructure."[22]

In early July 2021, Mr. Biden met with Senate Democrats to discuss another $3.5 trillion plan for "infrastructure."[23] The plan called for money for new electric vehicles and other pork-barrel projects, but it also suggested that infrastructure now included money to pay for childcare and for free community college for all Americans. At least it is not the "Medicare for All" plan that some Democratic candidates were pushing for in the 2020 campaign season.

In our other example of redefining language in America, the word *equality* is now out of fashion. It has now been replaced by what the Progressive New Left calls *equity*. Traditionally, the English word *equality* has meant that everyone is treated the same, or equally—"The state of being equal, especially in status, rights, and opportunities." The New Left seeks to replace this idea of equality with the notion of *equity*.

Equity, in the Progressive New Left view, is "the quality of being fair and impartial." What does this mean in the workplace or in society as a whole? It means that treating everyone the same in the pursuit of equality might not actually be fair or just. Another way to put this matter is to say that treatment should be given to what the individual needs rather than what he or she gets in relation to everyone else.

This is sometimes illustrated by three boys standing on the same kind of box so they can watch a baseball game over a fence. Because the two boys on the left are taller, they have an advantage over the shorter boy on the right. Equity would involve giving the shorter boy a second box that he might put atop the first so that now he could see the game over the fence like the other two boys. Thus, the shorter boy has now been given equity.

The additional box for the short boy gives the lad what he needs, in that he now has the same opportunity as the two other boys. The New Left would call the situation before the introduction of the second box for the short boy a case of equality, for all three boys received the same box. But the Progressive New Left would add that the introduction of the second box for the shortest boy now becomes an illustrative example of equity, for he now has the same "opportunity" to see the game as the other two boys.[24]

This shift from equality to equity, at least in practice, is also a shift in differing views about the nature of justice, or what Plato defined as "getting what one is due." Equality would demand that everyone is due the same, for all are equal, but the proponents of equity would say not everyone has the same needs, so they should not be treated equally.

What is left out of these two views of justice is the idea of getting what you are due in terms of your accomplishments or your merits. In this sense, justice becomes a matter of reward and punishment. One is rewarded or punished according to one's accomplishments. This is a very different view than the other two perspectives on Plato's "getting what one is due."

The replacement of the word *equality* with the word *equity*, on June 1, 2021, got to the point where Congresswoman Eleanor Holmes Norton, a Democrat from the District of Columbia and the chair of the Subcommittee on Highways and Transit, introduced a bill to require that car-crash dummies be modeled on both male and female bodies.[25] For Ms. Holmes Norton, this is not a matter of equality; it is a case of equity.

The discussion around equity replacing equality, then, appears to be nothing more than a movement away from equality and merit and in favor of equity and getting what one needs. Not only has the New Left redefined *infrastructure* and *justice*; it has also made changes in many other aspects of language when the traditional meanings of words do not fit their agenda, such as what a gender is or how many genders there are. In fact, the Progressive New Left is in favor of eliminating many sex and gender terms, such as mother, father, mister, Mrs., woman, female, and many others. Recently, it was suggested that the word *breastfeeding* should be scrubbed in favor of *chest milk*.

The Progressive New Left and their followers have proposed a form of surgery on many other words and their uses in contemporary America. We will speak of a few more of these throughout the essays of this study. For now, it is enough to point out that the surgery is going on.

IV

Finally, in this first chapter, we will make some observations about the name of this book, *The 1618 Project*. We have chosen this title to indicate that one of the goals of the book is to show that slavery in America did not begin in 1619, as the *New York Times* would have you believe.

There is sufficient evidence that shows that slavery was practiced in the Americas long before the year 1619, when twenty or so Africans were brought to the Virginia Colony on a ship called the *White Lion* in what would become the United States.

Several dates are important for understanding European participation in slavery in the Americas. Among these dates are 1513, 1528, the early 1530s, 1539, and 1564. For example, in 1513, while exploring the Bahamas, Ponce de León landed somewhere near present-day Cape Canaveral in Florida. He promptly dubbed the land he found there "La Florida."

In 1528, nearly a century before 1619, Pánfilo de Narváez landed near Tampa Bay. A decade later, in 1539, Hernando de Soto arrived on the Gulf Coast of Florida, which began a four-year trek across Florida from west to east. By the early 1630s, Spain had been transporting slaves across the Middle Passage for several years, many of them taken to Northern Florida and Southern Georgia.

In 1564, a group of French Huguenots, or Protestants, established a small colony along the Saint Johns River, near present-day Jacksonville. The following year, Pedro Menéndez expelled the Huguenots and founded a settlement at Saint Augustine. These dates are significant for our purposes because the Spanish had begun slavery in what would become the United States an entire century before 1619.[26]

In an interview with National Public Radio (NPR) in November 2017, after the publication of his book *The Other Slavery: The*

Uncovered Story of Indian Enslavement in America, scholar Andrés Reséndez suggested that from 1500 until 1900, there were as many as five million Native Americans enslaved in America.[27] But unlike African slavery, which was legal for centuries and sanctioned by the state and empires around the world, Native American slavery was made illegal by Spain in 1542. However, slavery existed in Florida beginning around the year 1500 and was continued by the Spanish until 1542.

In an article for the Gilder Lehrman Institute of American History, Professor David Wheat of Michigan State University chronicled the history of slavery conducted in Europe and North America. Dr. Wheat suggests that slavery was being conducted in North America by the year 1430. In fact, back in Spain and Portugal by the 1550s, 10 percent of the population of both countries were Black slaves. In southern Spain, Dr. Wheat tells us, there were "44,000 African slaves that made up 10 percent of the population."[28]

The Portuguese rounded the Cape of Good Hope in 1488. Although they had sent slaves to the New World before that time, by the time of Columbus, they were conducting slaves across the Middle Passage and to the Caribbean, to Brazil, and to North America.

The mention of these facts is significant because 1619 is a full century later than when the first African slaves were brought to America, not to mention the enslavement of Native Americans in that same period.

Meanwhile, in Mexico and South America, the Aztecs, the Mayans, and the Inca in Peru had practiced the slavery of rival tribes of Native Americans, going all the way back to at least the year 1500. The Aztec Empire in Mexico was an incredibly advanced agricultural empire that practiced both ritual sacrifice and slavery. Some even estimate that as many as 84,000 people were once sacrificed during a four-day period. But again, what is important here is that this sacrifice and slavery were going on in Mexico long before 1619.

The Mayans were another incredibly advanced American society. The Mayan people invented absolute zero and telepathy, as well as certain irrigation techniques, long before the Europeans. The Mayans practiced ritual sacrifice and slavery as well. And this Mayan slavery existed, as we know from archeological evidence, long before the year 1619.[29]

The Inca dominated a large area of land in what is now Peru. Francisco Pizarro conquered the Inca with only 180 men, one cannon, and twenty-seven horses. The Inca also had an advanced irrigation system. Among the things that Pizarro found in Peru was the practice of slavery. He made his expeditions to Peru in the late 1520s and early 1530s, again nearly an entire century before 1619.[30]

Brown University scholar Linford D. Fisher also wrote about the enslavement of Native Americans, saying, "It is a piece of history of slavery that has been glossed over." He added, "Between 1492 and 1880, between 2.5 and 5.5 million Native Americans were enslaved, in addition to the 12.5 million Africans."[31] A third scholar, Brett Rushforth, has also done extensive work on the enslavement of Native Americans. His estimated number of enslaved Native Americans from 1500 to 1800 was somewhere between two and five million.[32]

The conclusion about the research of Fisher and Rushforth should again be obvious. The earliest enslavement in the Americas by the Spanish can be shown to have existed as early as 1500—a full century before the *New York Times*' 1619 Project's date. If we add to this the fact that Portugal was conducting Black slavery in the Americas as early as the 1480s, then the year 1619 is far too late to find the first Black slaves in the Americas. Thus, I have picked the year 1618 to indicate that slavery was going on in the Americas long before 1619 and perhaps as early as the 1480s by the Portuguese.

One way to understand the study that is to follow is that it is an analysis of the Progressive New Left's ten fundamental ideas outlined earlier and how the implications for those ideas can be seen in contemporary American culture. To that end, we will speak of nine or ten main and controversial issues in today's America. These include the Defund the Police movement, the question of abortion, critical race theory, the origins of COVID-19, the crisis at the southern border, gun control and the Second Amendment, hate crime and hate speech in America, Big Tech censorship, the role of Marxism in the United States, and the 1619 Project.

What this study purports to be is nothing more than the philosophical and critical musings I have had over the past ten years or so regarding what the Progressive New Leftists have had to say about the issues listed in the previous summary. Indeed, the New Left has much to say about these contemporary controversies, especially since the death of George Floyd in the spring of 2020 and the protests that accompanied that event.

This brings us to the sources of this first essay, followed by Essay Two on what has come to be called the Defund the Police movement since the death of George Floyd in May of 2020.

ESSAY TWO

The Defund, or Abolish, the Police Movement

I

In this second essay and the others that follow it, I will write about what we see as the repercussions of believing in the Progressive New Left's ten fundamental philosophical beliefs I have introduced in the first essay of this study of implications of the governing of the New Left in the United States. In this essay, we will discuss the police and its possible defunding or abolishing in America, or its "reimagining," in the eyes of some on the Progressive New Left.

In subsequent essays, I will speak more about the 1619 Project, the repercussions for the idea of the family in the United States, the origins of the worldwide COVID-19 disease, and abortion, as well as several other issues.

Our first task in this second essay is to speak some about the distinctions made by various Americans on the Left about what they wish to do with the funds allocated to American police departments in the United States. Some want to reduce the budgets of the police and reallocate the money to other social issues, such as social services, youth services, housing, education, and many other possibilities.

On June 7, 2020, American singer-songwriter and music producer John Legend shared what the Defund the Police movement would mean. In Mr. Legend's view, the relocated police monies should go to "housing support, health care, education and child care, the arts, drug treatment, community centers, [and] all sorts of services that would actually reduce the problems that we ask the police to surveil and contain." Mr. Legend added the following:

> [Defunding] doesn't mean there will be no police; it means that there should be significantly fewer police and more professionals of other types with expertise in their fields, whether it's social work, health care, conflict resolution, drug treatment, etc.[1]

So one view of the Defund the Police movement we shall call the reallocation view. A second view, however, is from those who claim we should not defund the police; rather we should abolish the police altogether. This second perspective has been called both the Abolish the Police movement and the Reimagining the Police movement.

Since the death of George Floyd at the knee of a White Minnesotan police officer on May 25, 2020, both of our theories have been asserted, and the second one—the abolish view—has been around since the 1960s with thinkers such as activist Angela Davis.

The unrest in the summer of 2020 and the formation of the Black Lives Matter movement and Antifa, which Jerry Nadler told us is a myth,[2] have brought the two theories to the forefront in America, along with a belief that too many African Americans have died in America at the hands of White police officers.

In point of fact, about one thousand civilians are killed each year by law enforcement in America. By one estimate, Black men are 3.23 times more likely than White men to be killed by the police during their lifetimes.[3] According to another study, Black people who were shot fatally by the police were twice as likely as White citizens to be unarmed.[4]

Since 2015, at least according to the *Washington Post*, 6,211 people in the United States have been killed by the police. Ninety-four percent of those citizens were armed. Fifty-eight percent had a gun. Seventy-five percent were armed with either a gun or a knife or both. Eighty-seven percent were armed with a gun, knife, or some other lethal weapon, or they used a vehicle they were driving as a weapon.

Nearly every single person who has been shot by law enforcement since the *Washington Post* began their data collection in 2015 has been armed. Yet the popular misconception persists on the Left in America that the police are killing unarmed Black people at a staggering rate. In fact, only 2 percent of the total victims of deadly police shootings over the past six years were unarmed Black men. If we add to this fact that many of these Black men, like George Floyd, were enormous in size, that 2 percent figure gets even smaller. If we add the understanding that not all the officers who kill are White—and that Asian, Hispanic, and Black cops also have shot some Black people to death—then that 2 percent number gets smaller still. According to the *Washington Post*, of the 6,211 people shot to death by the police, 2,888 were White, or 46 percent, and 1,496 of these victims shot and killed by the police were Black, or 24 percent.

Only 6 percent of those shot and killed by American police officers were unarmed, and only 2 percent of the Americans killed by an officer were both unarmed and Black. In point of fact, since 2015, at least according to the *Washington Post*, thirty-three more unarmed White people have been shot to death by the police than unarmed Black people.[5]

One final relevant statistic is that of all the encounters that American citizens have with the police, of those meetings, only 0.0016 percent were murdered by American law enforcement. In 2015, the Obama Justice Department studied the Philadelphia Police Department's use-of-force behaviors.[6] In that study, researchers determined that White officers were less likely to shoot and kill an unarmed Black suspect in the City of Brotherly Love than either Black or Hispanic officers or Asian officers, as well.[7]

The conclusion of all of this should be clear. There is not an epidemic of White law enforcement killing Black citizens. It is a very infrequent event in America. And yet, when it does occur, those events are featured in the mostly progressive media, or these events are taken up by Al Sharpton and others to emphasize these very rare occurrences.

This brings us to the first section of Essay Two on the Defund the Police movement, in which we will speak of the attitudes of Americans about the movement that have been studied in three separate recent studies.

Public Perception of the Defund the Police Movement

Since May 25, 2020, the day that George Floyd died in Minneapolis, three major studies have been completed regarding the public perception of the movement. One of these was by the YouGov organization, a second was by an ABC News/Ipsos poll conducted in June of 2020, and a third was conducted by the Gallup Company in June and July of 2020.

The first of these polls of American attitudes toward the Defund the Police movement—the one by the YouGov website—was conducted on June 9 and 10 of 2020. The YouGov group found that most Americans opposed cutting police funding, and YouGov found similar results among those who identified themselves as Republicans and those who identified as Democrats.[8]

The ABC/Ipsos poll of 686 American citizens was conducted on June 10 and 11, 2020, two weeks after the death of Mr. Floyd. Thirty-four percent of the US adults polled supported the movement to defund the police, and 68 percent opposed it. Support for the idea was higher among Black Americans (57 percent) than among White Americans (26 percent) and Hispanic Americans (42 percent). And, in the ABC poll, support for the Defund the Police movement was much higher among Democrats, at 55 percent, than among Republicans and Independents (38 percent).[9]

The most startling of these three studies about American attitudes toward the Defund the Police movement was the Gallup study. The Gallup researchers, who conducted their survey from June 23 to July 6, 2020, found that 81 percent of African Americans indicated that they wished to spend the "same amount of money" in their neighborhoods or "slightly more" on the police.[10]

In fact, in the overall numbers of the attitudes of all races in the Gallup study, 86 percent were against the idea of defunding the police.

The results of these three polls of American attitudes toward the Defund the Police movement were remarkably consistent. Only somewhere between one-fifth and one-third of the Americans polled supported the movement. Similar findings can also be seen in attitudes toward the movement in polls conducted by Reuters/Ipsos, by *USA Today*, by the Pew Research Center, by the Siena pollsters in New York, and by Morning Consult/Politico.

In the Reuters/Ipsos poll, they found that only 39 percent supported the Defund the Police movement, while 57 percent opposed it.[11] In the Morning Consult/Politico study, researchers found that 29 percent were in favor of the Defund the Police movement and 57 percent were against it.[12] In an article published on March 7, 2021, in *USA Today*, the national newspaper revealed their findings of their polling of attitudes toward the movement. They found that only 18 percent of the adult Americans they polled were in favor of the goals of the Defund the Police movement.[13] The article did not indicate, however, what those goals are.

In polling of Americans conducted by the Pew Research Center in July of 2020 in regard to the movement, the researchers found that just 25 percent of those American citizens they polled were in favor of decreasing funding for police. Interestingly enough, however, Pew found that just 22 percent of the African Americans they interviewed wanted police funding to be "decreased a lot."[14]

Siena College researchers in New York published the results of a survey they had conducted on New Yorkers' attitudes toward police reform and the Defund the Police movement. The Siena poll suggested that 70 percent of all New Yorkers were in favor of "some police reform." And they also found that only 17 percent of the New Yorkers polled were in favor of a "significant reduction in the police budget." Thus, the representative New Yorkers who were polled were against the idea of defunding the police.

If we were to combine the polling data of all nine of the aforementioned organizations, which includes the attitudes of 13,000 Americans of all races, the average responses from those polls of Americans tell us this: 29 percent of the Americans polled supported the Defund the Police movement, while 61 percent of those same people opposed it.

This brings us to the second section of Essay Two, in which we will explore when, where, and why in America towns, cities, and counties have attempted or have in fact successfully "defunded the police."

Where, How, and Why the Police Have Been Defunded in America

Since the murder of George Floyd on May 25, 2020, forty-three police departments in America have reduced their public safety budgets, including several major cities of the United States as well as many towns and counties. In this third section of Essay Two, we will identify those cities, the monetary amounts by which their police departments' budgets have been reduced, and the repercussions of those reductions. The following police departments since May of 2020 have made significant reductions in their budgets:

1. Albuquerque (32.7 percent)
2. Atlanta (31.9 percent)
3. Austin (26.4 percent)
4. Baltimore (26 percent)
5. Boston (11.2 percent)
6. Camden, New Jersey (25 percent)
7. Charlotte (40.4 percent)
8. Garden City, Missouri (laid off all its officers and fired the chief)
9. Deposit, New York (17 percent)
10. Detroit (15 percent)
11. Hartford (2.85 percent increase)
12. Houston (34.4 percent)
13. Kansas City (37.5 percent)
14. Las Vegas (28.2 percent)
15. Louisville (29 percent)
16. Memphis (39.7 percent)
17. Mesa (41.5 percent)
18. Miami (32.8 percent)
19. Minneapolis (29 percent)
20. Nashville (8.6 percent)
21. New York (6 percent)
22. Norman (12 percent)
23. Oakland (45.3 percent)
24. Oklahoma City (33.4 percent)
25. Omaha (36.7 percent)
26. Philadelphia (15.1 percent)
27. Phoenix (41.5 percent)
28. Portland (34.4 percent)
29. Raleigh (22 percent)
30. Sacramento (25.1 percent)
31. Salt Lake City (10 percent)
32. San Antonio (37.5 percent)
33. San Diego (35.1 percent)
34. San Francisco ($120 million, percentage unknown)
35. San Jose (29.4 percent)
36. Seattle (10 percent)
37. Tucson (32.2 percent)
38. Tulsa (32.4 percent)
39. Virginia Beach (9 percent)
40. Washington, D.C. (5.7 percent)

According to *Forbes*, funding cuts of police departments in 2020 and 2021 ranged from $1 billion slashed in New York City's police budget to $3.5 million in Seattle and $865,000 in smaller cities like Norman, Oklahoma.[15] *Forbes* also reported, however, that some cities like Durham, North Carolina, for example, have increased their police budgets, as have the cities of Los Angeles and Hartford, Connecticut, for other examples.[16]

While anti-police advocates like to say that defunding the police does not affect violent crime in America, the statistics in many cities tell an entirely different story.

In our analysis, we will look at eleven of these cities that have reduced police department budgets in 2020 and some of the effects of those reductions. These cities are as follows:

Atlanta	Los Angeles
Baltimore	Minneapolis
Boston	New York
Chicago	Portland
Washington, DC	Seattle
Houston	

These eleven cities have several things in common, in addition to reducing their police departments' budgets. Among these are the following: First, each of these eleven cities is run by Progressives. Second, each city has instituted a new policy about bail for many violent crimes, in that they now have what might be called a "catch-and-release policy," in which criminals are released back into the community. In the city of New York, for example, between 2019 and 2020, the number of arrestees released without bail increased from 38 percent to 60 percent. In Baltimore, no one in the city is prosecuted for possession of marijuana or for prostitution,[17] and arrestees released without bail are now more than 60 percent.

Third, each of these cities has had to deal with the issues related to the COVID-19 pandemic while also responding to a wave of violent crime. It is very difficult, however, to measure the short-term and long-term effects of the pandemic.

In 2020, Atlanta, Georgia, saw the highest homicide rate in two decades. Drive-by shootings in Atlanta increased 100 percent from 2019 to 2020. The city also saw significant increases in other violent crimes from 2019 to 2020.

In Minneapolis, homicides increased by 58 percent in 2020.[18] With many of these crimes unsolved, there are fewer homicide detectives in the city because of the budget cuts. Things have become so bad in Minneapolis that a citizen group has filed a lawsuit against the city council to restore police funding. One of the plaintiffs in the suit, Cathy Spann, related, "As citizens, the City of Minneapolis owes us. We have the right to expect that we can be safe walking the streets, that our children can play in their yards. Enough is enough."[19]

The situation in Atlanta, Georgia, is much the same—the year 2020 was the city's most violent year ever recorded. Atlanta's police department investigated 157 homicides in 2020. That is up from 99 in 2019.[20] The 157 figure in Atlanta is the highest number in twenty years.

In Boston, we find the following increases in violent crime from 2019 to 2020:

- Homicide, up 54 percent
- Fatal shootings, up 61 percent
- Nonfatal shootings, up 42 percent
- Firearms arrests, up 13 percent
- Burglary, up 63 percent
- Larceny, up 24 percent

In the city of Baltimore, from 2019 to 2020, homicides were up 17 percent. Most of those added deaths came about from May to December, after the death of George Floyd. Of the nine police precincts in Baltimore, each of them saw an increase, with the northwest, south, southwest, and western districts seeing the largest increases in several violent crimes.

In the same period, in the city of Chicago, the police department investigated 774 murders in 2020. This was an increase of more than 50 percent over the 506 homicides from 2019. The number of shootings in Chicago also increased from 2,120 in 2019 to 3,237 as of December 2020. Twenty-five percent of all Chicago murders occurred in three West Side districts: Harrison, Ogden, and Austin. The year 2020 will go down as Chicago's second deadliest in the past two decades, only trailing 2016, when the city experienced 784 homicides.[21]

Meanwhile, in the nation's capital, Washington, DC, the homicide branch reported a 23 percent increase in murders from 2019 to 2020.[22] Washington, where guns are illegal, also experienced an increase in assaults, motor vehicle theft, arson, and recovered firearms during that same period. In fact, in 2020, Washington had its highest homicide number in fifteen years.

In Houston, Texas, the number of homicides in 2019 was 281. The *Houston Chronicle* reported, however, that by the year 2020, that figure was dwarfed, for Houston then had 400 homicides.[23] The city of Los Angeles also saw an alarming increase in violent crime. Homicide, assault shootings, car theft, and many other violent crimes have all increased from 2019 to 2020. Nearly two-thirds of all shootings occurred in South LA. In one six-week period in 2020, there were 110 shooting victims, compared to the same period in 2019, when there were only 24.

The state of violent crime in New York City was no better from 2019 to 2020. The homicide rate was up 41 percent, shooting victims in the city increased 103 percent, and shooting incidents increased 97 percent. New York's slide toward lawlessness was no different from the other seven cities we have reviewed so far in this analysis.

Violent crime in Portland, Oregon, and Seattle, Washington, from 2019 until the end of 2020 was no different from the other eight aforementioned cities, including a 60 percent increase in homicides in Portland and a nearly 250 percent increase in shootings from September of 2019 until September of 2020 in the Oregon city. The city of Seattle, Washington, from 2019 until the end of 2020, saw the highest number of homicides in the city for twenty-six years.[24] Seattle also saw the resignation of 270 cops in an eighteen-month period from 2020 to 2021.[25]

Violent crime in the city of Minneapolis in 2020 ballooned by 21 percent. In 2020, the city recorded 5,422 violent crime incidents, including homicides, rapes, robberies, and aggravated assaults, according to a preliminary report by the police department there. Minneapolis, in the five years before 2020, on average recorded 4,496 violent crimes.[26]

In the city of Saint Louis for the year 2020, the State's Attorney's Office has released 31 percent, nearly one-third, of all the people arrested for a felony in the Missouri city, and these would-be felons were allowed to reenter the society from which they had just been apprehended.

The Chicago police chief, David Brown, reported in July of 2021 that thirty-eight police officers in the city had been shot at or hit in the first six months of 2021. The number of total episodes of this kind may or may not top the 2010 all-time figure of seventy-nine incidents of Chicago police officers being shot at or actually being hit. Chief Brown also criticized the District Attorney's Office for letting suspected murderers back in the community without bail.

In the summer of 2020, the mayor and city council of Seattle reduced the police budget by 10 percent. In the demonstrations that arose from George Floyd's death, Mayor Durkan said it was like being "in a summer of love." Since that time, 250 officers in the Seattle department have resigned, and there's the promise of more in the offing. In late July of 2021, Mayor Durkan began to see the repercussions of these summer of 2020 decisions about public safety in the city of Seattle. Among the things the Seattle mayor said in her July 2021 press conference was, "We need more police officers."

Among these repercussions has been an extraordinary increase in violent crime in the city, including the highest rate of homicides in twenty-six years. There was an increase in homicides of 48.57 percent in 2020 over 2019.[27] Domestic violence deaths quadrupled in 2020 over 2019. And what was true in Seattle was also true in 2020 all over the United States.

In fact, in a review of sixty-six police jurisdictions in the US, sixty-three of them have seen an increase in at least one violent crime in the period from 2019 until the end of 2020. How are we to explain the findings about crime in American cities that we have outlined here?

Several social-scientific theories have been suggested to account for these statistics. This is the subject matter of the next section of this second essay.

Theories and Factors to Explain the Increase in Violence in American Cities

Many social scientists in the last year have offered several factors and theories that may help explain the increased violence in American cities from the beginning of 2019 until the end of 2020. In general, seven different factors and causes have been proffered to explain the increase. We will list these seven factors and causes here and then discuss them one at a time in order.

These seven factors and theories regarding the increase in violent crime in American cities are the following:

1. The COVID-19 pandemic.
2. Reduction of police budgets and subsequent depolicing in American cities.
3. Lack of trust in the police.
4. More guns lead to more violence.
5. The overwhelming of US hospitals led to more deaths.
6. Idle hands make more violence.
7. A downturn in the economy has led to more violence.

In the first of these factors/theories, researchers have pointed out that the COVID-19 pandemic has and will continue to effect and affect every aspect of human life in America. With many people being forced to stay home and live in fear of the new virus, all sorts of unpredictable behaviors must result, including violent behaviors.

Second, the reduction of many police budgets in cities across America, retirements of officers, and a reduction in actual policing in some areas may have contributed to the increase in violent crimes in America. If there are no cops on duty who may prevent crime, then crime becomes easier.

A June 2021 study by the Police Executive Research Forum (PERF), a nonprofit think tank, shows a startling 45 percent increase in the retirement rate among American police officers. In New York City alone, 2,600 officers permanently left the force in 2020. There was a 15 percent increase in police retirements in Chicago in 2020. And even the US Capitol Police in the year 2020 saw the retirement of seventy officers, a startling increase over the year 2019.[28]

A third factor or theory that may contribute to the increase in violent crime across America is what may be called a "lack of trust in the police." In response to the Ferguson case in 2015, some experts have offered the suggestion that certain demographics—like African Americans, for example—have lost their trust in the police. As a result, people have relied more on street justice and other illegal activities to resolve many interpersonal disputes. Thus, they do not call the police.

In the book, *Ghettoside*, one American researcher named Jill Leovy has offered some empirical support of this view. George Floyd's killing and the ensuing protests may have led to a similar phenomenon from May 25, 2020, to the present. Ms. Leovy refers to this factor as *legal cynicism*.[29]

As violent crime has become a more regular phenomenon in many American cities, we have also seen, as a response, an increase in the number of guns purchased since May of 2020. All told, twenty-three million guns were sold in the United States in 2020. This was a 64 percent increase over 2019.[30] More gun purchases, some experts argue, lead to more gun use and, thus, more gun violence. Some researchers at the University of California, Davis, have pointed to this fourth factor as a significant one in explaining the increase in violent crime and violent behavior in the cities we have outlined earlier in this analysis.

Another factor that may have contributed to the increase in violent crimes in American cities in 2020 and 2021 is the fact that many American hospitals in the early COVID-19 pandemic were overwhelmed. Doctors at these hospitals and their staff may not have been able to treat the victims of violent crime as thoroughly as they usually have in the past. That could easily translate to more deaths and more homicides, even if violent crime remained flat or decreased.

Similarly, throughout the pandemic, many people have become bored, with other forms of entertainment—such as restaurants, movie theaters—having closed down. Many schools have been limited or closed completely. Lack of these activities, as well as the anxieties associated with their absence, may have contributed to an increase in violent behavior or crime.

Finally, a bad economy may have forced people to take drastic measures to make ends meet. Disruptions in the flow of drugs in a bad economy may lead to more crime. The bad economy may also have led to less funding for social support that can keep people out of trouble. All this, and more, could have been contributing factors in the reality of more violence and more crime.

It may very well have been the case that the increase in violent crime in American cities across the country is only a short aberration and the high numbers will recede soon enough. Homicide numbers were quite high in 2005 and 2006. But they began to decline after that, and by 2014, they were at record lows.[31]

The notion that we were in a "down economy" from 2019 to 2020 is also suspect. On Donald Trump's watch, the stock market hit record highs many times. His bringing an end to the war in Afghanistan was boon for the economy, for we no longer had to spend all that money on weapons and manpower in the Middle East.

In the third quarter of 2020, while Mr. Trump was still president, the GDP grew a whopping 33.1 percent,[32] far greater than any quarter in the Obama administration, where the growth was never more than 5 percent. One might easily argue that 2020 was not a down economy in almost any sense. Meanwhile, inflation rates in the Biden administration have reached 8 percent and most likely are headed higher. We are waiting, of course, for this to be blamed on Donald Trump, as we can be sure it will be.

The blip on the scale in 2019 to 2021 in violent crime may be just that—a blip. The levels of violent crime spiked at that time, only to dip in the near future. Only time will tell. One set of explanations that has not been considered, however, is the Progressive, woke policies of the American New Left in many American cities.

Certainly, new attitudes toward bail and detention in many American cities, as well as the Biden administration's lack of solutions to solve the crisis at the southern border, may well be contributing factors in the rise of violent crime since Mr. Biden became president. Most adults captured or detained at the southern border are routinely released after two days, allowing them to assimilate into American culture without being tested for COVID-19. In most cases, these captives/detainees are allowed to enter American society with no vetting and no knowledge of whether these people had previously committed violent crimes.

Another factor that may have played a role in the increase in violence in American cities in the last couple of years is the changing attitudes in many legal communities about the idea of cash bail. Washington, DC; New Orleans; Tulsa, Oklahoma; Baltimore; Salt Lake City, Utah; and New York City have each turned to a policy of cashless bail. If implemented, of course, this would directly allow criminals immediately back into the community. If there is no bail, then there is no detention.

To cite one city, Baltimore, from 2014 to 2021, has reduced the number of people released on bonds from 35.6 percent to 14.4 percent. And where do these people go when they have no bonds? Right back into the community.

New York City, on the other hand, passed a new bail reform law that took effect in January of 2020. The goal of the bill was to reduce and eventually eliminate cash bail in New York State altogether.

The city of Saint Louis has instituted the Bail Project, which "combats mass incarceration by disrupting the money bail system." Nevertheless, in just one week in July of 2021, the State's Attorney's Office had an attorney fail to appear three times and fail to produce requested evidence, resulting in a murder case being dismissed.[33]

Among the advocates of cashless bail is President Joe Biden, who proposed the idea in his proposed justice policies that he revealed shortly after having taken office.[34] Indeed, for the most part, all the advocates for cashless bail are Progressive Democrats. Officials in New York, Washington, DC, Baltimore, Tulsa, New Orleans, and Salt Lake City have all followed Mr. Biden's lead, even though some of these legislators working on the issue are Republicans.

Bail reform has been an ongoing concern for several other police jurisdictions, as well as the states of New Jersey, Georgia, and Vermont and the city of Philadelphia, where they conducted something they called a Bail Experiment. Los Angeles district attorney George Gascón has said, "I think eliminating money bail is one of the moral imperatives of our generation."[35]

This may seem like a small matter, but if those denied bail are put back on the streets, then that certainly raises the moral issue of whether any of these detainees denied bail may have continued their crimes when released.

In short, I have argued in this section of Essay Two that the woke beliefs of the New Left in America, including now the Biden White House, may have contributed to the phenomenon of the increase in violent crimes in several cities in America. And among those beliefs are the crisis at the southern border, the New Progressive views on cashless bail, and the Ferguson effect in the George Floyd case in Minneapolis and other riots across America in the summer of 2020 in which both Mr. Biden and Kamala Harris referred to the participants as *protestors*, as well as some of the items in Mr. Biden's proposed economic policies about eliminating cash bail. These may all be relevant in discussing the factors and causes of the increase of violent crimes in American cities since Joe Biden was elected in November of 2020 and became president in January of 2021.

If President Donald Trump was held by some to be fomenting the people who assembled on January 6, 2021, in Washington, DC, then why can we not see Biden and Harris as having fomented the events of the summer of 2020? In short, I think it is not at all far-fetched to speak of the policies of the New Left Progressive woke establishment to be partially responsible for some of the increased violent crime from the end of the year 2019 until the present time.

We can add to the predicament at the southern border that the message about immigration to the United States is often contradictory. On January 20, 2017, Vice President Kamala Harris said, "Everyone is welcome in America." She repeated that same mantra in 2019.

But on June 7, 2021, while speaking in Guatemala, Ms. Harris simply said, "Do not come. Do not come."[36]

In New York City, from 1994 until 2001, when Rudy Giuliani was mayor, he reduced the number of violent crimes in the city by 56 percent.[37] This may be proof that urban violence is not an inevitability. His successor, Michael Bloomberg, presided over violent crimes being reduced even more in the city. During the time of Bill de Blasio in office, however, violent crime again skyrocketed in NYC. Certainly, we must ask if the difference between the Republican administration of Giuliani and the Progressive administration of Mr. de Blasio in regard to violent crime has any value in terms of the rate of violent crime in New York. Some have argued it is a factor to consider.

The city of Chicago has a reported more than one hundred thousand gang members and only an estimated eleven thousand police officers.[38] It will be very difficult to put an ebb in the city's crime if the gang members outnumber the cops by a factor of nearly ten to one.

This brings us to one final section of Essay Two, where we will discuss those advocates in America who have spoken of the idea of "reimagining the police in America," another idea that has gotten some recent play in several places.

Reimagining the Police in America

In this final section of Essay Two, we will describe and discuss what is now referred to as the Reimagining the Police movement or the Reimagining Public Safety approach in certain jurisdictions in the United States. This section will consist of three parts.

First, we will cover the four main elements of the movement/approach. Second, we will speak of some national organizations that have written and published policies on the movement/approach. And third, we will examine five locales in America that have reimagined, or have planned to reimagine, the police or public safety. In the third part, we will examine the efforts of Wilson County, North Carolina; Richmond, California; Northampton, Massachusetts; Berkeley, California; and Minneapolis, Minnesota.

We have chosen these five jurisdictions because our list contains one large city (Minneapolis), one suburban county (Wilson County), two midsize cities (Berkeley and Richmond), and one small jurisdiction (Northampton). Wherever the Reimagining the Police movement is found in the United States, that discussion inevitably involves four separate elements, some of which we have already mentioned in this essay.

These elements may be summarized in this way:

1. Defunding
2. Disbanding
3. Demilitarizing
4. Decriminalizing

In this second essay, we have already said enough about the idea of Defunding the Police and what that movement usually entails. In regard to Reimagining the Police, many jurisdictions are now calling for the complete disbanding of the police as well as the reallocation of those funds into things like housing, drug treatment, and other social services.

A third idea of Reimaging the Police or Public Safety in America calls for what might be called "demilitarizing the police." This refers to the penchant in some jurisdictions to add more and more military-style equipment to American police departments.

And finally, the Reimagining the Police movement also at times speaks about decriminalizing certain crimes in America, such as marijuana possession and distribution and prostitution, for example. I have spoken of this fourth element when we wrote about eliminating cash bail in many jurisdictions. Congressman Lee Zeldin, Republican from New York, wrote an op-ed piece on October 12, 2020, in which he related that in New York City in 2020, shootings were up "166 percent, murders rose by 34 percent and burglaries by 22 percent." The congressman added, "This summer, in one weekend alone, there were fifty-one people shot in New York City." Mr. Zeldin attributed much of that crime to the new provision in the state of New York for cashless bail.[39]

Many national organizations in the past few years have also joined the debate/discussion about the Reimagining the Police movement. Among these organizations are the following: the American Bar Association, the National Association of Social Workers, and the Center for Public Equity based in Los Angeles, California. Each of these three national organizations has developed written policies or suggestions about the Reimagining of Police in the United States.

We should point out, however, that each of these three organizations appears to be run by the New Progressive Left and woke culture, and what they have to say must be understood in that context.

Finally, in this final section of Essay Two, we will speak of five locales in America where the Reimagining the Police movement has been discussed in city, county, and town councils across the

United States. We will speak of each of these five jurisdictions and what they have had to say or have published or written about the issue at hand.

The first of our locales—Berkeley, California—has a population of 120,000; 60 percent of those are White, 21 percent are Asian, and 8 percent are Black. On July 14, 2020, the Berkeley City Council passed eight resolutions to reimagine the police in Berkeley. Berkeley increased its city budget for public safety by $320,000 for 2022. Violent crime increased by 5.86 percent in Berkeley for the year 2020. Its committee on reimagining the police has not yet made a report.

Northampton, Massachusetts, has a population of 29,000, of whom 82.7 percent are White, 8 percent are Hispanic, 3 percent are Black, and 13 percent are Native American or Native Alaskan. The city created the Police Review Commission in 2021, and the committee made several recommendations. Northampton increased its police budget by 3 percent in 2022. The violent crime rate in Northampton increased by 15 percent in 2020.

Wilson County, North Carolina, has a population of 82,000 people, of whom 56 percent are White, 40 percent are Black, and 10 percent are Hispanic. The county increased its police budget from $15 million to $16 million for 2022. The Wilson County Council created the Police Review Commission in 2020, which made several recommendations, mostly calling for increasing the budgets of social services to combat increases in violent crime, which increased 8 percent from 2019 to 2020.

Richmond, California, has a population of 110,000, of whom 37 percent are White, 24 percent are Black, 15 percent are Asian, and 5 percent are Hispanic. Richmond began its Reimagining Public Safety Committee in November of 2020. The committee, as of yet, has not issued a report. They slashed their police budget by $2.3 million for 2022. Violent crime increased by 9 percent from 2019 to 2020 in Richmond.

The population in Minneapolis, Minnesota, is 425,000, of whom 60 percent are White, 20 percent are Black, 6 percent are Asian, and 9 percent are Hispanic. The city formed the Community Safety and Violence Prevention Commission in the summer of 2020. Violent crime increased in Minneapolis in 2020 by 21 percent over 2019, most of that after May 25. Minneapolis cut its police budget for 2021 by $7.7 million. Most of that money has been reallocated to other social services after the death of George Floyd.

The trend in these five locales is that they have tended to decrease the police budget after the death of George Floyd. They have formed committees or commissions to respond to the protests that arose in light of Mr. Floyd's death, while at the same time violent crime has increased in the five jurisdictions mentioned here by an average of 12 percent from 2019 to 2020.

One thing is clear about the idea of reimagining the police. In the five jurisdictions we have mentioned here, residents in those places were polled about reimagining the police. Twenty-two percent of those residents believed their police department needed a "complete overhaul," while 37 percent in the poll preferred "major reforms." Twenty-seven percent, or slightly more than a quarter of the residents polled, said their police department needed a "minor overhaul," while only 5 percent believed the police did not need "any reform at all."

On June 23, 2021, President Joe Biden gave a speech on the rise of violent crime in America, in which he put the blame squarely on guns and gun dealers.[40] In his speech, however, he said nothing about gang violence in cities like Los Angeles and Chicago, where turf wars are likely responsible for many violent crimes. Mr. Biden also said nothing on the fact that the predominant number of people killed by guns in America in the past eighteen months were Black, most of whom were killed by other Black people.

In fact, Black-on-Black crime is rarely discussed in the traditional, mostly Leftist media. Mr. Biden also said nothing about the number of police officers in America who were retiring since the Black Lives Matter violence or "peaceful demonstrations," as the Left called them. As an aside, of the 486 arrests that the NYC Police Department made in regard to that violence/demonstration, half of them were dismissed by the District Attorney's Office, and many more were released without bail so they could return to the same communities from which they had just committed their crimes for which the arrests had occurred.

Contrast those arrests with those made in Washington, DC, on January 6, 2021, where 547 arrests were made and all of them have been, or will be, prosecuted. It is also interesting that homicides have increased by 18 percent since Joe Biden was elected. Mr. Biden did read his entire speech from a teleprompter, which he almost always has during his presidency.

Another interesting fact is that when citizens are polled in the cities where violent crime has soared in numbers recently—when asked in American inner cities about the added crime in a city like Chicago—72 percent still responded that they "trust" the police.

In short, there may be far more factors that go into the making of the increase in violent crime in America. Although Mr. Biden said a lot about guns and gun dealers, he said nothing about gangs, Black-on-Black crime, and the rash of police retirements in cities across the United States. Mr. Biden appears to have missed the boat regarding those factors.

What Mr. Biden did do in his June 23, 2021, address about gun violence, and even earlier in an early April speech in 2021 about the same subject, was deliver a six-point plan for how his administration proposes to deal with gun crime that kills thirty thousand people in the United States every year. These six provisions are as follows:

1. Stop the proliferation of "ghost guns"—guns with no serial numbers that cannot be traced.

2. Ban stabilizing braces that can turn a handgun into a short-barreled rifle.
3. Model red-flag legislature for states regarding people in crisis being barred from possessing guns.
4. Invest in evidence-based community violence interventions.
5. Issue an annual report on firearm trafficking.
6. The ATF and Biden's nominee for director, David Chipman, will take point on these provisions.[41]

There is nothing in these six strategies about guns regarding the fact that more than half of all deaths in America by firearms are suicides.[42] Nor is there anything in them about providing money for suicide prevention or counseling—two obvious needs.

Many of the aspects of these six provisions are in direct conflict with several provisions of the 1994 crime bill that Mr. Biden helped to write. Among these are the imposing of stricter sentencing terms on offenses involving crack versus powder cocaine and the elimination of the federal death penalty, which the legislature authorized as a potential punishment for the increase of crime in the early 1990s. Item number four listed previously is nothing more than the usual Biden-Harris approach—if there is a problem, throw money at it.

Leading up to the 2020 campaign trail, both Cory Booker and Kamala Harris, who later would become Biden's vice president, criticized the 1994 crime bill, essentially because it was not woke enough. In a tweet in July 2019, Mr. Booker wrote, "It's not enough to tell us what you're going to do for our communities. Show us what you have done for the last 40 years."

Ms. Harris, too, during the campaign trail chastised Mr. Biden's role in the 1994 bill. Among her 2019 criticisms was that Biden did not decriminalize marijuana and expunge the federal marijuana offenses, steps that President Biden now supports in his six-point plan. The new Biden-Harris plan on violent crime and guns in America may also be at odds with some of the recent Supreme Court decisions about guns.

In the District of Columbia v. Heller, 554 U.S. 570, decided in 2008, the Supreme Court ruled that the Second Amendment protects an individual's right to keep and bear arms unconnected with service in a militia for traditional lawful purposes, such as self-defense within the home, and that the District of Columbia's handgun ban and requirement that lawfully owned rifles and shotguns be kept "unloaded and disassembled or bound by a trigger lock" violated this guarantee.

The *Heller* decision was decided by a vote of five to four, and the majority opinion was written by Justice Scalia. A similar ruling was made two years later regarding the Second Amendment and due process concerns in the city of Chicago in the 2010 McDonald v. City of Chicago. That decision answered the question, "Does the Second Amendment apply to states because it is incorporated by the Fourteenth Amendment privileges and immunities or due process clauses and thereby made applicable to the states?"[43]

The *McDonald* decision was also made by a five-to-four vote, with Justice Samuel Alito writing the majority opinion. The court reversed the Seventh Circuit's holding that the Fourteenth Amendment makes the Second Amendment right to keep and bear arms for the purpose of self-defense applicable to the states.

The *McDonald* decision involved a Second Amendment challenge to a Chicago city ordinance that essentially banned private handgun ownership in the city. The court said that the citizen's right to bear arms is not absolute and that a wide range of gun control laws remain "presumptively lawful." These included laws that prohibited concealed carry, gun possession by felons and the mentally ill, carrying firearms in schools and government buildings, certain conditions for the commercial sale of guns, and what the Court called "dangerous and unusual weapons and promoted firearm storage to prevent accidents."[44]

In other words, the Supreme Court in the *Heller* and *McDonald* cases overruled the restrictions passed on handguns in both Washington, DC, and in the city of Chicago. Some Conservative commentators have suggested that parts of President Biden's six-point crime scheme announced in June of 2021 run counter to both the *Heller* and *McDonald* decisions.

One police chief who has begun to criticize the Defund or Reimagine the Police movement is LeRonne Armstrong from Oakland, California, where the city council recently slashed $20 million from the police operating budget.[45] On June 28, 2021, Chief Armstrong related that the council did not seem to understand that the move would have dire consequences. Since November 2020, the month when Biden and Harris were elected, carjackings are up 95 percent. Homicides are up 91 percent, nearly double the numbers from 2019 in Oakland. Assaults in the city of Oakland have increased 18 percent since November of 2020.

In the summer of 2021, Chief David Brown of the Chicago Police Department also made some searing comments about the State's Attorney's Office allowing suspected murderers to return to the community without bail.

It would not be at all surprising if other large cities in America run by the Progressive New Left began to see their police chiefs speak about the repercussions that surely will follow as a consequence of their budgets being slashed after the killing of George Floyd in the city of Minneapolis.

In late July of 2021, the state of Washington was the first to pass legislation that would require massive reform and accountability regarding the behavior of police officers. The new law will require background checks on officers before they are hired, dictate when they are authorized to use force, determine how they collect data about it, and establish a new state agency to review police use of deadly force.

Police Chief Rafael Padilla of Kent, Washington, among many

others in the state, observed this regarding the new regulations of police conduct: "When you take the legislation and apply it, that is when you really learn how effective it's going to be."[46] He added:

> The challenge is—and I am going to be very frank here—the laws were written very poorly, and the combination of them all at the same time has led to there being conflicts in clarity and what was intended versus what was written.

It is likely that Washington is only the first state to enact reforms in regard to police behavior. My guess is that many other states—particularly the Democratic-led states—will soon follow, if the Washington reforms and accountability statutes have some success. We will soon see.

This brings us to the main sources for Essay Two, followed by Essay Three, in which I will discuss the topic of abortion in the United States, including the suggestion of a compromise on that issue.

ESSAY THREE

Abortion, the New Left, and a Compromise Position

I

The central purposes of this third essay are to do the following things. First, I will give an account of the American history of abortion. Next, we will examine the provisions of the 1973 Supreme Court case known as Roe v. Wade. Finally, I will examine the Progressive New Left's view of abortion since Roe v. Wade, give a critique of that position, and then, finally, offer a compromise view on abortion between those who say human life begins at conception (the right-to-life view) and those who say abortion is a matter of choice (the Progressive New Left perspective).

Before we move to a summary of the history of abortion in America, I must first point to two qualifications I possess in writing this essay. For several years at the Johns Hopkins University, I taught a course called Death, the Individual, and Society. A full one-third of that course dealt with moral issues related to death in American culture, including suicide, euthanasia, and abortion.

The other qualification I have in constructing this essay is a similar chapter I wrote in my book *Ronald Reagan's Religious Beliefs*, published in 2020 by Crosslinks Publishing.[1] In that volume, I first sketched out the compromise view on abortion that will appear at the end of Essay Three. This brings us to a summary of the history of attitudes toward abortion in America from 1821 to the Supreme Court's controversial decision in Roe v. Wade in January 1973.

The History of Abortion in the United States: 1821 to 1972

The first state in the United States to pass an abortion law was Connecticut in 1821. At that time, Connecticut banned all abortions after what was called *quickening*, the point at which the mother can first feel the fetus in the womb. In 1856, this law was followed by Dr. Horatio Storer of the American Medical Association (AMA), who began a movement to ban abortion in the United States. Prior to that time, first-trimester abortions were considered to be misdemeanors in most states.

By the year 1860, twenty American states had laws limiting abortion. By 1890, the AMA supported a position that abortion should be outlawed unless it was necessary to save the mother's life. This was followed by the American Law Institute (ALI) proposing a model penal code for state abortion laws in America. The ALI code recommended legalizing abortion for reasons including mental or physical health, pregnancy due to rape or incest, or if fetal deformities could be detected.

On April 25, 1967, the state of Colorado issued the first "liberalized" abortion bill in the United States. It, too, allowed abortions in the cases of poor mental or physical health of the mother or fetus as well as those pregnancies resulting from rape or incest. A short time later, other states followed, with bills being passed in California, Oregon, and North Carolina.

Gone from this Colorado bill was any mention of the rights of the fetus to its mental and physical health. This was clearly the beginning of the movement to deny these rights to the fetus in the womb.

The following year, 1968, several other states began to liberalize their views on abortion. The National Right to Life Committee was also formed in the summer of 1968. On April 11, 1970, the state of New York passed a law signed by Governor Nelson Rockefeller that allowed abortion on demand up to the twenty-fourth week of pregnancy. This 1970 New York bill repealed that state's 1830 law that had banned abortion.

Similar laws were passed in Alaska, Hawaii, and Washington State in 1970. On April 21, 1971, the US Supreme Court ruled on its first modern abortion case in the United States v. Vuitch case. The high court upheld a District of Columbia law that permitted abortion to preserve the mother's life or health. The Supreme Court also made it clear that *health* meant "psychological and physical well-being," which effectively allowed abortion for any reason.[2]

Again, there was nothing in these new state abortion laws that spoke of the preservation of the rights of the fetus to its mental and physical health. This is also true in the Roe v. Wade decision, which we will discuss in the next section of this essay.

By the end of 1972, thirteen states had adopted ALI-type abortion laws. Four states now allowed abortion on demand. Mississippi allowed abortion only for rape and incest. Alabama allowed abortion for the mother's physical health, and thirty-one states allowed abortion only to "save the mother's life."[3]

This brings us to the second section of Essay Three, in which we will delineate and discuss the provisions of the 1973 Supreme Court decision, Roe v. Wade, as well as other abortion developments in that same year and afterward.

The Provisions of Roe v. Wade and Other Developments on Abortion

On January 22, 1973, the United States Supreme Court issued its ruling on the Roe v. Wade case. In that ruling, the court found that a "right to privacy," of the Fourteenth Amendment, which the court had established earlier, "was also broad enough to encompass a right to abortion." The court also established a trimester scheme for pregnancy in regard to abortion. In the first trimester, the court suggested, the state could enact no restrictions on abortion. In the second trimester, the government could regulate some provisions but only if "the mother's health was at risk." Roe v. Wade, however, says nothing about the rights of the fetus.

In the third trimester, after viability, a state could ostensibly "proscribe abortion," provided that it made exceptions to preserve the life and health of the woman seeking an abortion. On that same day in 1973, the Supreme Court also issued its decision on a case known as Doe v. Bolton, in which the court defined *health* to mean "All factors that affect the woman, including physical, emotional, psychological, familial, and the woman's age."

In the Roe v. Wade case, Jane Roe was an unmarried pregnant woman in Texas who filed a suit on behalf of herself and others to challenge the abortion laws in Texas. A Texas physician joined Roe's lawsuit arguing that the state's abortion laws were too vague for doctors to follow. The physician in question had previously been arrested for violating the state of Texas's statute.

At the time, abortion was against the law in Texas unless it was done to save the woman's life. It was a crime in Texas to get an abortion or even to seek one. The US Supreme Court, as we have indicated, provided a fundamental "right to privacy" that protected the woman's "right to choose" whether to have an abortion. But the court did not say that this right was absolute. It must be balanced against the government's interests in protecting women's health and prenatal life.

Both sides in the Roe v. Wade case employed several arguments before the Supreme Court. The state of Texas, which defended its abortion restrictions, made three fundamental arguments. These may be summarized this way:

1. The state has an interest in safeguarding health, maintaining medical standards, and protecting prenatal life.
2. A fetus is a person protected by the Fourteenth Amendment.
3. Protecting prenatal life from the time of conception is a compelling interest for the state of Texas.

In these arguments, the state of Texas appears to have suggested that a fetus becomes a person at conception and that person is protected by the Fourteenth Amendment. Ms. Roe and her colleagues, however, made these three arguments before the Supreme Court:

1. The Texas law invaded the individual's right to "liberty" under the Fourteenth Amendment.
2. The Texas law infringed on women's rights to marital, familial, and sexual privacy that are guaranteed by the Bill of Rights.
3. The right to an abortion is absolute—women are entitled to end a pregnancy at any time, and for any reason, and in any way they choose.

In essence, Ms. Roe's attorneys argued that there is no way to establish when a fetus becomes a person, so a woman's right to privacy to do what she wants with her own body becomes paramount.[4]

In the court's decision, it took a compromise position, in that it argued that after the arrival of the third trimester, the state could prohibit abortion. It was a compromise because it was halfway between personhood at conception (the state of Texas's view) and personhood at birth (Ms. Roe's perspective).

The Supreme Court in the Roe v. Wade decision, by a vote of seven to two, decided that unduly restrictive state regulations of abortion were unconstitutional. The majority decision opinion was written by Justice Harry A. Blackmun. He wrote that a set of Texas statutes criminalizing abortion in most instances violated a woman's constitutional right of privacy, which was found to be implicit in the liberty guarantee of the due process clause of the Fourteenth Amendment, which says, "nor shall any state deprive any person of life, liberty, or property without due process of the law."

Since the month of the Roe v. Wade decision, there have been sixty-two million abortions in the United States. Many of these—about two-thirds—have been in the first sixteen weeks of pregnancy. About 45 percent of Americans still see abortion as a form of murder. This must be kept in mind throughout the remainder of this essay.

This brings us to the third section of Essay Three, in which we will examine the views of the Progressive New Left in America in regard to the issue of abortion, as well as a critique of that position.

The Progressive View on Abortion

The general Progressive view of abortion in America can be seen in places like the National Association for the Repeal of Abortion Laws (NARAL) Pro-Choice America's "Statement of Principles." Listed in those principles are the following:

1. As progressives, we stand united in understanding that policies that limit access to abortion and force medically unnecessary procedures are oppressive to women, especially low-income women and women of color.
2. As progressives, we stand united in the belief that a woman's autonomy over her own body is not a secondary issue or a "social justice" issue, but rather a human right

and a necessity in order to attain and preserve economic security in her life.

3. As progressives, we acknowledge that the current economic system is exceptionally punishing to mothers, single mothers, and mothers of color whose wages, job opportunities, and economic advancement suffer due to the "motherhood penalty."

This is followed by three other "principles" on the NARAL website, followed by this conclusion:

> Thus, as progressives, we know to organize, mobilize, and win elections we must field candidates who understand the integral nature of these core values and bring the full power of our collective base to win.[5]

Another way to see the Progressive New Left's position on abortion is to see that every Democratic candidate for president in the 2020 election wanted to repeal the Hyde Amendment, which prohibits federal Medicaid money from covering the costs of abortion.[*6] All ten candidates also agreed that they would use the Roe v. Wade decision as a litmus test when selecting Supreme Court justices. Only two of those ten candidates—Joe Sestak and Representative Tulsi Gabbard—were willing to say that they support restrictions on third-trimester abortions.

Another of the ten candidates for president, Joe Biden, who had supported the Hyde Amendment when it was first proposed, reversed his position in June of 2019 and now said that he was in opposition to the Hyde Amendment and would seek to eliminate it if he were elected. In June of 2019, Mr. Biden is reported to have said, "If I believe that health care is a right, as I do, I can no

* The Hyde Amendment was passed by Congress in 2013.

longer support an amendment that makes that right dependent on someone's zip code."

It is also significant that at the Democratic Party debates leading up to the 2020 election, then-candidate Biden did not support Joe Sestak and Representative Gabbard, who were the only two to outright state that they "support restrictions on third-trimester abortions."

Another example of the Progressive New Left's view on abortion can be seen in Virginia governor Ralph Northam's January 2019 interview with WTOP about third-term abortions. In that interview, Mr. Northam, who was both the governor and a physician, observed:

> Third term abortions are done in cases where there may be severe deformities. There may be a fetus that is nonviable. So, in this particular example, if a mother is in labor, I can tell you exactly what would happen.

Then Governor Northam added:

> The infant would be delivered. The infant would be kept comfortable. The infant would be resuscitated if that's what the mother and family desired. And then a discussion would ensue between the physicians and the mother.[7]

The radio interview with Governor Northam came within the context of HB 2491, introduced in the Virginia state legislature by Democratic delegate Kathy Tran, whose aim was to ease some of the restrictions for abortions in Virginia. Her bill called for the number of doctors who must certify the need for the abortion to be reduced from three to one. It also required that the procedure be done in a hospital; it would also require that any danger to the mother must be "substantial and irremediable."

When Ms. Tran's bill was proposed, she was questioned by Republican delegate Todd Gilbert about whether HB 2941 would allow a live-birth abortion if it was indicated that the mother's mental or physical health would be impaired.

After short hesitation, Ms. Tran said, "My bill would allow that." Later, Ms. Tran corrected herself when she told the *Washington Post*, "I misspoke . . . I should have said: 'Clearly, no, because infanticide is not allowed in Virginia, and what would happened in that moment would be a live birth.'"[8]

The implications for the remarks by Governor Northam and Virginia state delegate Kathy Tran are multiple, but what they have in common is that Northam and Tran were in favor of the perspective that personhood begins at birth, as opposed to the more Conservative understanding that personhood begins at conception.*

President Joe Biden, caving in to the farther Left Progressives of his party, has changed his views about abortion many times over the years. On January 28, 2021, a week after being sworn in to office, President Biden signed an executive order that officially repealed President Trump's global gag order, which restricted health organizations around the world from receiving US assistance in performing abortions or information about abortion procedures as a form of family planning.† Biden's act went directly against public opinion, which showed 77 percent of Americans disagree with the idea of using public funds for foreign abortions.

---

* Ten of the Democratic candidates for president in 2020, during their campaigns, expressed their support of Roe v. Wade, including Joe Biden and Kamala Harris. Mr. Biden's views on abortion have changed several times over the years, but Ms. Harris's perspective has always been that she supports abortion.

† Donald Trump's global ban on using American funds for abortion came in January of 2016. President Biden, in his first day in office, rescinded it.

The Biden-Harris administration also dropped the Hyde Amendment's provision to restrict the allowance of public funding on abortion. Indeed, the announced proposed 2022 Biden budget has taken the Hyde Amendment money out of the forty-sixth president's budget. It must be pointed out, however, that Mr. Biden voted for the Hyde Amendment in 1977, when it was passed.

In 1981, Mr. Biden supported a constitutional amendment that would enable states to overturn Roe v. Wade. In his book *Promises to Keep*, published in 2007, Joe Biden wrote, "While I am personally opposed to abortion, I don't feel I have the right to impose my view on the rest of society."[9] In 2006, Biden called himself the "odd man out" of his party because he did not support federal funding for abortion and voted for bans on the procedure in the third trimester. In an interview with CNN, Mr. Biden related, "I did not vote for funding for abortion . . . I voted against partial-birth abortion—to limit it—and I voted for no restrictions on a woman's right to be able to have an abortion under Roe v. Wade."[10]

Mr. Biden continued in the same interview:

> And so, I made everybody angry. I made the right-to-life people angry because I won't support a constitutional amendment or limitation on a woman's right to exercise her constitutional right as defined by Roe v. Wade. And I have made the groups—the women's groups and others—very angry because I won't support public funding and I won't support partial-birth abortion.

Presumably, the comment about public funding is a reference to Biden's vote for the Hyde Amendment, which had restricted abortion funds for recipients of Medicare and Medicaid, federal employees, women in the armed services, and Washington, DC, residents. Since the Hyde Amendment, however, Mr. Biden has changed his tune about federal funds for abortions, in that he is now in favor of it.

Mr. Biden's proposed 2022 budget omits a ban on federal funding for most abortions, which has been part of government spending bills for decades. Mr. Biden's 2022 budget was released in May of 2021. Mr. Biden, a lifelong Catholic, supported the Hyde Amendment for most of his political career, but he changed his position in the summer of 2019 while campaigning for president, saying the right to an abortion was under assault in many states and increasingly inaccessible to lower-income women.

Mr. Biden's nomination for Health and Human Services secretary, Xavier Becerra, was grilled in late February of 2021 about his views on abortion. Senator Mitt Romney asked the nominee about his views on partial-birth abortion, which refers to a late-term abortion that is medically known as "dilation and extraction."[11] During the procedure, a pregnant woman partially delivers an unborn child "for the purposes of performing an overt act that the person knows will kill the partially delivered, living fetus," the law says.

The Partial-Birth Abortion Ban Act was passed in 2003, at a time when Mr. Becerra was representing the state of California in the US Congress. He voted against the act alongside 132 of the 205 Democrats who were present in the chamber at that time. The bill, which was passed, was subsequently challenged in 2007, at which time the US Supreme Court upheld the partial-birth ban.

It is important to point out, however, that the Progressive New Left in America prefers the name *late-term abortion* to the Conservative moniker of *partial-birth abortion*. This, among other things, makes the procedure politically acceptable under the large umbrella of the Roe v. Wade decision in their view.

Mr. Biden, in his life in Congress, supported the Partial-Birth Abortion Ban Act. But in the summer of 2019, during his presidential campaign, he backed the idea of scrapping the ban as well as the Hyde Amendment, reversing his long-standing position in favor of both the partial-birth bill and the Hyde Amendment.

Needless to say, Mr. Biden's views on the question of abortion in America have undergone a rebirth of sorts. He now appears to be in favor of the Progressive view that a fetus is not a person with rights until that fetus is born. In his 2022 proposed plan for health care, Mr. Biden said he wants to build on the progress made by the Affordable Care Act, which covers access to preventive care and contraceptives. In the new budget plan for 2022, Mr. Biden proposed that "the public option will cover contraceptives and a woman's constitutional right to choose."[12]

This view of Mr. Biden's was contradicted, however, during remarks leading up to the presidential election of 2020 when, in the context of speaking of "codifying" Roe v. Wade, Mr. Biden said, "it is not included in the Constitution." Mr. Biden appears to be contradictory when it comes to whether the right to an abortion is in the US Constitution. This is another example of his long series of contradictions about issues related to abortion rights.

One final issue in this section of Essay Three revolves around the Catholicism of Mr. Biden and other Catholic Democrats, like Nancy Pelosi. The question must be raised: Should the American Catholic bishops allow Catholics like Biden and Pelosi to receive the sacrament of Communion in their churches? The Catholic bishops of America appear to be split on the matter.

On the one hand, there are people like Archbishop Joseph Naumann of Kansas City, who wrote, "Because President Biden is Catholic, it presents a unique problem for us." The archbishop added in an interview with the Associated Press, "It can create confusion . . . How can he say he's a devout Catholic and he's doing these things that are contrary to the church's teaching?"

San Francisco archbishop Salvatore Cordileone has said about the issue at hand, "Abortion is not just one among many important issues . . . it is a direct attack on human life."

American cardinal Raymond Burke has gone so far as calling to mind the Roman Catholic Church's ultimate sanction—

excommunication—when he said politicians "who 'publicly and obstinately' support abortion are 'apostates' who not only should be barred from receiving Communion but deserve excommunication."

The Catholic bishops of America were supposed to meet this month to vote on a resolution on barring Catholic politicians like Pelosi and Biden from receiving Communion. But Bishop Wilton Gregory of Washington, DC, organized a group of bishops who wished to delay or postpone the vote on the resolution. The pastor at the Catholic church in Wilmington, Delaware, where Mr. Biden and his wife also attend, has made it clear that Mr. and Mrs. Biden are welcome to receive Communion in the churches of the bishop's diocese. Father Gillespie, the pastor at the Wilmington church attended by the Bidens, has also indicated that the president has and will be welcome to receive the Holy Eucharist at his church.

A recent editorial in the *National Catholic Reporter*, however, has pointed out that barring Biden from Communion, "will seal the deal on the branding of Catholicism in the United States as a culture war project."[13]

On January 21, 2021, Salvatore Cordileone—the archbishop of San Francisco, Nancy Pelosi's home district—said in a statement about the abortion issue, "Our land is soaked with the blood of the innocent, and it must stop."

In 2010, the previous archbishop of San Francisco—George Niederauer—called Ms. Pelosi's support for abortion "entirely incompatible with Catholic teaching."[14]

In a letter to President Biden congratulating him on his victory, Archbishop José Gómez, the president of the US Bishops Conference, outlined areas of agreement and disagreement between the two. But he also reiterated, however, that the ending of abortion in America is the "preeminent priority." Other American bishops, however, like Chicago's cardinal, Blase Cupich, have issued scathing criticisms of Bishop Gomez's missive to President Biden.

A third American politician who claims to be Roman Catholic is New York congresswoman Alexandria Ocasio-Cortez (AOC). It is clear that she was raised as a Catholic, but there is very little evidence that she still considers it her faith. In an article for the *Huffington Post*, she did identify herself as Catholic, and she frequently refers to her religious beliefs on her Twitter account.[15]

On December 10, 2018, for example, she called herself a "raised Catholic," a way that ex-Catholics often refer to themselves when they are not still practicing their faith.

The staff of the Catholic League did a Nexis search of AOC to learn how often she said or wrote "as a Catholic" or "my Catholic." They found zero references. The sole reference to her being Catholic in the Nexis search was in an interview she gave for an article in *America* magazine, a Jesuit publication, on June 27, 2018. The article was titled, "Alexandria Ocasio-Cortez on Her Catholic Faith and the Urgency of Criminal Justice Reform."[16]

In the article, she indicated that she believes that "all people are holy," which, of course, is polar opposite to the core Catholic doctrine of original sin, which says that all people are depraved by their very natures. Then there is also the question of abortion; again, the view of the right to life is a central belief of the Catholic faith. Ms. Ocasio-Cortez's views on the matter, however, are in line with the New Progressive Left's point of view that a woman has a right to an abortion until the time of birth.[17]

One thing that is clear about the Democratic Party's stance on abortion rights is that Mr. Biden, Ms. Ocasio-Cortez, and Ms. Pelosi all support the idea of the right to an abortion that extends, as Vice President Harris has indicated, "until the moment of birth." This puts all four of these prominent Democrats in the camp that personhood, for moral purposes, begins at birth.[*]

---

* The platform of the Democratic Party mentions the abortion issue and how they support the Roe v. Wade decision. They also support the

Another thing that appears to be true is that many members of the Progressive New Left in America have no idea what the provisions of Roe v. Wade actually are, specifically in regard to the third trimester.

On June 16, after the vote on politicians and Communion was delayed, it was rescheduled. Conservative American bishops again pushed for a statement to signal that President Biden and other American Catholic politicians who support abortion rights should disqualify themselves from receiving Communion.

When the issue finally came to a vote, the bishops passed the Conservatives' proposal, and henceforth, the president should be denied receiving the sacrament. But this was not the first time Joe Biden was refused Communion. In 2020, the pastor of Saint Anthony Church, Father Robert Morey, denied communion at his South Carolina church.

Canon 915 of the *Code of Canon Law* is the theological support of the bishops' view. This canon states:

> Those who have been excommunicated or interdicted after the imposition or declaration of the penalty and others obstinately preserving in manifestly grave sin are not to be admitted to Holy Communion.[18]

Canon 916 requires a believer not to approach to receive Holy Communion with a guilty conscience. And Canon 915 requires ministers who distribute the sacrament to withhold that sacra-

view that a fetus is a person at birth. Only two of the Democratic presidential candidates expressed any reservations about third-trimester limitations on abortion: Tulsi Gabbard and Joe Sestak. The Republican Party's platform also mentions abortion. It opposes the Roe v. Wade decision and tends toward the person-at-conception view, as well as the right-to-life perspective.

ment from those who obstinately practice manifestly grave sin. The support of abortion rights would appear, according to the American bishops, to be one of those sins.

This brings us to the final section of Essay Three, in which we will introduce a compromise view on the abortion question—a compromise that suggests that "personhood" and the acquisition of moral rights in the United States may be found between the traditional Roman Catholic view that one is a person at conception and the Democratic Party's perspective that one becomes a person with moral rights at birth.

One issue in regard to the New Left Progressive view among contemporary Democrats is that they have no idea that the Supreme Court banned abortion after the beginning of the third trimester. Because this fact is not widely known among the Progressives, they go on to believe that an abortion is morally permissible right up to the moment of birth.[19]

The interface of politics and religion should also be raised in regard to Ilhan Omar and Rashida Tlaib, both of whom claim to be observant Muslims. The traditional view in Islam, however, is that a fetus is believed to be a living soul after 120 days of gestation.* If that is true, then it follows that the fetus becomes a person, at least in hadith literature, at seventeen weeks. This, of course, is very far from the forty weeks of gestation—or personhood at the moment of birth—that the Progressive New Left often advocates.

One might ask, then, how Ms. Omar and Ms. Tlaib square their Progressive view on abortion with hadith from al-Bukhārī and other scholars who say abortion is permissible until the 120th day of gestation.

This brings us to the fourth section of this essay on the New Left Progressives and the question of abortion, in which we will

* *Sahih al-Bukhari*, Vol. 4, Book 55, Number 549; Koran 2:228; Koran 5:31.

sketch out a compromise position between the pro-life advocates, who say a fetus is a person at the moment of conception, and the pro-choice believers, who claim that personhood begins at birth.

A Compromise View on Personhood and Abortion

In order to understand my compromise position on abortion about when the fetus becomes a person, we must first make some introductory remarks about how we define *death*—that is, what the American culture now believes about when an individual is no longer a person.

For over three hundred years in the United States, a person was thought to be dead when he or she no longer possessed what were called the "vital signs" of life. This meant no heartbeat, no respiration, and fixed and dilated pupils.

This vital-signs definition of death can be seen in a number of passages in the Old and New Testaments, including Genesis 35:18; 1 Kings 17:21; and Jonah 4:3 as well as Acts 5:10; Mark 15:37; and Luke 23:46. These final two passages use the expression "breathed his last," indicating no longer having respiration. In the 1611 translation of the Bible, the King James Version, the translators employed the expression "giving up the ghost," a view that suggests that death occurs when the soul or spirit separates from the body.

The KJV translators employed that expression in several places in the scriptures, including Genesis 25:8 and 25:17; Genesis 35:29; Lamentations 1:19; and, as we indicated earlier, Mark 15:39; Luke 23:46; and John 19:30. Not to mention Acts 5:5 and 12:23. The same view of death can also be seen in the article on death in the first edition of the *Encyclopedia Britannica* from the mid-eighteenth century in 1768. The encyclopedia related:

> Death is generally considered as the separation of the soul and body; in which sense, it stands opposite to life which consists in the union thereof.

By the nineteenth century, the vital-signs definition of *death* made a comeback, principally because it is difficult to determine when the soul or spirit has departed from the body. Indeed, physicians in the nineteenth century pointed out that the loss of respiration, lowered body temperature, lack of heartbeat, and fixed and dilated pupils were much better signs for the determination of death. That is, until December of 1967.

In early December of 1967, a surgery took place in Cape Town, South Africa, performed by surgeon Christiaan Barnard on a grocer named Louis Washkansky, resulting in the first successful human-to-human heart transplant in human history. The donor was a twenty-five-year-old woman who had been killed in an automobile accident. The surgery is important for our purposes because if the vital-signs definition of death had been used, the surgery would have been prohibited. In fact, using the old definition of death, the surgeon would be killing two people at the same time and then making one of them, miraculously, alive again.

A month later, in January of 1968, this set of facts occasioned the formation of an *ad hoc* committee at the Harvard Medical School in Cambridge, Massachusetts, chaired by Dr. Henry Beecher. His committee's purpose was to redefine death. If American medical facilities were going to continue heart transplants, then adjustments needed to be made to the vital-signs definition.

The Harvard committee issued a report in the summer of 1968. The Harvard committee to redefine death suggested four characteristics to indicate that a human being is dead. These were the following:

1. Unresponsiveness to stimuli.
2. No heartbeat.
3. No respiration.
4. A flat EEG.

The Harvard criteria also said that, "The fourth criterion, the flat EEG, is of the most confirmatory value."[20] What that meant in essence was that the locus of life was no longer to be found in the heart; rather, it was to be found in the brain, as well as the brain stem. What happened next in US history is that states began to adopt a new definition of death, with the Harvard criteria at the center of those new definitions.

The state of Kansas was the first to develop a new statute on death in 1970, followed by Massachusetts, Connecticut, Minnesota, Maryland, Texas, and California, all locations where heart transplants were now being performed—Harvard, Yale, Johns Hopkins, the Mayo Clinic, the University of Texas at Austin, and the University of California, Los Angeles.

In July and August of 1980, a national Conference of Commissioners on Uniform State Laws was appointed and formed in Kauai, Hawaii. The purpose of this conference, among other things, was to develop what was later to become the Uniform Determination of Death Act, which was approved by the AMA on October 19, 1980. The act was subsequently approved by the American Bar Association on February 10, 1981.

In the preface to the act, the National Conference of Commissioners observed: This Act provides a comprehensive basis for determining death in all situations. It is based on a ten-year evolution of statutory language on the subject.

At the end of the same document, the provisions for the Uniform Determination of Death Act were sketched out. These criteria were more or less the same as those the Harvard committee had suggested twelve years earlier. Thus, by the year 1980, all states of the United States had adopted the new Uniform Determination of Death criteria. In other words, the definition of death in America had moved from the vital-signs definition to a definition based on electrical activity in the whole brain and brain stem.

Now, it may be of some importance in the next step of this analysis to ask, "What has this to do with the question of abortion?" The answer is very simple. If we have decided as a culture that what it means to be dead in America is that the brain and brain stem no longer conduct electricity, then why is it not the case that what it means to be a living person in America is when a fetus's brain begins to conduct electricity? In other words, why is a fetus not a living person when its brain initially begins to conduct electricity?

The next step in our analysis should be obvious. When does the fetal brain begin to conduct electricity? The evidence to answer that question is somewhat ambiguous in the medical literature. Ronald Munson, in his book *Intervention and Reflection: Basic Issues in Bioethics*, wrote this about the issue at hand: By the end of the eighth week, some brain activity usually becomes detectable. At this time, the embryo is about the size of a kidney bean, and it now becomes known as a fetus.[21]

Materials found on a website produced by the Mayo Clinic in Minnesota suggest that the fetal brain begins to conduct electricity at "about eleven weeks." Literature from the BabyCenter staff, in an article titled "Fetal Development Week by Week," puts the magic number at twelve weeks. And the Cleveland Clinic website on "Fetal Development: Stages of Growth" suggests that the nervous system and brain and brain stem of the fetus begin "to conduct electricity at sixteen weeks."[22]

Needless to say, we have a range of opinions, from eight weeks to sixteen weeks. For the sake of our analysis, we will take the average of these opinions: twelve weeks. This twelve-week point, of course, is exactly in the middle between the Conservative view of personhood at conception and the Supreme Court view in Roe v.

Wade, which suggested that the cutoff point should be the beginning of the third trimester, or weeks twenty-four to twenty-seven.

This compromise view we have introduced here now occasions another question. Why do we not say that a fetus is a person at thirteen weeks? This would allow a woman to make her decision about abortion up to and including the thirteenth week of pregnancy. Interestingly enough, nearly two-thirds of all American abortions occur before the ninth week (64.5 percent), and 91 percent of all American abortions occur by the thirteenth week of gestation. Only 9 percent of American women have abortions between the fifteenth and twenty-second weeks of pregnancy.

One interesting question about abortion in America is the fact that nowhere is the view of the father ever taken into consideration in the decision-making process of abortion. In America, the father, it seems, has no rights with respect to the fetus, although a philosophical argument from the Progressive Left about that position has not, as of yet, been presented.

The compromise perspective we have presented here is between the conception view of personhood held by many Conservatives and the Catholic Church and the beginning-of-the-third-trimester perspective on personhood held in the Roe v. Wade decision, which would do nothing to satisfy most Progressives of the New Left in America, who argue that personhood begins at birth, even though Governor Northam seems to think it applies in some cases even after birth.

The US Supreme Court announced in mid-May 2021 that they would reconsider the right to an abortion under a Mississippi statute that may drag President Biden into the incendiary political fight that would loom large heading into the midterm election. As a presidential candidate, Mr. Biden largely stayed quiet on the issue, while Elizabeth Warren, Kamala Harris, and other Democratic contenders took the lead in putting forward sweeping abortion-rights policy platforms.

Mr. Biden did concede when pressed, however, that the landmark Roe v. Wade decision that legalized abortion nationwide should be written into federal law and, as we have indicated, the longtime ban on federal funding for abortion, the Hyde Amendment, and President Trump's gag order to limit funding for abortion overseas should both be abolished.

Pressed in mid-May about how the Biden administration will respond to the court taking up Mississippi's ban on abortion after fifteen weeks—a statute that is similar to our compromise view—White House press secretary Jen Psaki told reporters that the administration is "committed to codifying Roe," but she declined to say how such legislation could get through an almost evenly divided Congress.

Ms. Psaki's response, of course, was in line with the administration's general reticence on the subject of abortion. Some Progressive members of Congress and outside groups say they have been struck by President Biden's own silence on the issue of abortion. Since taking office in January of 2021, Mr. Biden has not mentioned abortion in any speeches, videos, or social media posts.

Now the New Progressive Left is calling on Mr. Biden to speak up—and to lay out how he will safeguard abortion access when it faces challenges at the Supreme Court and the states that are pushing for more restrictions.

Samuel Lau, a spokesperson for Planned Parenthood, told *Politico* recently, "It's incumbent on them to use the bully pulpit to shine a light on these attacks and to show that they are standing up for access to sexual and reproductive health care, including abortion."[23] Some Progressives also have called for the Biden Justice Department to submit an *amicus* brief in the Mississippi case, while urging the US Supreme Court to uphold the long-standing precedent protecting access to abortion in America.

Mississippi's attorney general, Lynn Fitch, filed a petition for certiorari with the Supreme Court in June of 2020 to ask the court to review her state's Gestational Age Act, which preserves the right to an abortion before fifteen weeks of gestation. Attorney General Fitch said she hoped that the court would accept the case and "allow Mississippi to defend innocent life as the Legislature and people of this great State intend."

The Supreme Court will not hear the Mississippi case until the fall, and any decision on the case likely will not come down until the following spring or summer. That is, during the run-up to the midterm elections. Mary Ziegler, a law professor at Florida State University who specializes in abortion law, said recently that the court's taking of the Mississippi case will likely accelerate conversations about "expanding the court," or what some might call "packing the court."

Any of these steps, however, from packing the court or passing legislation that would codify Roe v. Wade, would have to involve abolishing the Senate filibuster that would require sixty votes to pass any of these measures.

Ms. Ziegler remarked, "The Biden administration seems to have concluded, up until now, that there was no reason for them to say something about abortion . . . Until now, it was something easier for him to finesse and sidestep. But when the Supreme Court puts it front and center, he can no longer do that."[24]

Since the Roe v. Wade decision in January of 1973, there have been sixty-two million abortions in the United States—that is an average of more than ten million abortions a decade. I grew up in a religious tradition—the same one that Joe Biden and Nancy Pelosi grew up in, Roman Catholicism—to believe that abortion is murder. I know the president and the speaker were taught the same thing, as was Representative Alexandria Ocasio-Cortez. It is difficult for me to see how these three square their religious beliefs with their political points of view on abortion. In fact, I wonder if we should agree with the claim that each of them remains a Catholic in light of their views on the abortion issue.

Some groups of Americans require certain beliefs for membership. In my mind, one of those requirements for being Catholic is that one must be opposed to the practice of abortion. Geraldine Ferraro, while running for president in 1984, reported that there are "many views of Catholic women about abortion." But Bishop James C. Timlin of Scranton, just an hour after Ferraro's speech, rejected her attempt to justify her Catholic faith and her pro-choice beliefs about abortion. The bishop called Ms. Ferraro's position "absurd" and "not a rational position."[25]

The bishop of Scranton related that there is only one view on abortion for Roman Catholics, and that is that it is a form of homicide, exactly the view that Ms. Ferraro must have learned as a child. The same can also be said about Joe Biden, Nancy Pelosi, and Alexandra Ocasio-Cortez.

One of the days when I was most proud of my son, Jack, was when he went with a teacher and some classmates to Washington, DC, to protest against the passing of Roe v. Wade in January of 2018—the Roe v. Wade anniversary. This was the same event where student Nick Sandmann of Covington Catholic High School, who was wearing a MAGA hat, had an encounter with Nathan Phillips, a Native American activist who was playing a drum and singing.

Nick Sandmann was smart enough not to shout or say anything. A few months later, Mr. Sandmann and his family sued the *Washington Post*, NBC, and CNN for libel and defamation. NBC settled their suit with an undisclosed settlement. The other suits are still pending.[26]

It is my guess that Nick Sandmann was there that day because, as a committed Catholic, he believes that abortion is murder and thus is morally wrong. I entirely agree on the matter, and he knew that saying or doing anything that day would ruin the experience. So he demurred, as did my son, of whom I am very proud.

At any rate, the treatment of Nick Sandmann and the Progressive New Left's views on the issue of abortion may be another sign that the United States is now in the midst of a second civil war.

In the year 2017—the most recent available year—there were 862,301 abortions in the United States. That is a rate of 18.3 per every 100,000 of the population. That is less than the rate in 1973, the year of the Roe v. Wade decision, when the rate was 19.3 per 100,000 in the US. The rate in 2014 was over 20 per 100,000, when there were 926,000 abortions in the United States.

Many years ago, in a lecture at the Johns Hopkins University Medical School, I asked 125 medical students how many of them were in favor of killing innocent people. Nearly no one raised his or her hand. But then I asked, "How many of you are in favor of a right to choose abortion?" More than one hundred raised their hands. It was clear that for those medical students, the debate centered on what counted as an *innocent person*.*

More recent polls of Americans on abortion show that 60 percent favored a woman's right to an abortion in the first two trimesters. But when asked about the third trimester, the numbers were fifty-fifty. As many Americans would ban third-trimester abortions as people who would allow them. This is probably the best picture of the contemporary views of abortion in the United States.

This brings us to the sources of this third essay, followed by Essay Four, on the origins of the coronavirus.

---

* The lecture I refer to at the Johns Hopkins Medical School was to second-year medical students in the Robert Wood Johnson Program on May 18, 1995, in Baltimore.

ESSAY FOUR

The Origins of the Coronavirus, China, and the New Left

I

The purpose of Essay Four is to examine the question of the origins of the COVID-19 disease that emerged in China in December of 2019. This essay will be divided into four sections. In the first of these, we will speak of the history of the virus since December of 2019 until the present.

In the second section of the essay, we shall introduce the work of writer Nicholas Wade, who has, perhaps, written more extensively on COVID-19 than any other writer to date. In section three of Essay Four, we will identify and discuss the many cases of lab leaks of diseases into the human population over the last sixty years or so.

In the fourth and final section of Essay Four, we will examine and discuss what the Biden administration has had to say about China and COVID-19, since the forty-sixth president was campaigning for his post in the summer of 2019 until the present time.

International efforts to discover the true origins of the COVID-19 disease have been stymied by the lack of cooperation from the People's Republic of China. Nevertheless, as we shall see in this essay, significant circumstantial evidence raises serious concerns that the COVID-19 outbreak may have been leaked from a Wuhan virology lab. This is the view that I will take in this fourth essay.

In America, Republican officials have pointed to China's "history of research lab leaks resulting in infections" and the warning of US diplomats in China as early as 2017 that the Wuhan labs were conducting "dangerous research" on coronaviruses without following "necessary safety protocols, pricking the accidental outbreak of a pandemic."[1] Republicans have also pointed to public reports that "several researchers in the Wuhan labs were sickened by COVID-19-like symptoms in the fall of 2019, in October and November, two months before the first cases of the virus in the city of Wuhan were reported."

On the other hand, as we shall see in this essay, very little circumstantial evidence has emerged to support the theory that the virus emerged in a natural setting from another species, such as the bat. To date, Chinese scientists "have failed to identify the original species that allegedly spread the virus to humans," which, of course, is critical to the zoonotic transfer theory—that is, that the virus appeared with a natural cause from another species.

This brings us to the first section of this essay, in which we shall provide a short history of what we know of the COVID-19 disease, beginning in the fall of 1999 until the fall and winter of 2021, when Joe Biden was elected and then inaugurated as the forty-sixth president of the United States.

The History of COVID-19

SARS-CoV-2, the official name of the virus, made its appearance in Wuhan, China, in the fall of 2019. The CDC began screening for the coronavirus in three US airports. And the following day, a Washington State resident became the first confirmed person in the United States with the virus. By the end of 2020, the United States had surpassed 20 million infections and nearly 350,000 deaths. Globally, at that time, the number of cases stood at eighty-four million, and the number of deaths worldwide was around two million.

On the final day of January 2020, the World Health Organization (WHO) declared the virus to be a "public health emergency."[2] President Trump followed a couple of days later on February 2, 2020, and declared the disease in America to be a public health emergency, and he also restricted much global air travel to the United States. Passengers on a California cruise ship tested positive for COVID-19 between March 6 and 21. In all, twenty-one people tested positive.

During that same time, the director general of the WHO issued a brief statement in Geneva that the coronavirus was now a worldwide pandemic.

On March 26, 2020, the US Senate passed the CARES Act—the Coronavirus Aid, Relief, and Economic Security Act—that provided $2 trillion in all to hospitals, small businesses, and state and local governments. The following day, President Trump signed the CARES Act into law as the largest economic-recovery package in history. The bipartisan act provided direct payments to Americans as well as expansions in states' unemployment insurance programs.

On May 12, 2020, Dr. Anthony Fauci of the National Institute of Allergy and Infectious Diseases (NIAID) testified before the US Senate and reported that the US death toll of eighty thousand people was most likely an underestimate of the actual figure. A couple of weeks later, on May 21, 2020, AstraZeneca announced a collaboration to speed up the development of a COVID-19 vaccine.

They said they expected the first doses of the vaccine to be available by October of 2020.

By June 10, 2020, the number of confirmed cases of the virus had reached two million in the US, and the number of cases was rising in twenty states at that time. Two weeks later, a study in *Science Translational Medicine* suggested that up to twenty million cases of the flu from March to May 2020 were actually cases of COVID-19. By the end of June 2020, Dr. Fauci warned that the number of new cases in America would soon reach one hundred thousand a day. Meanwhile, several states around the country had put restrictions on the activities of their residents. Most Americans now wore masks, and by July 7, the United States had surpassed three million infections. The United States also began its removal from the World Health Organization. On July 16, the US reported a new record of daily cases of the pandemic, with 76,600 new cases of COVID-19 across America.

By July 22, Health and Human Services (HHS) and the Department of Defense (DoD) announced a vaccination-distribution system agreement with Pfizer and AstraZeneca as well as BioNTech for a December 2020 delivery of one hundred million doses of their COVID-19 vaccines.

One thing that is now frequently overlooked in the Biden-Harris administration is how quickly President Donald Trump, through what he called "Operation Warp Speed," was able to make these vaccines available to the American people. This, of course, along with a secure southern border and energy independence, among other things, was the inheritance of Mr. Biden from Donald Trump.

Some findings from the *New England Journal of Medicine* indicated that the level of antibodies against the virus dropped dramatically from May to July of 2020. A few days later, on July 27, the US Senate introduced the HEALS Act, which provided provisions for new stimulus checks as well as more money for small businesses.

In early August 2020, hospitals faced a shortage of intensive care beds as well as a lack of ventilators for COVID-19 patients. On August 7, talks stalled between Republicans and Democrats on the second stimulus checks, and the unemployment rate in America had added two million people since the beginning of the pandemic.

A week later, on August 13, candidate Joe Biden asked for a three-month mask mandate, and two days later, the Food and Drug Administration (FDA) approved a saliva test. By that same date, COVID-19 had become the third leading cause of death in the United States, and by September 1, the US rejected the WHO global COVID-19 vaccine effort. September 2020 saw a sharp rise in the number of virus cases in Europe. And in early October, both President Trump and his wife tested positive for COVID-19.

The following month, on October 19, worldwide cases hit the forty-million mark, and Joe Biden was elected the forty-sixth president of the United States a few weeks later. A week later, on November 17, 2020, Dr. Fauci highlighted the need for a long-term follow-up on the effects of the COVID-19 disease.

By early December 2020, the FDA had established that both vaccines developed by the Trump administration were at least 90 percent effective, and Americans were now widely vaccinated.

In late December 2020, the United Kingdom experienced another surge of pandemic cases, and by the final day of 2020, the CDC had told us that about 2.8 million people so far had been vaccinated. The CDC also reported that fourteen million doses had been distributed out of a total of twenty million that had been allocated.

In 2014, a group of American scientists who called themselves the Cambridge Working Group had urged caution in the creation of new viruses. In very prescient words, they had specified the risks of creating a SARS-like virus when they wrote, "Accident risks with newly created potential pandemic pathogens raise grave new concerns." The Cambridge Group went on to say:

> Laboratory creation of highly transmissible, novel strains of dangerous viruses, especially but not limited to influenza, poses a substantially increased risks. An accidental infection in such a setting could trigger outbreaks that would be difficult or impossible to control.[3]

In 1975, at a public conference held at Asilomar, the subject matter of the conference was the techniques for moving genes from one species to another. Despite much internal opposition, the molecular biologists of the Asilomar group drew up a list of stringent safety measures that could be relaxed in the future—and duly were—when possible hazards had been better assessed.

The conference center at Asilomar was originally built as a hotel in 1911, but it became a conference center a year later. It is located east of Moss Bay on the Monterey Peninsula in California. The conference there on genetic techniques was held in the spring of 1975. The conference was held to begin to discuss the moral implications of recombinant DNA research.

This brings us to the second section of Essay Four, in which we will explore the two main theories about the origins of the COVID-19 disease by looking at the work of writer Nicholas Wade, the most informed and cogent American writer on the question of the virus's origins.

Nicholas Wade on COVID-19 Origins

Nicholas Wade (born 1942) is a British-born journalist who immigrated to the United States in 1970 at the age of twenty-eight. He has served as a staff writer and editor for *Nature* and *Science* and as a science writer for the *New York Times*, whose staff he joined in 1982 and retired from in 2012. He now writes occasional pieces for various publications.

On May 5, 2021, Mr. Wade published a lengthy essay in the *Bulletin of the Atomic Scientists*. In this essay, Mr. Wade sketched out the two most likely views on the origin of the COVID-19 disease: that it came from nature or that it was from a laboratory leak. Mr. Wade suggested in the essay that a leak from the Wuhan Institute of Virology was the most likely theory.

In his essay, Mr. Wade began by telling his readers:

> In what follows, I will sort through the available scientific facts, which hold many clues as to what happened, and provide readers with the evidence to make their own judgments.

Mr. Wade went on to say the following in the essay:

> I'll describe the two theories, explain why each is plausible, and then ask which provides the better explanation of the available facts. It's important to note that so far there is *no direct evidence* for either theory . . . So I have only clues, not conclusions, to offer. But those clues point in a specific direction. And having inferred that direction, I am going to delineate some of the strands in this tangled skein of disaster.[4]

For the most part, Dr. Anthony Fauci, as well as the worldwide Progressive press, has favored the theory that COVID-19 began in the natural world. In an article in the journal *Lancet* from February 19, 2020, the signers of a letter wrote: "scientists . . . overwhelmingly conclude that this coronavirus originated in wildlife." It later turned out that the *Lancet* letter had been organized and drafted by Peter Daszak, president of the EcoHealth Alliance of New York. Mr. Daszak's organization had funded "gain-of-function" coronavirus research at the Wuhan Institute of Virology in China. Gain-of-function research is medical research that genetically alters an organism that enhances the biological functions of gene products. In other words, it is a process that makes pathogens such as the coronavirus more deadly in a human population. Both the US and the European Union strictly regulate such research.

Mr. Daszak and his company had much at stake. If the COVID-19 disease escaped from a Wuhan lab that he had funded, then Mr. Daszak may be potentially culpable. This obvious conflict of interest was not declared to the *Lancet*'s editors, nor to their readers. On the contrary, the letter to *Lancet* concluded this way: "We declare no competing interests."*

In the March 17, 2020, edition of the journal *Nature Medicine*, an opinion piece written by Kristian G. Andersen of the Scripps Research Institute and others concluded, "Our analyses clearly shows that the SARS-CoV-2 is not a laboratory construct or a purposefully manipulated virus."[5]

Mr. Wade goes on in his essay to describe the two arguments that Dr. Andersen and his group employed in their opinion piece, and Mr. Wade's conclusion about those two arguments was that they were "grounded in two major speculations." The natural-emergence theory remained the media's preferred theory until February of 2021, when the WHO made a trip to the Wuhan labs. Among the group of scientists who were on the WHO commission that visited China was the ubiquitous Peter Daszak.

When the WHO asked the US government to submit three names for the fact-finding mission in Wuhan, they did so. An FDA veterinarian, a CDC epidemiologist, and an NIAID virologist. None of these was deemed acceptable by China. Instead, only one representative from the United States made the cut—and that was, not surprisingly, Peter Daszak.

Afterward, the commissioner who visited Wuhan for the WHO asserted before, during, and after their trip that the COVID-19 disease began as a natural event. Both SARS and MERS had been shown to have had origins in nature. But similar evidence for the SARS-CoV-2 pandemic has yet to be found.

By February of 2021, the lab-leak theory had made a comeback. Among the reasons for that was the revelation that a few Wuhan lab workers had exhibited COVD-19-like symptoms in

* The comments on Mr. Daszak and his role in the funding of the COVID-19 research in China are covered extensively in Nicholas Wade's essay.

October and November of 2020, when they had been hospitalized. The proliferation of lab leaks in major labs throughout the world, going all the way back to the 1960s, also began to be studied. We will take up this issue of lab leaks in the third section of this essay.

In the meantime, Nicholas Wade went on in his *Bulletin of the Atomic Scientists* article to give a plethora of evidence for the lab-leak hypothesis. Mr. Wade also pointed out in the essay regarding the Chinese authorities that "They had suppressed all records at the Wuhan Institute of Virology and had closed down its virus databases completely." Mr. Wade also wrote about the Chinese:

> They released a trickle of information, much of which may have been outright false or designed to misdirect and mislead. They did their best to manipulate the WHO's inquiry into the virus's origins and led the commission's members on a fruitless run-around. So far, they have proved far more interested in deflecting blame than in taking steps necessary to prevent a second pandemic.

At any rate, Mr. Wade remained strongly behind the lab-leak theory, though he never came out directly to suggest that the leak of SARS-CoV-2 may have been deliberate. What did follow, however, was an effort from the Liberal American media to discredit Nicholas Wade.

Indeed, in articles in the *New York Times* and the *Washington Post* as well as the *Wall Street Journal*, all published editorials or opinion pieces endorsed the "credibility" of the theory that COVID-19 was released from the Wuhan Institute of Virology. Marc Thiessen's article in the *Washington Post* included a headline that said: "The case that the virus emerged from nature, not a lab, is falling apart."[6]

Nicholas Wade also began to be criticized for a book he published in 2014 titled *A Troublesome Inheritance: Genes, Race, and*

Human History. Many critics began calling Mr. Wade a racist. One of many examples of this phenomenon is a review of Wade's book by Eric Michael Jonson in the *Scientific American* called "On the Origin of White Power." In his review, it is perfectly clear to me that Eric Jonson believes that Nicholas Wade is a racist.

It seems to me that the same conclusion was made by *New York Times* columnist Bret Stephens, in comments about Mr. Wade in an article about his book, as well as many other Left-leaning reviews of the work. Included in these other perspectives was a May 29, 2020, op-ed piece in the *New York Times* with a headline that said, "Why the Lab Leak Theory Matters."

Other critics of Mr. Wade's book and essay also began to emerge. A number of the geneticists whose work Wade used in his book began to call the journalist to account for misrepresenting their research. A group of these scientists, in a letter to the *New York Times*, wrote:

> Wade juxtaposes an incomplete and inaccurate account of our research on human genetic differences with speculation that recent natural selection has led to worldwide differences in I.Q. test results, political institutions, and economic development. We reject Wade's implications that our findings substantiate his guesswork. They do not. We are in full agreement that there is no support from the field of population genetics for Wade's conjectures.[7]

One final aspect about China and the origins of the coronavirus is that Chinese officials and news outlets have suggested three different times that some entity of the United States is responsible for the virus. The first of these theories is that SARS-CoV-2 came from infected frozen food from the United States. A second theory suggested by China in late 2020 is that the virus came from an American military laboratory. In an article on the virus by Lily Kuo in Hong Kong, she quoted a Chinese official who related, "It might be the US Army who brought the epidemic to Wuhan." Foreign Ministry spokesperson Zhao Lijian, in mid-March 2020, in a headline-grabbing moment, suggested the virus "might have been brought to Wuhan, the original center of the pandemic by the US military."

In late 2020, Chinese officials and scientists put the blame on American biolabs where virus research was being conducted. "It may have escaped from a US biological research facility." And finally, Chinese officials also blamed the United States for its supposed overreaction and falsely claiming that Washington was the first to impose travel bans. But there is also a clear desire on the part of the Chinese to divert anger away from officialdom and toward an external foe—the United States of America. In early February 2020, Chinese Foreign Ministry spokesperson, Hua Chunying, said, "The US actions could only create and spread fear, instead of offering assistance."[8]

Needless to say, there is no evidence that any of these three suggestions made by the Chinese government could be true.* One thing that is true is that in the four years in which Donald J. Trump was in office, the Chinese government increased the number of political rants about America by a factor of at least three times.

This brings us to the third section of this essay on the origins of the COVID-19 disease, in which we will make a number of other observations about just how frequently laboratory leaks occur in major labs across the globe.

---

* I have also viewed a December 9, 2016, YouTube interview of Peter Daszak of EcoHealth with Kani Everington of *Taiwan News*, just a few days before the Wuhan Institute announced the outbreak of COVID-19. The same interview was aired a second time on January 18, 2021, but Mr. Daszak's comments on the gain-of-function research that he sponsored in Wuhan were heavily edited from their original form. This is perhaps another example of the secrecy of the People's Republic of China.

World History of Lab Leaks: 1960 to Present

One question that has to be raised about the origins of the coronavirus is: Just how often do leaks occur in labs all over the world? The answer to that question is that every year since the 1960s, hundreds and perhaps thousands of diseases and viruses have escaped labs all over the world. The smallpox virus, for example, escaped three times from labs in England in the 1960s and '70s. They caused one hundred infections and several deaths.

Dangerous viruses and diseases have leaked out of labs almost every year since then. The US government has controlled research into "select agents and toxins" that pose serious threats to human health, from the bubonic plague to anthrax, for example. There are sixty-six select agents and toxins regulated under a program, and nearly three hundred labs are approved to work with these diseases and toxins.

The researching of these pathogens and toxins allows us to develop vaccines, diagnostic tests, and clinical treatments. Advanced biological techniques also allow for more controversial forms of research, including making diseases more virulent and deadly to anticipate how they may perform and mutate in the wild. This kind of research, then, can be a very important and critical part of public health. Unfortunately, the facilities that do this kind of research are sometimes also plagued by a serious problem—human error.

The 1978 smallpox leak was caused by carelessness, poor lab safety procedures, and badly designed ventilation in the lab where the leak occurred. We would like to think that these kinds of errors are things of the past. But scary accidents—caused by human errors, software failures, maintenance problems, or a combination of all these things—are hardly a thing of the past.

In 2014, the FDA found unclaimed vials of virus samples in a cardboard box in the corner of a cold storage room. Six of those vials were smallpox. No one had kept track of them. No one knew they were there. They may have been there since the 1960s, when the first modern smallpox leak happened. In an investigation that followed, the FDA found persistent and horrifying shortcomings in the handling of these incredibly dangerous substances.

Also in 2014, a lab researcher accidentally contaminated a vial of fairly harmless bird flu with a far deadlier strain. The deadlier bird flu was shipped across the United States to a lab that did not have proper lab restrictions in place.

The CDC's Select Agents Program requires that all examples of "theft, loss, release, causing of an occupational exposure, or release outside the primary biocontainment barriers" of agents and toxins on its watchlist must immediately be reported. Between 2005 and 2012, the CDC received 1,059 reports, or an average of an incident every few days. Here are a few examples:

- In 2008, a sterilization device malfunctioned, unexpectedly opened, and exposed a nearby unvaccinated worker to undisclosed pathogens.
- In 2009, a high-security bioresearch facility that was rated to handle the Ebola virus, smallpox, and other dangerous pathogens had its decontamination showers fail. The pressurized chamber kept losing pressure, and a door back into the lab kept bursting open while researchers leaned against it to keep it closed. Building engineers were eventually called to handle the chemical showers manually.
- In 2011, a worker at a lab that studied dangerous strains of bird flu found herself unable to shower after a construction contractor accidentally shut off the water in the building. She removed her protective equipment and then left without having a decontamination shower that was required by protocol. She was then escorted to another building and had a contamination shower there, but pathogens certainly could have been released in the meantime.

The vast majority of these and other mistakes like them infect no one. And while 1,509 is an eye-popping number of accidents, it also reflects a low number of those working in controlled biological labs.

These kinds of mishaps do not occur only in labs in America. Between June of 2015 and July of 2017, for example, British labs reported forty incidents at special laboratories. This amounted to one lab leak every two or three weeks.

The condition known as Severe Acute Respiratory Syndrome, or SARS, had an outbreak in 2003. Since then, we have not found the disease in the wild, but there have been six separate incidents of SARS escaping labs—one in Singapore, one in Taiwan, and four at a lab in Beijing.[9]

USA Today had a reporter on the biohazard beat for five years. Her name was Alison Young. Ms. Young's stories had headlines like "Hundreds of Bioterror Lab Mishaps Cloaked in Secrecy" (8/17/14) and "CDC Failed to Disclose Lab Incidents With Biotech Pathogens to Congress" (6/23/16).

Alison Young no longer writes for *USA Today*. Will we ever know the truth about the origins of the COVID-19 disease? Dr. David Relman, of Stanford University Medical School, has been advocating for a 9/11-type commission to examine the origins of the virus responsible for the pandemic. But 9/11 took place on a single day, whereas, "This has so many manifestations, consequences, and responses across nations. All of that makes it a hundred-dimensional problem."[10]

Viruses that escaped from American labs in the last forty years include the following:

- 1978: Foot-and-mouth disease
- 2001: Anthrax
- 2004: Foot-and-mouth disease
- 2005–2015: Anthrax

- 2009: Scrub typhus
- 2010: Hog cholera (swine fever)
- Cowpox
- 2013: H5N1
- 2014: H1N1
- 2014: Anthrax
- 2014: Smallpox
- 2016: Zika virus

Lab leaks in international labs over the same period include:

- 1966: Smallpox (UK)
- 1967: Marburg virus (West Germany)
- 1971: Smallpox (Soviet Union)
- 1972: Smallpox (UK)
- 1976: Ebola virus (UK)
- 1977: H1N1 (Soviet Union/China)
- 1978: Anthrax (Soviet Union)
- 2005: Ebola virus (Russia)
- 2007: Foot-and-mouth disease (UK)
- 2008: SARS (Singapore)
- 2009: Ebola virus (Germany)
- 2011: Dengue (Australia)
- 2012: SARS (Taiwan)
- SARS (China)
- Anthrax (UK)
- 2014: Ebola virus (Sierra Leone)
- Dengue (South Korea)
- 2018: Ebola virus (Hungary)
- 2019: Prions (France)
- Brucellosis (China)[11]

These many narratives of escaped pathogens have a number of common themes.* In an article for the *Bulletin of the Atomic Scientists*, medical historian Martin Furmanski spoke of some of these themes when he wrote:

> There are unrecognized technical flaws in standard biocontainment, as demonstrated in the UK smallpox and FMD cases . . . The first infection, or index case, happens in a person not working directly with the pathogen that infects him or her, as in the smallpox and SARS escapes. Poor training of personnel and slack oversight of laboratory procedures negate policy efforts by national and international bodies to achieve biosecurity, as also shown in the SARS and smallpox escapes.[12]

The search for the origins of the COVID-19 disease is made more complicated when the laboratory involved takes place in a closed, secretive society. The difficult job of confirming the source of a virus outbreak becomes much more complicated. One good case in point is an infamous anthrax outbreak in Sverdlovsk in the Soviet Union in the late 1970s. In early 1979, many rumors of anthrax killing dozens and even thousands of Russians began to trickle out to the West.[13]

Recently, White House press secretary Jen Psaki, in early May 2021, also called on China and the WHO to allow international experts "unfettered access" and to allow them to ask questions of people on the ground at the time of the outbreak. Ms. Psaki also said that these medical experts are still reviewing the WHO report,

---

* We have said nothing about how the Russian smallpox leaks from the late 1970s were as secretive as the COVID-19 disease in 2019 to the present. Ronald Reagan believed the Russian event was a "deliberate, military weapon." One only wonders about that possibility in regard to the current virus.

but the White House believes it "doesn't meet it at the moment."[14]

Later that same year, 1979, the Soviet journals began to confirm some of these rumors, even confirming that upward of hundreds of people had contracted anthrax after ingesting contaminated meat. More than sixty people died. But perhaps this tragedy was inevitable, for anthrax had been discovered in local animal populations for years. Some of Ronald Reagan's CIA analysts in 1980 hypothesized that the Soviets had mistakenly released a weaponized form of anthrax. The secrecy and privacy of the Soviet society did not help the effort to get to the bottom of the outbreak. Mr. Reagan was convinced that the anthrax outbreak was intentional and came from a "closed society." Perhaps we are in a similar situation today in regard to COVID-19.

China's closing of any access to the records of the Wuhan labs, as well as the closing down of its databases in viral research, has not aided international scientists in making a final judgment about the origins of the COVID-19 worldwide pandemic. We must take the Chinese secrecy and privacy into account when making a final judgment about the origins of the COVID-19 disease.

Needless to say, the lab-leak theory suggested by Nicholas Wade appears to be alive and well. And his theory must be kept in mind when the Biden administration speaks and writes about the issue in the future. Indeed, the final section of this essay is on what President Joe Biden's relationship with China has been over the years, as well as those of his family members. We will also, in the final section of this essay, discuss what the Biden-Harris administration has said and written about the COVID-19 outbreak.

The Bidens on China and the COVID-19 Outbreak

In 1997, at a time when the United States enjoined supreme power in regard to the rest of the world, National Security Advisor

Zbigniew Brzezinski, in his book *The Grand Chessboard: American Primacy and Its Geostrategic Imperatives*, observed that:

> Potentially, the most dangerous scenario would be a grand coalition of China, Russia and perhaps Iran, an antihegemonic coalition united not by ideology but by complementary grievances. It would be reminiscent in scale and scope with the challenges once posed by the Sino-Soviet Bloc, though this time China would be the likely leader and Russia the follower.[15]

It should be clear that Mr. Brzezinski's fear has now come true. But a number of issues have arisen about China-US relations, particularly since Joe Biden has become president of the United States and while he was running for that office as well.

One issue has to do with how Mr. Biden views China. In early May 2019, while running for president, Mr. Biden related that, "China is not competition for the US. They are not bad folks, folks." He told an audience this while campaigning in Iowa.[16] By April of 2021, however, the forty-sixth president appeared to have changed his tune about China. A senior adviser said at the time, "When Biden announces a package of spending proposals to Congress, he will talk about the investments necessary for our economy to compete with China."[17] I thought Mr. Biden said they were not competition!

The pairing of domestic policy and international policy is not new—most recent US presidents have done the same thing. Mr. Biden has ratcheted up the stakes by suggesting that the US's survival as a democracy depends on competition with China and how that competition plays out.

The notion is that in a space of two years, Mr. Biden appears to have changed his view about whether China is competition with the US. Several other issues with China should also remain on the front burner. Among these is, what are the implications of the dealings of Joe Biden's son, Hunter, in China and the Ukraine?[18]

In several interviews, Hunter Biden has related that the laptop left in a Delaware pawn shop in 2019 may have been his laptop, or, as he also related, "part of a Russian misinformation scheme." In regard to the latter possibility, the *Daily Mail* on April 8, 2021, said that the contents of the laptop "have been verified by cyber forensic experts."[19] The paper hired the firm of Maryman & Associates, a California company that says on its website that it has over twenty years of experience.

The *Daily Mail* also said that the company had matched the content of the laptop with email addresses, content from an iPad and iPhone, and a serial number on the phone connected to Hunter Biden.[20]

In the fall of 2020, a former partner of Hunter Biden, a man named Tony Bobulinski, told Fox News, contrary to the president's statements that he had nothing to do with Hunter's business affairs, that Hunter had frequently asked for his sign-off or advice on various deals in China. Mr. Bobulinski went on in the interview to say that he had met Joe Biden on two separate occasions to discuss business deals with China. The first time was in May of 2017, when Mr. Biden was a private citizen.

Mr. Bobulinski also related that when he asked the president's brother, James, whether the family was concerned about possible scrutiny of the former vice president's business deals with China, James Biden replied, "Plausible deniability." Mr. Bobulinski also said in the interview that he was invited by Mr. Trump to be his guest at the final presidential debate in Nashville on October 22, 2019.[21]

A third issue about Joe Biden and China has to do with his stated belief that the international policies will be "drastically different from those of my predecessor."[22] In an article for the *Wall Street Journal*, however, written by Alex Leary and Bob Davis on June 10, 2021, the pair wrote under the headline "Biden's China Policy Is Emerging—and It Looks a Lot Like Trump's."

Two examples that Leary and Davis gave in their article were Mr. Trump's attempt to crack down on Chinese platforms, such as TikTok, and a list of sixty-seven companies that Trump has black-listed for maybe stealing military secrets and technology. Mr. Biden's retention of the latter issue was confirmed in early June 2021, when he signed a presidential order that amended the Trump ban to fifty-nine firms involved in China's defense and surveillance technology sectors, and fifteen names were added on a Pentagon list of Chinese military-controlled companies. But unlike Mr. Trump's list, the Biden list does not affect subsidiary companies on the list.[23]

Finally, another issue continued over the central claim of this essay—the origins of the COVID-19 disease. On May 26, 2021, in the briefing room, President Joe Biden made a statement on the investigation into the origins of COVID-19. Mr. Biden announced that in early 2020, he had his national security advisor task the Intelligence Community to prepare a report on the most up-to-date analysis of the origins of COVID-19, "including whether it emerged from human contact with an infected animal or from a laboratory accident."[24]

In the statement, Mr. Biden went on about having received that report earlier in May and asking for "additional follow-up." The president also suggested that he expected to receive the follow-up report within ninety days. That would mean the second report would be finished sometime in August of 2021. But this raises the question of what Mr. Biden will do if the second report's findings lean in the direction of Nicholas Wade's lab-leak theory.

At the recent G7 summit in early June 2021, the United States and its allies called for a "timely, transparent, expert-led and science-based" study on how the virus first emerged. WHO Director-General Tedros Adhanom Ghebreyesus also has reiterated that China should be more forthcoming about the matter.[25] But at that point, in the summer of 2021, that would seem most unlikely.

History, it would appear, lends credibility to the idea that our current disaster, COVID-19, may not have a natural origin—that some as-of-yet undetermined combination of human error or reckless research may account for the initial spread of the coronavirus. But there is something else to remember as well—something that history can also tell us. When it comes to lab leaks of viruses across the world, it often takes a long time to tell the story. And sometimes the answers about a virus are profoundly unsatisfying and incomplete. In the case of the COVID-19 disease, we must prepare ourselves for the possibility that we may never know the precise origins of a pandemic that has killed millions, including 650,000 Americans.

By 2021, a growing number of American scientists had begun to adopt the lab-leak theory of Nicholas Wade. One of those scientists is the former head of the CDC, Dr. Robert Redfield. Speaking to CNN in an interview on March 26, 2021, Dr. Redfield observed that the most likely etiology is the virus escaped from a lab and that it is not unusual for respiratory pathogens to infect laboratory workers.[26]

Dr. Redfield added in the interview, "But I am not implying any intentionality in regard to the escape of the virus." At any rate, the toll on the world at that time included three million deaths worldwide and nearly 650,000 in the United States, to say nothing of the losses to businesses, hospitals, and other industries that have been adversely affected by COVID-19.

In a letter published in early May 2021 in the journal *Science*, eighteen scientists wrote, "We must take hypotheses about both natural and laboratory spill-overs seriously until we have sufficient data. Public health agencies and research laboratories alike need to open their records to the public."[27] Among the signers of that letter was Dr. Alina Chan, a geneticist at MIT's Broad Institute who has long argued for the laboratory theory—Nicholas Wade's theory—to be more thoroughly considered. In an interview with

NPR in May of 2021, Dr. Chan said, "Our lives depend on finding out how this virus got started, so we can prevent another one from getting started five or ten years from now."[28]

Another of the signers of the *Science* letter was Dr. David Relman, professor of microbiology at the Stanford University Medical School. He criticized the WHO report that indicated that the pandemic virus was caused by a lab leak when he said, "The report dedicated only 4 of its 313 pages to the possibility of a laboratory scenario, much of it under the heading titled 'Conspiracy Theories.'" Dr. Relman added, "Multiple statements by one of the investigators lambasted any discussion of a laboratory origin as the work of dark conspiracy theorists."[29]

A third signer of the letter to *Science* was Dr. Gregory Gray, a Duke University professor, has also called for a more thorough evaluation of the lab-leak hypothesis.[30]

Another factor to be considered when evaluating the lab-leak theory is that President Donald Trump supported that view while president. Since most medical academics tend to be Democrats, and perhaps haters of President Trump, then it makes good sense to those scientists to say the lab-leak theory is part of a conspiracy as well as racist toward the Chinese people.

President Trump was criticized for calling COVID-19 the "China virus." And yet, the Ebola virus got its name from the Ebola River, to say nothing of German Measles, the Spanish Flu, and many other diseases that got their names from where they began.

Indeed, these eighteen scientists who signed the letter to *Science* and a *Wall Street Journal* story in May of 2021 put the Nicholas Wade lab-leak theory back in the medical mainstream. This is precisely where it should be.

One final scholar who supports the lab-leak theory is Chinese virologist Dr. Li-Meng Yang, who, in an interview on the Tucker Carlson show on June 30, 2021, not only supported Nicholas Wade's theory but also argued that the COVID-19 disease was made and paid for by a Chinese military lab. After being hassled in her own country, she came to the United States in April of 2020, where she now lives in hiding.[31]

In 2015, when Mr. Obama was president and Joe Biden was vice president, the French government warned the United States that the Chinese military and scientists at the Wuhan Institute of Virology—which the French helped them to build—were in the process of creating deadly new viruses in their labs, labs that would later be given US money for some of the research. One wonders how much Joe Biden knew about the messages from France. But maybe he was more concerned about the multimillion dollars that he; his son, Hunter; and his brother James appear to have made from the Chinese. This may be why we have seen a change from the "They are not bad folks, folks" on Mr. Biden's part in 2019 to his current view that the Chinese are the rivals of the United States.

The comments of Dr. Li-Meng Yang look eerily familiar to what the French government told the Obama administration in 2015. We wonder how much and what Joe knew on the matter—and when. In the meantime, the ninety-day timeline to get back to the president about the cause of COVID-19 is rapidly approaching in August of 2021. What will Mr. Biden do if his Intelligence Community tells him that the best theory of explanation is the lab-leak theory?

Finally, in late July 2021, the US Border Patrol in the city of La Joya, Texas, released into the custody of a charity there a large group of migrants. The families were taken to a hotel to live, even though many of them were COVID-19 positive. When they were discovered coughing and sneezing at a La Joya restaurant without masks, the police were called. They were told that the group had come to America two days before and had tested positive for COVID-19. This raises the question of how many immigrants with the COVID-19 disease are crossing the southern border. This is an issue that I will discuss more in the following essay, number five.

In fact, it turns out that the Biden administration is spending $86 million on hotel rooms for migrants across America.[32] In fact, the Biden administration has secured a contract with hotels near the southern border in Arizona and Texas to house 1,200 migrants. The contract is to last six months.

Hotels and motels have been used by immigration officials before, including in 2020, when hundreds of migrants—including children—were held and housed in major hotel chains before being deported under President Trump's pandemic border ban.

In a widely shared tweet, Republican representative Lauren Boebert of Colorado claimed the funds allocated by the hotel contract resulted in migrant families staying in hotel rooms costing $395.00 a night. Ms. Boebert said in her tweet:

> So Biden is spending $86 million to purchase hotel rooms for 1,200 illegal alien families for six months. By that math, he's spending around $395.00 a night per room. How many of you have stayed in a $395.00 a night hotel room?[33]

One only wonders if this is the only "contract" that the government has secured to house immigrants. It would also be interesting to know how these 1,200 immigrants eat their meals and who pays for them. A statement from the US Immigration and Customs Enforcement (ICE) suggests that the contract also covers "other necessary services," so it is not just the cost of the rooms being provided by the US government.

The WHO, which in 2020 called a lab leak "highly unlikely," a year later, in the summer of 2021, said that the lab-leak theory was "probable." Quite a change in a span of fourteen months. It will be of some interest to see what the ninety-day Intelligence Community study ordered by President Biden will have to say later in August of 2021, particularly since the president said about the Chinese, "They are not bad folks, folks."

One final item and a question about the COVID-19 vaccination and the possible mandates that seem to be coming next: What ever happened to the "My body, my choice" view? If the Fourteenth Amendment secures the right to an abortion, why does it not also secure the right to not be vaccinated? Do I not have bodily autonomy as well? This seems like a double standard about the issue of autonomy.

Another important question to be raised about the unvaccinated in the United States is why so many Black males in the United States are among those not yet vaccinated. Some reports say less than 40 percent of young African American males in the United States are vaccinated.[34] In New York City alone, only 28 percent of Black males have received a COVID-19 vaccination.[35] Why is that? How can we explain it, and, more importantly, how can we fix it?[36]

This brings us to the main sources for Essay Four, followed by Essay Five. The central subject matter of Essay Five of this study of attitudes and responses from the New Left Progressives shall be the crisis at the southern border of the United States.

ESSAY FIVE

The Crisis at the Southern Border of the US

I

The main purpose of this fifth essay of this study is to discuss what has come to be called the "crisis at the southern border" of the United States. We will begin this essay by making some very general comments about the history of the US-Mexico border. This will be followed by a discussion of the history of events at the two-thousand-mile southern border since the Obama administration, including the fact that Mr. Biden's press secretary, Jen Psaki, even refuses to call it a *crisis*.

These two opening sections of Essay Five will be followed by a discussion of policies on the southern border that have been put into place since the election of Joe Biden and Kamala Harris to become the president and vice president of the United States. These three sections of Essay Five will be followed by a careful evaluation of those Biden-Harris policies in regard to the southern border.

A History of the Southern Border

After the US victory in the Mexican-American War of 1848, Mexico was forced to sign over 525,000 square miles of territory, including what is now California, Nevada, and Utah as well as parts of

Arizona, New Mexico, Colorado, and Wyoming. Five years later, the US purchased an additional 29,000 square miles of land that included present-day Southern Arizona and Southwestern New Mexico. This more or less established the present-day border with Mexico.[1]

In the nineteenth century, illegal immigration was not considered a problem by the US. Thus, the US essentially had open borders. Would-be immigrants did not need "papers." In 1882, Congress passed the first major immigration restrictions. The principal reason for those restrictions was to bar illegal Chinese workers from entering the United States. Chinese migrants had begun to slip over the southwestern border, often learning a few words in Spanish so they could pass as Mexicans when entering the US.

The first federally funded border fence went up in 1911, but it was not erected to keep people out. Instead, it was meant to keep tick-infested cattle from wandering into the US from Mexico. The disease caused by the ticks was called Texas Fever, and it killed large parts of many herds of cattle in the Southwest in the beginning of the twentieth century. While the disease was eradicated in the US, it remained prevalent in Mexico. The *Saturday Evening Post* at the time described the fence as "the finest barb-wire boundary line in the history of the world."

The Border Patrol was created by an act of Congress in 1924, primarily to crack down on Chinese immigration and to stem the flow of illegal alcohol under the Prohibition era. In the 1920s and '30s, the southern border was lightly patrolled by a few hundred officers on horseback. Aside from a handful of private fences built during the Mexican Revolution in the first two decades of the twentieth century, the boundary between the US and Mexico remained largely unfortified.

Because of a surge in Mexican immigration during World War II, a Temporary Guest Worker Program, or TGWP, was created to send Mexican workers to places in the United States that needed labor.* The TGWP ended in 1964, but the need for Mexican cheap labor did not end. When the Mexican economy slumped in the 1970s and early 1980s, millions of Mexican laborers headed north, still without papers.

By 1986, an estimated 3.2 million undocumented immigrants were living in the United States, up from 550,000 in 1969. The war on drugs, instituted by President Nixon in 1971, also focused attention on the southern border, for it would become the main conduit for cocaine and marijuana into the United States.

During the administration of Jimmy Carter, the construction of a fence or wall was suggested at the southern border, particularly among the most heavily trafficked parts of the border. In 1979, however, the idea was scrapped after backlash at home and in Mexico. Carter's Republican opponent, Ronald Reagan, during a debate in 1980 said, "You don't build a nine-foot fence along the border between two friendly nations." In 1986, President Reagan supported the passage of the 1986 Immigration Reform and Control Act, which increased the Border Patrol's numbers by 50 percent to over five thousand officers. The Border Patrol officers were also equipped with night-vision goggles, new helicopters, and high-tech surveillance systems. The 1986 law also provided amnesty and legal status to some 2.7 million undocumented immigrants who had lived and worked in the United States for at least three years.[2]

The sections of wall added in the Clinton administration were limited to the cities of El Paso and San Diego, where poor farmers were displaced by the North American Free Trade Agreement, and large numbers of immigrants increased in number in the mid-1990s. The Clinton efforts did not stop the migrants; they simply rerouted them, often to harsh terrain in the Southwest.

---

* The Temporary Guest Worker Program was established by US 1/2A and US 1/2B. It ended in 1964.

After 9/11, with the country in a state of fear, Congress passed the REAL ID Act of 2005, which allowed the head of the newly created Department of Homeland Security to waive all laws that could hinder the construction of a wall on the southern border. This was followed by the Secure Fence Act of 2006, which mandated the construction of seven hundred miles of border wall and other barriers on the US-Mexico border.

The first major physical barriers at the southern border were constructed in the 1990s under Presidents George H. W. Bush and Bill Clinton. These barriers included a fourteen-mile stretch that separated San Diego and Tijuana. The fence was built using steel helicopter landing pads left over from the Vietnam War.

George W. Bush, through the Secure Fence Act in 2006, added 548 miles of fencing at a cost of $2.3 billion. An additional 137 miles of fencing at the southern border were erected under President Barack Obama, when Joe Biden was vice president. When Donald Trump left office, just over seven hundred miles of the border wall, of the possible two thousand miles, had been constructed.[3]

This brings us to the second section of Essay Five, in which we shall discuss policies in regard to the southern border in the Obama and Trump administrations. As we shall see, in 2014, the former referred to the increase in undocumented immigrants as a *crisis*.

History of Immigration at the Southern Border: Obama, Trump, and Biden Administrations

A *New York Times* story by Michael Shear and Jeremy Peters from July 8, 2014, with a headline that read, "Obama Asks for $3.7 billion to Aid Border," suggested that the forty-fourth president of the United States went before a joint session of Congress to request almost $4 billion to handle a surge of young migrants from Central America crossing the border into Texas, calling it an "urgent humanitarian situation and crisis."

Mr. Obama's request quickly became entangled in the fierce political debate over immigration. Republicans said they were wary of Mr. Obama's request and could not immediately support it. Mr. Obama said he needed the money to set up "new detention facilities, conduct more aerial surveillance and hire immigration judges and Border Patrol agents to respond to the flood of 52,000 children."

This sudden flood of children at the southern border overwhelmed local resources and touched off protests of local residents who were angry about the impact on the local economy. In a letter to Congress, Mr. Obama urged them to "act expeditiously" in regard to his request.

In a 2014 interview with George Stephanopoulos, Mr. Obama was told he needed directly to tell people, "Don't come; if you come you, will be deported."[4]

Mr. Obama answered by saying, "Actually, we've done that. The problem is that under current law, once those kids come across the border, there is a system in which we are supposed to process them, take care of them until we can send them back."

Then Mr. Stephanopoulos asked, "Is your message 'don't come'?"

President Obama answered, "Our message absolutely is: Don't send your children unaccompanied on trains . . . Do not send your children to the borders."

In addition to calling out the migration of children to the southern border in another 2014 interview, there is also another aspect of the Obama-Biden immigration policies that is relevant for our purposes, and it is this: The Obama-Biden administration, from 2008 to 2016, oversaw the construction of an additional 128 miles of border wall. In order to complete these portions of the barriers between Mexico and the US, many properties had to have been condemned. These condemnations began under the second

Bush administration, but they continued without a pause under the Obama-Biden watch.

Among the barriers where existing walls and fences were replaced under the Obama-Biden administration were parts of a wall in El Paso, Texas; other fencing in Naco, Arizona; and where the wall between San Diego and Tijuana enters the Pacific Ocean. Sections of border wall that were swept away by flooding at Organ Pipe Cactus National Monument; near Nogales, Arizona; and through Andrade, California, were also rebuilt during the Obama-Biden years.

One interesting aspect of the Obama-Biden view of a border fence or wall is that on May 10, 2011, in his first term, Mr. Obama told reporter Robert Farley, "The fence along the border with Mexico is now basically complete."

Thus, from the historical record, two points about Obama and the border are significant. First, in 2014, he declared a "humanitarian crisis" occurring at the southern border. Second, during the eight-year Obama-Biden administration, nearly 130 miles of border-wall fences were constructed on their watch.

While in office, the Trump administration proposed and implemented policies on a wide range of immigration issues, touching on everything from asylum to deportation policy, refugee resettlement, and denial of admissions to certain majority Muslim countries.

Below, we have assembled a short history of these border actions of the Trump administration. It is by no means an exhaustive list, but it does give the flavor of the forty-fifth president's approach to the issues:

- January 25, 2017: Trump issued an executive order on sanctuary cities and border wall.
- January 27, 2017: Trump issued an executive order on refugee admissions and immigration bans.

- September 24, 2017: Trump administration released updated rules for refugees and capped the number of migrants at forty-five thousand.
- January 25, 2018: Trump released the initial framework for immigration.
- February 15, 2018: Trump signed a bill to fund parts of the government border barrier and declared a state of emergency.
- October 30, 2018: Trump proposed ending birthright citizenship.
- February 3, 2019: Trump announced more troops would be sent to the southern border.
- February 15, 2019: Trump signed a bill to fund parts of the border wall.
- February 19, 2019: Trump signed a $328 billion spending bill that included $1.375 billion for barriers on the southern border.
- March to December 2019: Trump visited the southern border several times to examine the construction of the wall.

In January 2021, Joe Biden became president of the United States. Two months later, on March 20, 2021, Senator Tom Cotton accused Mr. Biden of inviting a recent surge of migrants to the United States, "claiming that the border is wide open." In an interview on *Fox News Sunday*, the Arkansas Republican said Biden had "dismantled highly effective policies" in securing the southern border with Mexico.

In the interview with Fox, Senator Cotton also criticized Homeland Security secretary Alejandro Mayorkas, who also made the Sunday talk shows to speak about the Biden-Harris plans for the southern border. A repeated talking point by the secretary was that the Trump administration, which took a hard line on border policy, was to blame for the surge at the border because Mr. Trump was expelling families and adults. He also said that the Biden administration was working to address the issue with Mexico and Central American countries where the asylum seekers were coming from.

We will say more about the Biden-Harris border policies in the next section of this essay. First, however, we shall take a look at the numbers to make better sense of the southern border crisis. In December of 2020, the final month that Mr. Trump was in office, 74,019 were detained at the border by the United States. The following month, January of 2021, when Mr. Biden was in charge, the numbers stayed relatively stable with 78,442 immigrants.

In February of 2021, that number ballooned to 101,117, followed by March, with 173,337. April's figure was 178,854, and in May, immigrants detained at the southern border reached 180,034. By June, the number had nearly reached 190,000. Thus, we went from 74,000-a-month migrant apprehensions on the Trump watch to 190,000 apprehensions at the southern border six months into the Biden-Harris administration.

The figures for unaccompanied minors, children under the age of eighteen, are no better. In May of 2014, the month when President Obama called the surge of children at the southern border a *crisis*, there were 10,600 children detained. By May of 2019, that number had reduced to 8,475 minors. In March of 2021, Mr. Biden's third month in office, the number of children under eighteen apprehended by Biden border authorities was 18,656. More than double President Trump's numbers during his watch. This figure for March 2021 far exceeded those in 2014, during Obama, and 2019, during Trump. By July of 2021, the number of unaccompanied minors at the southern border increased to 25,000.

In the month of June 2021, 188,000 immigrants were detained at the American southern border by state, local, and federal agents. That was a 450 percent increase from June of 2020 and

10,000 more than May of 2021 on the Biden-Harris watch. By the end of July, the number of migrants at the southern border had increased to 212,000 in a single month.[5]

It is not entirely clear what to make of these numbers. The president of Mexico, when asked about them, recently observed, "What do you expect? Biden is the migrant president." Many accounts of migrants themselves have been recorded since Biden took office. And when they were asked why they came north, they often said that the smugglers and coyotes told them, "It is easier at the border now that Biden is president."

This brings us to the third section of Essay Five, in which we will outline and discuss the Biden-Harris administration's policies in regard to the southern border. This third section of Essay Five will then be followed by a fourth section in which we shall critique the Democratic and Progressive New Left policies regarding the southern border.

The Biden-Harris Administration on the Southern Border

To begin our discussion of Joe Biden and his administration's views on the southern border, we must point to two dates: August 5, 2020, and January 20, 2021. The first of these concerns an interview he did with NPR's Lulu Garcia-Navarro, who asked the soon-to-be forty-sixth president whether he would continue the border wall. Biden's response was clear: "Not another foot."[6] The other date, January 20, 2021, was Mr. Biden's inauguration day. On that day, the forty-sixth president signed an executive order that called for the elimination of Section 202 of the National Emergencies Act. Additionally, the "national emergency declared by Proclamation 9844, and continued on February 13, 2020, and January 15, 2021," was terminated. Biden's proclamation continued: "the authorities invoked in that proclamation will no longer be used to construct a wall at the southern border."

Mr. Biden went on in his proclamation from January 20, 2021, to give detailed directions for how the general order was to come about. In a February 10, 2021, letter to Speaker to the House Nancy Pelosi, President Biden also wrote, "I have determined that the declaration of an emergency at our southern border was unwarranted." Mr. Biden added the following in the letter to Pelosi:

> I have also announced that it shall be the policy of my administration that no more American taxpayer dollars be diverted to construct a border wall, and that I am directing a careful review of all of the resources appropriated or redirected to that end.[7]

It is not clear whether the animus for the actions on these two dates in his early presidency was a reaction of Mr. Biden to the wall being a symbol of his predecessor's time in office or if Mr. Biden wanted to end construction on the wall for other reasons. What is clear is that while Joe Biden was vice president of the United States, the Obama administration oversaw the construction of 130 miles of fences and other kinds of barriers at the US southern border, as we have indicated earlier in this essay.

A number of other factors have gone into the Biden-Harris policies pertaining to the southern border, including the fact that President Biden appointed his vice president to be in charge of issues related to the border on March 24, 2021. Ms. Harris did not actually go to the southern border, however, for another ninety-two days until June 25, 2021.[8] When she was interviewed by Lester Holt in Guatemala in early June, Mr. Holt repeatedly asked Ms. Harris if she had any plans to go to the border. When the NBC reporter told the vice president that she had not specifically been to the southern border, Ms. Harris replied by laughing and then said, "I have not been to Europe. I mean, I don't understand the point you are making."[9] Ms. Harris may not have understood Mr. Holt's point, but the American people certainly did, and what Europe has to do with our southern border is not at all clear.

Regarding her trip to Guatemala and Mexico, Ms. Harris told Lester Holt that the purpose of her trip was "to address the reasons that people leave for the US." Later, the vice president referred to these reasons as the "root causes."[10] When her staff was asked what these root causes were, they responded by pointing to:

1. Civil wars in the 1980s
2. Two hurricanes in November of 2020
3. Hunger
4. Poverty
5. Unemployment
6. Violence
7. Corruption
8. Climate issues

Ms. Harris herself, when asked the same question about the nature of the root causes, answered: a lack of economic opportunity (or number five from her staff's list), violence (number six from her staff), corruption (item seven), food insecurity (item three), and basic needs not being met (number four). Nowhere in the Harris materials can be found any explanation for how climate change may be a cause of migration to America from Central America.

There is also little explanation for how civil wars from more than thirty years ago are connected to the migration issue. Harris did say in Guatemala, "So the work we have to do is the work of addressing the causes . . . otherwise, we will continue to see the effects, and that is what is happening at the border. It is going to require a comprehensive approach that acknowledges each piece of this."

One way the Biden-Harris administration has responded to the root causes is by doing what the Democratic Party usually does when they wish to solve a problem—throw money at it. Between 2016 and 2020, President Trump gradually reduced the foreign aid to Central American countries from a high of $750 million in 2016 to $520 million in 2020.

The proposed 2022 Biden-Harris budget has allocated $861 million. We may ask, "Where will this money go, and how will it help to ameliorate the root causes at the southern border?"

Another aspect of the border crisis in terms of the Biden-Harris administration is what has happened to ICE from their election in November of 2020 to July of 2021, their first six months in office. The arm of the American government known as ICE was essentially shut down after Mr. Biden took office, chiefly because of the shouts during his campaign to "Abolish ICE."* In fact, the American Civil Liberties Union (ACLU) sued the Trump

* The Abolish ICE movement began in the late summer of 2018. One poll at that time indicated that 25 percent of all American Democrats supported calls to dismantle ICE, and more than 50 percent of those same people polled viewed the agency in a negative way. These figures are consistent, of course, with those we have summarized in Essay Two about the Defund the Police movement. Since the Trump administration, a number of American politicians and national organizations have called for the abolishing of ICE. The American Friends Service Committee, for example, has called for the abolishment of ICE, as has the North American Congress on Latin America (NACLA) in an article by Rennie Rose Nelson of NACLA called, "Abolish Ice: Fighting for Humanity Over Profit in Immigration Policy" in *NACLA Reports* from June 6, 2019. Alexandria Ocasio-Cortez has been the driving force behind the Abolish ICE movement. This was bucking the prevailing mainstream Democratic view, like Joe Biden and Kamala Harris, who have called for keeping the agency intact while reforming it. Senator Bernie Sanders and New York City mayor Bill de Blasio have also called for the breaking up of ICE as well as the redistribution of its functions to other agencies.

administration over whether detention centers operated by ICE should be closed.[11]

Many of the Progressive New Left during the Trump administration—like the members of the "Squad," including Alexandria Ocasio-Cortez, as well as Senators Kirsten Gillibrand and Elizabeth Warren, during their bids for president—joined the Abolish ICE movement. Even Kamala Harris, while a California senator, told MSNBC, regarding ICE, "We need to probably think about starting from scratch."

During his presidential campaign, Mr. Biden also promised a path to citizenship for eleven million undocumented immigrants, whom he called the "dreamers." However, a recent study at Yale University conducted by Mohammad Fazel-Zarandi suggested that the number is much closer to twenty-two million.[12] One wonders if Mr. Biden still wishes to continue his plan for the undocumented in America.

When the Biden-Harris team took office, they continually made six claims about President Trump and border issues. We will identify and then examine these six claims in the next section of this essay.

Biden's Claims about Trump and the Border: An Evaluation

From the time of his election to the presidency until July 2021, the Biden-Harris administration continually made six separate claims about Mr. Trump and his treatment of the southern border issues. We will list these six claims here and then evaluate them one at a time in this section of Essay Five.

1. Biden inherited "one God-awful mess at the border from the Trump administration."[13]

2. The border crisis is receiving urgent action now.
3. A month ago, there were thousands of young kids in custody in places that they should not be and controlled by the Border Patrol. Biden has cut that down dramatically.
4. There was a failure to have a real transition. Biden did not find out what was happening in immigration and the DOD—that is, that they fired many people and now they are left understaffed.
5. About immigration numbers, the Biden-Harris administration says, "Well, look, it is way down now. We now have it under control."
6. Trump did not plan for the transition. They did not have enough beds for the children, who were often placed in the hands of people who could not take care of them.[14]

Although all six of these claims have been made over and over again, none of these claims are, in fact, true. About the first claim listed, it is true that in the final six months of the Trump administration, the number of border apprehensions increased dramatically, mostly because people were coming illegally in the hopes of a Biden election victory. When the Biden administration took office, however, the monthly apprehensions exploded.

The Biden administration inherited a border that was under control thanks to a strong and effective system of the Trump administration. In May of 2019, 140,000 illegal aliens were caught crossing the border. By November 2019, the number was down to 42,000. And by April of 2020, apprehensions were down to a level under 17,000. By July 2021, on Biden's watch, the number of unaccompanied children at the southern border had ballooned to 25,000.

This decrease occurred, one might argue, because of the migrant protection protocols that essentially eliminated fraudulent asylum claims at the southern border, as well as asylum cooperative agreements with the Central American countries of the Northern Triangle. This gave individuals the right to apply for protection closer to their home country instead of at the southern border.

Every one of these effective border policies was still in place until January 20, 2021, when President Biden, as we have shown earlier in this essay, undid all of them with a single stroke of the pen. We have seen the numbers skyrocket since then. Joe Biden and Kamala Harris, in fact, inherited the most secure border in US history, and then they promptly blew it apart.

The second claim—that the border is receiving urgent action now—is a fatuous notion on its face. It took Ms. Harris, who was tapped with being responsible for the border, ninety-two days to visit the border. Even then, she went to El Paso rather than the Rio Grande Valley Sector, where the traffic in migration is the heaviest.

Holding Zoom calls and calling for amnesty is not "urgent action," nor is abolishing ICE. Urgent action would be resuming the construction of the wall that even the Border Patrol has said is urgently needed and effective. The Biden administration appears to be fiddling while the southern border of the United States burns.

The third claim made by the Biden administration mostly has to do with unaccompanied minors, children under the age of eighteen. In the summer of 2021, nearly 25,000 unaccompanied minors were in federal custody—more than 21,000 of whom were transferred to HHS. By March of 2021, that figure was 19,000, and by July it had ballooned to above 25,000. We went from eight hundred minors in custody on the Trump watch to 25,000 under the Biden-Harris administration just six months later.

The fourth claim on our list was uttered by Mr. Biden himself—that the transition was nowhere near good enough. What Mr. Biden said is simply false. Trump's Department of Homeland Security provided the transition team with more than two hundred extensive briefings on Homeland Security issues. The majority of these were about securing the border, immigration policy, and the processes and procedures that were in place up to and until January 20, 2021.

These transition meetings were available then, and still are now, for any reporter or American citizen to attend or examine. The minutes of those meetings may be acquired through the Freedom of Information Act. During the transition period, the Biden administration was made fully aware of the consequences of undoing the effective border policies implemented under Mr. Trump. Trump's border officials warned the incoming administration of the consequences if the Trump protocols were eliminated. The Biden-Harris clan ignored those warnings, and now they are reaping the effects of them.

It may have been that Biden and Harris simply wished to take down the symbol of Mr. Trump's presidency—the wall. But now we are seeing the consequences of not having the wall.

Biden's claim that lots of employees were fired during the transition—particularly in the DOD and immigration—is simply not true. Not only that—it is illegal to remove any senior executive service employees from their jobs for 120 days after the change of administration.

The fifth claim—that they now have it under control—is not only false, but it is also absurd. We have gone from 74,019 apprehensions in the final month of Mr. Trump's tenure to nearly 190,000 in just six months, and that number appears to be continuing to rise. In what sense can the Biden administration say, "We have it under control"?

The Biden-Harris administration, as well as many members of Congress, refuses to be honest with the American people about the state of the border crisis or to acknowledge the reality concerning the immense cost to our law enforcement officers, to working Americans, and to our communities. The Democrats appear to just see the electoral gold mine since most of these migrants who settle in America will become voting Democrats. Or maybe it is because, as Secretary Mayorkas said at the time, "The border is closed."[15]

The Biden administration is not being truthful, except for the one day when President Biden made the mistake of calling what was happening at the southern border a *crisis*. It came on April 17, 2021, when he said, "We're gonna increase the numbers [of refugees allowed into the country]. The problem was that the refugee part was working on the crisis that ended up on the border with young people, and we couldn't do two things at once."

Not surprisingly, the White House the following Monday backtracked on Biden's statement from April 17. When asked about the matter by CNN, a White House official said, "The president does not feel that children coming to the border seeking refuge from violence, economic hardship, and other dire circumstances is a crisis."[16] Again, we must remember that when Mr. Obama was president in 2014, he did call the number of children arriving at the southern border a *crisis*, despite the fact that Jen Psaki, White House press secretary, refuses to call it by that name, even though her boss, Joe Biden, did exactly that.

This leaves us with the sixth and final claim that has been made repeatedly by the Biden administration since November of 2020—that the transition plan did not allow for things like the number of beds that will be needed for children in the new administration or where these minor children will be housed and for how long. These claims are nothing short of outrageous.

In November of 2020, under the Trump administration, there were fewer than eight hundred unaccompanied minors in US custody. By March of 2021, that number had increased to more than 10,000. By the end of July 2021, the number of unaccompanied minors in custody from the southern border had increased to 25,000.

The Border Patrol, on August 6, 2021, reported the highest number of unaccompanied minor children crossing the southern border in a single day when more than eight hundred children were taken into US custody.[17] At that rate, we would be adding 292,000 children to the migration numbers in a year, not to mention those adults and families who are apprehended at the southern border.

Even though apprehensions began increasing at the border in 2020 as a growing number of illegal migrants gambled on a potential Biden victory and perhaps subsequent amnesty, the Trump administration had put strong policies in place by quickly and responsibly processing and deporting most of these migrants. This meant that there were no extensive backlogs or overcrowding at Customs and Border Protection (CBP) and HHS facilities.

The Biden-Harris administration broke this system and now has the temerity to blame it on President Trump for not implementing restrictive policies in anticipation of its reckless behavior. This is truly astounding.

Biden and Harris are correct about one thing in regard to the southern border. The circumstances for children at the border have significantly changed. The open-door policy is encouraging more unaccompanied minors and families to make the dangerous journey to the US-Mexico border. This has also created a windfall for the drug cartels and smugglers who profit off human misery. And this sadly has involved an increasing number of minor and unaccompanied children—by July of 2021, 25,000 of them.

Former acting commissioner of CBP Mark Morgan and his assistant, Lora Ries, have summed up the state of the border in the Biden administration. They wrote about the cartels and smugglers:

> These vicious organizations are banking profits of $14 million a day, and likely more, from trafficking women, children, and families through Central America and across the border. Many of these women and children suffer from horrific abuse, malnourishment, exposure, and sickness along the route, and others are left to die in the wilderness if they get lost or can't keep up. The large numbers of people surging to the border are a serious public health risk, and are facilitating the spread of COVID among vulnerable populations, and if individuals do not catch the virus during the trip, they are likely to do so while packed on top of each other in overcrowded Border Patrol facilities.[18]

In the Biden administration, children are often kept in these conditions for up to ten days or more because the Border Patrol simply does not have the capacity to handle the surge created by the Biden administration's southern border policies. When these children are sent to HHS facilities or overflow border facilities, the results are often just as disastrous. In short, this sixth claim about the southern border made by the Biden-Harris administration has no more vestiges of truth than the other five claims in the discussion.

Indeed, in this fourth section of this fifth essay, we have argued that none of the six major claims that the Biden-Harris administration has made about what can only be called the crisis at the southern border appear to be true, whether these claims were made by the president, the vice president, or the secretary of Homeland Security for the Biden administration, Alejandro Mayorkas.

Of these three officials, the latter has had the most to say about the southern border since November of 2020. Secretary Mayorkas has been guilty of two sins with regard to the southern border of the United States. First, he has repeatedly, since February of 2021, assented to the first erroneous claim we mentioned earlier in this section—that is, that the Trump administration has left the border situation in a mess.

On many occasions since January 20, 2021, Mr. Mayorkas has said or written things like this statement he made on March 14, 2021:

> The prior administration completely dismantled the asylum system. The system was gutted, facilities were closed, and they cruelly expelled young children into the hands of traffickers. We have had to rebuild the entire system, including the policies and procedures required to administer the asylum laws that Congress passed long ago.[19]

Two months later, on March 21, 2021, the current secretary of Homeland Security told ABC News' Martha Raddatz, when asked about the southern border and unaccompanied minors, "Martha, it takes time. The Trump administration would have turned these minors away. When I say it takes time, I mean it, because we are dealing with a dismantled system. And we did not have the ordinary safe and just transition from one administration to another."

Here, Secretary Mayorkas repeated the fourth claim of the Biden administration that we have dismissed earlier in this essay. On Friday, May 7, 2021, when Alejandro Mayorkas led congressional delegation to Donna, Texas, to receive an update on unaccompanied children arriving at the southern border and to review conditions at the CBP facilities there, the secretary began his remarks by saying:

> The Biden-Harris administration inherited a dismantled system plagued by chaos and cruelty, and I was proud today to show members of Congress who have been leading the effort to reform our immigration system the dramatic progress we've made so far.[20]

Again, Secretary Mayorkas alluded to claims one and four discussed earlier in this essay. Mr. Mayorkas said nothing, however, about what public opinion says about the Biden administration's treatment of the southern border crisis. In an ABC News/*Washington Post* poll from early June of 2021, the administration had only a 37 percent approval rating for his work on the immigration situation at the US-Mexico border.

The other "sin" we believe Secretary Mayorkas is guilty of is that when it comes to the southern border, he often has made many contradictory statements about the issues there.

For example, beginning on May 7, 2021, five months into the Biden administration, Mr. Mayorkas began to say, "The border remains closed."[21] A June 15, 2021, article from the Reuters news agency records Secretary Mayorkas as saying, "The US southern border is not open."[22]

Apparently, no one told the 178,000 migrants who came to the southern border weeks before the comments of Mr. Mayorkas in April of 2021, nor the 181,000 migrants to the southern border that followed in May of 2021, or the nearly 190,000 immigrants who came to the border in June. And the secretary told us, "The border is closed."

Perhaps there is a disconnect about what counts as *open*, much like President Bill Clinton's remark he made on August 17, 1998: "It depends on what the meaning of the word *is* is." This may have been another example, as with *infrastructure*, of when the Biden administration decided to redefine what is meant by *open* and *closed* in regard to the southern border.

Despite Mr. Mayorkas's repetitions of his playbook about Trump and the immigration crisis at the southern border, the secretary of Homeland Security and the Biden administration have experienced much criticism on border issues since January 20, 2021. We will end this analysis by looking at some of these criticisms.

Not surprisingly, many of the criticisms directed at Secretary Mayorkas and his border policies, as well as those of the Biden administration in general, have come from two sources: Republican senators and Conservative thinkers and columnists.

When Mr. Mayorkas appeared before the Senate on May 13, 2021, to discuss border issues, ranking member Senator Rob Portman sketched out some figures on the border in 2021 compared to previous years. He then asked the secretary how much of the surge could be explained by the infusing of drugs into the US from Mexico. The secretary dodged the question. Then Mr. Portman asked Mr. Mayorkas about smuggling and human trafficking, but again, Mr. Mayorkas had no answer to the question.

Senator Portman, Ohio Republican, then went on to remind the secretary that we knew only of the ones we caught. "How many other migrants come to the US that we don't catch?"

Mr. Mayorkas responded by saying, "Senator, I have no idea."[23]

Republican senator of Alabama, Tommy Tuberville, on February 16, 2021, during the discussion about the southern border with Mr. Mayorkas, asked a series of relevant questions about the border with Mexico. Among those questions, for which Senator Tuberville got no acceptable answers, were the following:

- How does the Department of Homeland Security plan to prioritize the health, safety, and security of our law enforcement officers at the border?
- Is every person at the border being screened for credible fear, which the Biden administration believes is a cause of the border crisis?
- Please explain how the rescinding of executive orders of the Trump administration has made our border stronger, the American people safer, and our lawful immigration system more secure.

These and other queries were directed by Senator Tuberville to the secretary during the discussion as well as in remarks the senator made about the southern border in a letter to Mr. Mayorkas sent around the same time.[24]

Senator Rick Scott of Florida has also been aggressive in questioning Mr. Mayorkas about Biden's policies on the southern border. One remark he made to the secretary was from the same hearing as Mr. Tuberville's questions. Senator Scott observed:

> As I talk to sheriffs in Florida, what they are seeing since Joe Biden's inauguration is an unbelievable increase in fentanyl coming across, coming into Florida. And the only thing they can say is it must be coming from the border.

Senator Scott went on to say, "If record low drug seizures are because Customs and Border Patrol agents are being diverted to manage the humanitarian crisis at the southern border, are there other reasons for the lack of these drug arrests?" One of the answers to Senator Scott's question, of course, is that President Biden has denuded the power of ICE and changed their rules about arrests and taking people into custody. But that factor did not come into play when Mr. Scott questioned Mr. Mayorkas.

A number of American Conservative scholars and writers have also criticized the current Homeland Security secretary in regard to the southern border. One of these scholars is Ken Cuccinelli, a former visiting fellow at the Davis Institute. In an essay titled "Commentary Homeland Security," published on March 22, 2021, the scholar made a number of direct criticisms of the Homeland Security secretary.

One of the most strident and direct criticisms of the secretary can be seen in this paragraph by Mr. Cuccinelli:

> [Mayorkas's statement] uses small children as political props, implying that they comprise the bulk of under-18 illegal aliens arriving without family. This is not true, as three-fourths of those arriving are between 15 and 17 years old—teenagers on the brink of adulthood.[25]

Mr. Cuccinelli goes on in his essay to point out that in one speech, Secretary Mayorkas made comments on three different categories of migrants: single adults, families, and unaccompanied minors. In his discussion of these three categories, Mr. Cuccinelli pointed out, Secretary Mayorkas used one paragraph to speak of the first two categories and three full pages to speak of the children.

This observation is clearly consistent with Mr. Cuccinelli's observation that Secretary Mayorkas uses the idea of small children as pawns in trying to achieve his political goals regarding the government's actions and policies at the southern border. Mr. Cuccinelli also pointed out that Mr. Mayorkas always "begins by comparing the Biden administration's treatment of unaccompanied children to that of the Trump administration that was 'much more punitive.'"

In June of 2021, former Border Patrol Council president Brandon Judd remarked that, "[The crisis at the southern border] is a man-made crisis."[26] If he is correct, then the obvious question is, "Who is that 'man'?" The answer to that question is clearly "Joe Biden."

One final issue about the crisis at the southern border is what the Biden administration has done in regard to what is called Title 42. This is a US health law, specifically Section 262 of *United States Code* Title 42, that prohibits entry into the US when the director of the CDC believes "there is a serious danger to the introduction of a communicable disease into the US."

On March 20, 2020, the Trump administration invoked Title 42 when the COVID-19 pandemic began to escalate globally.

The question began to be raised, "How many migrants coming to America are tested for COVID-19, and what happens to those who test positive?" Since March of 2020, the testing of migrants for COVID-19 has been mixed. Some centers do it, while others do not. Those that do COVID-19 testing have reported a significant number of COVID-19-positive cases since Joe Biden became president.

At this point, we have no idea what the overall numbers are of immigrants coming to the United States who have, or have had, COVID-19. This does not help us to decide the question about the source of the virus, but it is another manifestation of the problem as the pandemic manifests itself in the United States. Since testing by the US government for COVID-19 varies from place to place, we have no idea how many COVID-19-positive individuals and families have been released into the general American culture.

In 2021, when Vice President Kamala Harris finally made her trip to the southern border, she related, "We are making progress." In early August 2021, we were on schedule to process more than 212,000 migrants at the border. At that rate, we would add more than 2.1 million migrants a year, many of whom are released back into the United States. This is progress indeed.

Even Secretary Mayorkas, when he believed he was off camera and away from the microphone, admitted that the Rio Grande Sector "can't continue like this . . . our system isn't built for it."[27]

One might even call that a *crisis*!

I have said nothing about guns and drugs that have been confiscated since November of 2020 at the American southern border. In the fiscal year 2020, California Border Patrol saw a 30 percent increase in guns confiscated, as well as many more drug confiscations than on the Trump watch—particularly the drug fentanyl. Traditionally, guns go south from the US, and drugs come north from the southern border. But now it seems that the guns go south and then back north from where they came, including a recent cache of .50-caliber rifles—what the Progressive New Left would even call *assault weapons* or *weapons of war*.

Since the Biden-Harris election, the Border Patrol has seized 5,500 more pounds of heroin, 325,000 more pounds of marijuana, and 43,000 more pounds of cocaine than the comparable period in 2020 when Donald Trump was in charge.[28]

This brings us to the major sources for Essay Five, followed by Essay Six. The subject matter of the sixth essay of this work is the Progressive New Left's views on the Second Amendment and the right to bear arms. After the sources, then, I will turn our attention to guns in the US.[29]

ESSAY SIX

Progressives on Gun Control and the Second Amendment

I

The purpose of this essay is to do the following things. First, we will describe and discuss the Second Amendment of the US Constitution—what it says and what it means. Second, we will explore what the US Supreme Court has had to say about guns and the Second Amendment in the modern age. Third, we will examine the political opinions of the Democratic Party in contemporary America on guns and the Second Amendment. A fourth goal in this essay is to give an account of what Joe Biden and Kamala Harris have had to say and write about guns and the Second Amendment. The final goal of the sixth essay is to offer a critique of the Biden-Harris plan in responding to gun deaths and violence. Before we move to these goals, however, we will first give a short report on gun deaths in the United States. As we shall see, these figures will be surprising for most anti-gun Americans.

The most-recent available statistics on gun violence and gun deaths in the United States come from the CDC and the Pew Research Center from 2017. In that year, 39,773 people died in the US from gun-related incidents. This figure includes homicides, suicides by guns, accidental deaths by guns, deaths by law enforcement using guns, and those deaths by guns that cannot be determined.*

* One factor that the Pew Research Center has pointed to is that positive

In 2017, six out of ten gun deaths in America were suicides (23,854); 37 percent comprised homicides (14,542), accidental deaths (486), those that involved law enforcement (553), and undetermined deaths by guns (338). Three-quarters of all US murders in 2017—that is, 14,542 of 19,510—involved a firearm. About half of all suicides in 2017 in the United States, or 51 percent, involved one gun or more.

The 39,773 gun deaths in America in 2017 were the most since the year 1968, the earliest year that the CDC began to collect its data. Both gun murders and gun suicides have increased in recent years. The number of gun homicides rose 32 percent between 2006 and 2017. Gun suicides reached their highest level in 2017, while the number of gun suicides rose each year between 2006 and 2017, or a 41 percent increase overall.

The states with the highest number of gun deaths tracked by the CDC in terms of events per every 100,000 of the population were the following in 2017:

---

attitudes toward gun control tend to increase after a shooting event in the news. Shortly after the following incidents, the numbers in favor of gun control usually rose to somewhere between 63 and 92 percent:

- Shooting in a middle school in Jonesboro, Arkansas (1998)
- Shooting at a high school in Springfield, Oregon (1998)
- Shooting at a Jewish community center in Los Angeles (1999)
- Snipers shooting near Washington, DC (2002)
- Shooting at a fitness club in Pennsylvania (2009)
- Shooting at Virginia Tech (2007)
- Shooting at an elementary school in Connecticut (2012)
- Shooting at a Sikh temple in Wisconsin (2012)
- Shooting at a mall in Portland (2012)
- Shooting at Navy Yard in Washington, DC (2013)

1. Alaska (24.5/100,000)
2. Alabama (22.9)
3. Montana (22.5)
4. Louisiana (21.7)
5. Missouri (21.5)
6. Mississippi (21.5)
7. Arkansas (20.3)

The states with the lowest rates of gun deaths per every 100,000 of the population were:

1. New Jersey (5.3/100,000)
2. Connecticut (5.1)
3. Rhode Island (3.9)
4. New York (3.7)
5. Massachusetts (3.7)
6. Hawaii (2.5)

Nationwide, the US gun death rate per 100,000 was 12. This is much higher than:

1. Canada (2.1/100,000)
2. Australia (1.0)
3. France (2.7)
4. Germany (0.9)
5. Spain (0.6)

The rate of gun deaths in the United States, however, was much lower than:

1. El Salvador (39.2/100,000)
2. Venezuela (38.7)
3. Guatemala (32.3)

4. Colombia (25.9)
5. Honduras (22.5)

Worldwide, the United States in 2017 ranked twentieth in its gun mortality rate. In terms of the kinds of weapon used, handguns in 2017 were involved in 64 percent of the US gun murders. Long guns, or rifles and shotguns, accounted for 6 percent of all gun deaths in America. The remaining 30 percent involved guns that were classified by the CDC as "other guns or types not stated."[1]

One final figure related to American gun deaths from 2017 involves the question, "How many people are killed in mass shootings every year?" The FBI collects data on what it calls *active shooter incidents*, which it defines as "one or more people actively engaged in killing or attempting to kill people in a populated area."

Another question to ask about gun deaths in America is whether the rate of US gun deaths has changed over time. In 2017, there were 12 gun deaths per 100,000 population, the highest rate in more than two decades but still way below the 16.3 gun deaths per 100,000 in 1974, when the highest rate in the CDC database was recorded. Both the gun murder rate and the suicide murder rate are lower today than they were in the mid-1970s. There were 4.6 per 100,000 gun murder deaths in 2017, far below the 7.2 rate from 1976.

Using the FBI definition of *active shooter incidents*, in 2017 eighty-five people—excluding the shooters—died in such incidents. The Gun Violence Archive, an online database on gun-violence incidents in the United States, defines a *mass shooting* as four or more people—excluding the shooters themselves. Using that definition, in 2017, 373 Americans died in this kind of gun incident.

The FBI's database on American gun deaths is based on information submitted by state and local police departments. Not all departments participate. In any given year, nine out of ten departments do.

On average, yearly, between six hundred and seven hundred American children under the age of eleven die to gun violence. 2017 was high, with 733, and 2014 was low, with only 603. The number of murder-suicides in the US has been pretty constant in the last eight years, with a low in 2015 with 530 and a high in 2018 with 621 murder-suicides. Mass shootings are on the rise in the US. In 2014, there were 269 incidents, and in 2017, there were 417.

One final element of this introduction of this sixth essay of this study has to do with my qualifications for writing this essay. Many years ago, at the John Hopkins University Medical School, I was the faculty sponsor for a graduate student project in which the student, a fellow in the university's Robert Wood Johnson (RWJ) Fellows Program, wanted to determine how young Black men in Baltimore acquired guns in that population.

I learned a great deal from that research, especially about the acquisition of firearms in the Baltimore community. I was also the faculty sponsor for a number of other projects in the RWJ Fellows Program. We will discuss some of these other projects over the course of this study.

This brings us to the first section of this sixth essay, in which we will discuss the wording of the Second Amendment of the US Constitution and how its words are to be interpreted.

The Second Amendment and What It Means

The Second Amendment was part of the US Bill of Rights, which was added to the US Constitution on December 15, 1791. This amendment protects the rights of citizens to "bear arms" or to own weapons such as guns. The Second Amendment has become controversial in recent years in America. Many people want more laws to prevent citizens from owning guns. They believe this will help reduce gun killings and keep mentally ill people from owning firearms. Other Americans think the Second Amendment is perfectly clear when it speaks of:

> A well-regulated militia, being necessary to the security of a free state, the right of the people to keep and bear arms, shall not be infringed.[2]

Many people today believe that the Second Amendment was added so that people in Revolutionary times could have weapons to go hunting, but this was not why the Amendment was added. The Second Amendment was written to help the people protect themselves from a tyrannical government, like the one from which they had just rid themselves—the British. The American people—and particularly the Founding Fathers—wanted to maintain the right to "bear arms" in case the new government began to take away their rights.

In Revolutionary times, citizens owning guns was also important for other reasons, including organizing a local militia, fighting off invasions from foreign powers, self-defense in things like Indian raids, and helping with law enforcement.[3]

A *militia* was a group of local men who acted as a military force in times of emergency. The members of the militia were trained, organized, and disciplined. They were not simply a bunch of guys with guns.

The expression *to bear arms* means to carry a weapon. Although there is no description of what kind of arms, the writers of the amendment at the time certainly thought to include handguns, rifles, and shotguns. Some question whether the Amendment means that individuals can bear arms or only the militia. This question and what kind of arms are acceptable to bear have been two of the foci of recent discussions in the United States about guns and gun control.

Later in this essay, we will see that President Joe Biden, in the past few years, has raised both of these kinds of queries about guns in America, including the claim, as we shall see, that individuals in Revolutionary times could not own cannons. The US Supreme Court also has weighed in on these two questions. We will move to their views in the second section of this sixth essay.

The Supreme Court on Guns and the Second Amendment

Since 1939, the US Supreme Court has made eight major decisions related to firearms and the Second Amendment. We will list these eight cases here and then speak of each of them one after the next. These Supreme Court cases and the years they were decided were the following:

1. United States v. Miller (1939)
2. District of Columbia v. Heller (2008)
3. United States v. Hayes (2009)
4. McDonald v. Chicago (2010)
5. United States v. Castleman (2014)
6. Henderson v. United States (2015)
7. Caetano v. Massachusetts (2016)
8. New York State Rifle & Pistol Association v. Corlett (2021)

In the United States v. Miller decision of 1939, the court explained that the "obvious purpose" of the Second Amendment was to "render possible the effectiveness" of militias.

Thus, the amendment must be "interpreted and applied with that in mind." In the same decision, the Supreme Court also upheld a ban on sawed-off shotguns and again implied that the Founding Fathers adopted the amendment to ensure that the then-new federal government could not disarm state militias.

In 1976, the Washington, DC, City Council barred the city's residents from owning a handgun. In 2007, however, the US Court of Appeals for the District of Columbia ruled in favor of Dick Anthony Heller, a sixty-six-year-old armed security guard who sued the district after it rejected his application to keep a handgun at home in Capitol Hill. The district appealed the case to the US Supreme Court.

In June of 2008, the Supreme Court upheld the lower court ruling, striking down the District of Columbia's handgun ban as being unconstitutional in the *Heller* case. In the US v. Hayes (2009), the Supreme Court affirmed the use of a federal law barring people convicted of domestic violence from owning guns. The court held that state laws against battery need not specifically mention domestic violence to fall under the domestic violence gun ban that was enacted in 1996. The victim of such a crime need only be involved in a domestic relationship with the attacker.

A year later, in 2010, in its McDonald v. Chicago decision, the US Supreme Court reversed the Seventh Circuit, holding that the Fourteenth Amendment makes the Second Amendment's right to keep and bear arms for the purpose of self-defense applicable to the states. Justice Samuel A. Alito wrote the majority opinion. He said that "rights are fundamental to the nation's scheme of ordered liberty" and are "deeply rooted in this nation's history and tradition," which are appropriately applied to the states through the Fourteenth Amendment.

In the United States v. Castleman case of 2014, the opinion was a unanimous decision. In that case, the court ruled that a state conviction for misdemeanor domestic assault qualifies for a "misdemeanor crime of domestic violence for the purposes of possessing a firearm." The court recognized that domestic violence can include acts that do not always adhere to everyone's idea of what *violence* is.

In the 2015 Henderson v. United States case, the Supreme Court addressed whether federal law gives felons the right to transfer their lawfully owned firearms to a third party. In a unanimous decision, the court held that the transfer of a felon's lawfully owned firearms from government custody to a third party is not barred if the court is satisfied that the recipient will not give the felon control over the firearms during or after the transfer. The court's ruling in the *Henderson* case allowed felons to ask the government to transfer their firearms to an independent third party, including transfers to dealers for sale on the open market as well as direct transfers to particular people.

In the 2016 Caetano v. Massachusetts decision, the Supreme Court ruled that a Massachusetts state law prohibiting the personal possession of a stun gun contradicted the precedent established in the *Heller* and *McDonald* cases. The court did not address the question, however, of whether a stun gun constitutes "arms" for the purposes of the Second Amendment. The court concluded that the Second Amendment extends to "all instruments that constitute bearable arms, even those that were not in existence at the time of the founding."

Finally, the Supreme Court has agreed to consider the New York State Rifle & Pistol Association v. Corlett case in its next session. In this case, the court will review a New York law, upheld by the lower courts, that requires individuals to get a license to carry a concealed weapon outside the home. The case will likely be heard in the fall. The issue at hand in the New York case is "whether the Second Amendment allows the government to prohibit ordinary law-abiding citizens from carrying a handgun outside the home for self-defense."

Immediately after the court's announcement that they would hear the case, New York governor, Andrew M. Cuomo, released a statement about the court's decision. In that statement, the governor's office related on April 26, 2021:

> In light of the Supreme Court's announcement this morning that they will take up New York State Rifle & Pistol Association v. Corlett in the next term, it's worth remembering that New York's nation-leading gun violence prevention laws . . .

The statement from the New York governor continued this way:

> This NRA-backed case is a massive threat to that security. Imagine someone carrying a gun through Times Square, onto the subway, or to a tailgate outside of a Bills game. The NRA's goal here is to shift the onus onto regular New Yorkers, police officers, security guards, and first responders to determine whether an armed individual poses a threat or is simply carrying for self-defense.

The final paragraph of Mr. Cuomo's statement said this:

> While we have to respect the role of the courts, we don't have to play along with the NRA's strategy of using them to roll back strong gun safety laws passed by individual states, turning the lowest common denominator into the law of the land. We can keep all Americans safe through federal action. Changing the law to require background checks on all gun sales, ban assault weapons and high-capacity magazines . . .[4]

There certainly is no question where Governor Cuomo stands on gun control, the NRA, and the Supreme Court's decision to hear the New York case. Mr. Cuomo's remarks were in consort with other contemporary Democrats, as we shall see in the next section of this sixth essay.

Other Prominent Democrats on Gun Control

The first attempt to enact gun control by the Democratic Party in the modern era was the Gun Control Act of 1968, in response to the assassinations of public officials such as JFK, RFK, and MLK.[5] The legislation restricted the sale of guns as well as who could buy them. This is perhaps the final bipartisan effort toward gun control in America. It was the final time to date that there was an uneasy détente between those who wanted to keep their guns and those who wished to keep restrictions on owning guns.

By the late 1970s, and during the Carter administration, gun control had all but disappeared in America as well as in the Democratic Party's platform. Gun control was not even nominally a part of Mr. Carter's agenda.

Both Walter Mondale and Michael Dukakis—the Democratic candidates for president in 1984 and 1988—in their platforms leading up to those elections, made no references to guns or to gun control.

In the election of 1992, things began to change for the Democrats. In that year, Congress passed the Federal Assault Weapons Ban, but nowhere in the bill does it provide the definition of an *assault weapon*. For many Democrats, this legislation did not go far enough. One added fact was that a federal law banning assault weapons in Chicago or New York City might not play out well in Cheyenne, Wyoming, or Boise, Idaho.

At any rate, by 1996, the Democratic Party's platform celebrated Mr. Clinton's passing of gun control legislation and his ability to "defy the gun lobby . . . to make Americans safer."

Indeed, Bill Clinton was happy to show off his record as the "gun controller in chief," in contrast to the more Liberal members of his party who did not comment about the issue one way or the other. Candidate John Kerry in 2004 devised a similar moderate platform on gun control, as did Mr. Obama in 2008.

The issues of guns and their control became very important, however, in most of the Democratic presidential candidates leading up to the 2020 election. Candidate Cory Booker, a senator from New Jersey, carved out the most ambitious path in the gun control debate. He said about his plan at the time that it was the most comprehensive gun violence prevention plan of any candidate for president in decades.[6]

Mr. Booker's plan was announced in May of 2019. It would have required all gun owners to acquire a license through the federal government. At the time, only sixteen states had a similar requirement to varying degrees. Senator Booker's plan was a catalyst for other presidential candidates to develop gun control policies as well.

Senator Elizabeth Warren; former Housing and Urban Development secretary in the Obama administration, Julian Castro; South Bend, Indiana, mayor Pete Buttigieg; and former Texas representative Beto O'Rourke all echoed their support for a national licensing plan. Mr. O'Rourke even went as far as demanding banks and credit card companies stop processing assault weapons sales and firearms transactions without background checks.[7] But neither Ms. Warren nor Mr. O'Rourke defined what they meant by *assault weapon.*

Mr. Castro unveiled a gun policy after an El Paso shooting, and he also came out at the time in favor of a buyback program that was first suggested by candidates Joe Biden and Senator Bernie Sanders. Ms. Warren did not support the buyback plan, but she was in favor, like Governor Cuomo, of reducing the power of the NRA in America. The Massachusetts senator also proposed putting $100 million annually toward gun-safety research. This, of course, is the usual Democratic strategy of "Throw money at it."

Senator Warren said during her campaign:

> Historically, when Congress works to address big national issues, we do not simply pass one law and cross our fingers. Instead, we continue to research . . . into new policies around the consequences of our existing policies . . . and then come back on a regular basis to update the law . . . We don't do this with guns.[8]

Senator Warren also echoed Senator Kamala Harris's plan in pledging to act on gun control within the first hundred days of their administrations through executive actions. Shortly thereafter, Ms. Harris ended her bid for president. We will say more about Kamala Harris on guns and gun control in the next section of this sixth essay.

Democratic candidate Amy Klobuchar, Democrat from Minnesota, said on the campaign trail that she would not want to "hurt my uncle Dick in his deer stand."[9] She added, "So I come at this from a little different perspective than some of my colleagues running for this office."

Like Ms. Klobuchar, Senator Bernie Sanders has many constituents who hunt. According to the Vermont Department of Fish and Wildlife, there are sixty-six thousand residents who hunt, and the state rakes in $4 million in hunting and fishing licenses every year. During his 2016 presidential candidacy, Mr. Sanders was frequently attacked for voting against the 1993 law that established federal background checks. During the 2020 campaign, on February 20, 2019, Bernie Sanders said the following about semiautomatic assault weapons via his Twitter account:

> I am running for president because we must end the epidemic of gun violence in this country. We need to take on the NRA, expand background checks, end the gun show loophole, and ban the sale and distribution of assault weapons.[10]

Like the other Democratic candidates, there is nothing in Mr. Sanders's remark about how to define an *assault weapon*. Of all the more than two dozen Democratic candidates for president in 2020, only one had not seen a mass shooting take place in his or her state. This was Representative Tulsi Gabbard of Hawaii. Ms. Gabbard has been criticized on the campaign trail by other candidates for not supporting gun control measures that are widely supported by other Democrats. Perhaps this is due to Ms. Gabbard's military background.

Some Democratic candidates for president in 2020 also changed their minds during the campaign trail leading up to the election in November of 2020. In May of 2020, Beto O'Rourke, for example, told reporters that the federal gun licensing idea "went too far." But the next day, and after what he called a "night of reflection," he changed his mind, and he credited Senator Booker for changing his mind about the issue.

Senator Kirsten Gillibrand, who dropped out of the presidential race in late August of 2020, went from an A rating from the NRA to an F rating. Later, she called this a point of pride. Another 2020 Democratic candidate, Tim Ryan of Ohio, also went from an A rating to an F from the NRA. Mr. Ryan later shifted his stance and made many contributions to gun control organizations.

Finally, the mayor of South Bend, Indiana, Pete Buttigieg, at a townhall meeting in 2020, followed the Democratic Party line, including this comment he made about serving in the military in Afghanistan:

> I did not carry an assault weapon around a foreign country so I could come home and see them used to massacre my countrymen.[11]

The mayor is certainly correct that the M16 he was carrying in the war was an assault weapon. But he said nothing about how an assault weapon might be defined. When a Democrat does define it, it is usually by the number of bullets that the rifle carries, as we will discuss later in this essay.

This brings us to the two final sections of this essay, in which we will sketch out the Biden-Harris administration's statements on the Second Amendment and on gun control and provide a critique of those views.

The Biden-Harris Administration on the Second Amendment and Gun Control

Both Joe Biden and Kamala Harris have had extensive records on the Second Amendment and gun control before their election in November of 2020. Nevertheless, there are two sources to glean their administration's views on these issues: one is in a document, and the other is a speech given recently by Mr. Biden.

The document is titled "The Biden Plan to End Our Gun Violence Epidemic."[12] It was issued by the Biden administration on June 23, 2021, six months into the Biden-Harris first term. The other source for discerning the forty-sixth president's current views on the Second Amendment and gun control is a speech the president gave on the third anniversary of the shooting at Marjory Stoneman Douglas High School in Parkland, Florida, on June 9, 2021. Mr. Biden's remarks were taped. He was not present in Florida that day.

From both of these two sources, Mr. Biden indicates his administration's plan in regard to the issues of this essay. These may be summarized in the following way:

1. First, a ban on so-called assault weapons.
2. Second, a ban on high-capacity magazines.
3. Third, a mandate for background checks on all gun sales.
4. Fourth, eliminating immunity for gun manufacturers.

About this fourth issue, Mr. Biden said on June 9 that he wanted to clamp down on "whoever knowingly put weapons of war on our streets."

Mr. Biden did not, however, supply a definition of what he meant by *weapons of war on our streets* or by *assault weapon*. This appears to be nothing more than another scare tactic that the Left often employs to put the seeds of dissention into the hearts of Americans in regard to guns.

None of these four Democrat points concentrating on guns and gun control, however, are particularly new in the sense that they have not been suggested previously by Democrats for the last twenty-five years. But these two sources were the first times as president that Biden was calling on Congress to take up these issues.

Amy Swearer, in an article for the Heritage Foundation on March 7, 2021, commented on these four proposals from the Biden-Harris administration. Ms. Swearer wrote, "As usual, instead of addressing the real, underlying problems when it comes to gun violence, President Biden is pushing politically divisive measures that could seriously damage our right to keep and bear arms without making the nation any safer."[13]

In the same interview/article, Ms. Swearer also gave some telling criticisms of each of Mr. Biden's proposals. Most of those we will refer to in the final section of this sixth essay on the Progressive New Left and their views on guns and the Second Amendment.

The Biden plan tells us, "It is within our grasp to end our gun violence epidemic and respect the Second Amendment, which is limited. As president, Biden will pursue constitutional, common-sense gun safety policies." The plan goes on to list and discuss several examples of what the Biden-Harris team has in mind when it comes to guns. Among those plans and examples are the following:

1. Hold gun manufacturers accountable.
2. Regulate possession of existing assault weapons under the National Firearms Act.
3. Buy back the assault weapons and high-capacity magazines already in our communities.
4. Reduce the stockpiling of weapons.
5. Keep guns out of dangerous hands.
6. Require background checks for all gun sales.
7. Close the "hate crime loophole."
8. Close the "Charleston loophole."
9. Close the "fugitive from justice loophole."
10. Give states incentives to set up gun licensing programs.

In regard to number seven in the list, the plan tells us, "Biden will enact legislation prohibiting an individual 'who has been convicted of a misdemeanor hate crime, or received an enhanced sentence for a misdemeanor because of hate or bias in its commission' from purchasing or possessing a firearm." As we shall see in the next essay of this study, what counts as a *hate crime* is not an easy question to answer.

In regard to the Charleston loophole—number eight—the Biden plan observes:

> The Charleston loophole allows people to complete a firearms purchase if their background check is not completed within three business days. Biden supports the proposal in the Enhanced Background Checks Act of 2019, which extends the timeline from three to 10 business days.

Still under the heading of "Charleston loophole," the document continues:

> Biden will also direct the Federal Bureau of Investigation (FBI) to put on his desk within his first 100 days as president a report detailing the cases in which background checks are not completed within 10 days and steps the federal government can take to reduce or eliminate this occurrence.

The "fugitive from justice loophole," or item number nine of the plan, refers to an action taken by the Donald Trump administration. Mr. Biden's suggestion in this regard is to "enact legislation to prohibit online sales of firearms, ammunition, kits, and gun parts."

About incentives to states, number ten in the list, the plan tells us, "Mr. Biden will enact legislation to give states and local governments grants to require individuals to obtain a license prior to purchasing a gun." Once again, the normal Democratic strategy—if there is a problem, throw money at it.

In addition to the ten proposals, the Biden plan also speaks of other proposals related to online harassment and abuse as well as violence against women. It also calls on law enforcement to "expand the use of evidence-based lethality assessments" in cases of domestic violence.[14]

Additionally, Mr. Biden's plan also sketches out observations about the storing of weapons, the access of minor children to weapons, and ghost guns (guns without serial numbers), and it calls on the Bureau of Alcohol, Tobacco, Firearms and Explosives (ATF) to report on gun trafficking every year. All of these additional proposals, however, for the most part, refer to the strategies in the four points discussed at the beginning of this section of this sixth essay, which brings us to a critique of those four ideas, the final section of this sixth essay.

Before we get to that critique, however, we must discuss a few gaffes that Mr. Biden has made over the past few years in regard to the Second Amendment and gun control. He has related on at least two occasions that in the Founding Fathers' time, the individual citizen had no right to own a cannon.

On June 23, 2021, and again earlier during his presidential campaign, Mr. Biden said:

> The Second Amendment, from the day it was passed, limited the type of people who could own a gun. You could not buy a cannon.

The *Washington Post*, citing experts on the Second Amendment and historical documents, reported that Mr. Biden's assertion about cannons relative to the right to bear and keep arms is demonstrably false. The *Post* awarded Mr. Biden four "Pinocchios" for the remarks about cannons and the Second Amendment, the highest number possible in their rating system.[15]

On another occasion during his campaign leading to his election to president, Joe Biden observed, "Like most rights, the right secured by the Second Amendment is not unlimited. From Blackstone through the 19th-century cases, commentators and courts routinely explained that the right was not a right to keep and carry any weapon whatsoever in any manner whatsoever and for whatever purpose."

In fact, the Bill of Rights and the Second Amendment do endorse a right to bear and keep arms, both in terms of individual citizens and in the context of a militia. This brings us to our critique of the Biden plan on guns, the subject matter of the final section of this essay of this work on the Progressive New Left's views on contemporary issues.

During the run-up to the 2020 election for president of the United States, both Senator Cory Booker and Kamala Harris chastised Joe Biden on his role in the 1994 crime bill. Ms. Harris herself has been criticized by criminal justice reform advocates as being too tough on the accused during her tenure as the San Francisco district attorney and as California's attorney general before she was elected senator.

This brings us to the final section of this essay, in which we will outline and discuss a critique of the Biden-Harris plan on what they call the "epidemic of gun violence in America."

A Critique of the Biden Plan

In regard to the ban on so-called assault weapons, it is important to point out that nowhere in Mr. Biden's speech, nor in his plan, do we find a definition for what *assault weapons* or *weapons of war* are, like with the other Democrats mentioned earlier in this essay.[16] Are these bans to be only "future bans" and not on the guns Americans already own? This is what Mr. Biden appears to have called for during his campaign. "You can keep the guns you have now, but we are going to ban future sales"? Or is Mr. Biden suggesting a full-on Australian-style confiscation of weapons? Thus, Mr. Biden's first proposal is pretty vague on assault weapons.

In regard to high-capacity magazines, we must begin with the Second Amendment. If it protects them, then it does not matter what anyone's particular opinion is on the matter. If the Second Amendment protects it, then that is the end of the matter. Something like twenty to fifty million of what Mr. Biden calls *assault weapons* are in circulation among civilians in this country. When the New Left begins to use phrases like *weapons of war*, these are not useful or meaningful constitutional tests.

If we look at what the Supreme Court has said in cases like *Heller* and *McDonald* in Washington and Chicago, and when we simply look at the original meaning of the words of the Second Amendment, there is nothing in the Constitution and the Bill of Rights saying that if some people think this is a *weapon of war*, then it is not covered. The Supreme Court in the two cases provided a test that essentially said, "If it is a weapon that is commonly used by law-abiding citizens for lawful purposes, then that weapon is protected under the Second Amendment."

If one looks at the weapons that were commonly employed when the Second Amendment was written, they would find there are several. These would have included single-shot pistols or dueling handguns, muskets, the Brown Bess musket, and the Kentucky long rifle used by the Continental Army. Some of these, at times, were used as "weapons of war" and were often used in service to the militia.

The idea of *weapons of war* is nothing more than an attempt to scare people. It has no constitutional significance. But beyond that, if we could snap our fingers and all twenty million semiautomatic rifles in America would disappear, would that make a big difference to gun violence in America? The short answer to that question is no.

When one looks at the characteristics of *assault weapons*, it is never things like caliber, muzzle velocity, and rate of fire that are mentioned by the Leftists. It is almost always cosmetic features, like collapsing stocks and pistol grips. And if you ask how often these guns are used to commit crimes, the answer is not very often. To be more specific, these weapons are employed in only about 3 percent of gun crimes in America.

In regard to high-capacity magazines, we must begin again with the Second Amendment. Plus, it is an arbitrary definition to begin with. Some states say it refers to ten rounds; other states say twelve; some states even say fifteen rounds—but there are no statistical reasons for picking any of these numbers. The more we get beneath these numbers, the more we see visceral reactions, particularly in relation to mass killings. The media coverage of these events goes well beyond the small number of these events every year in America.

We must add to this the fact that in the great majority of mass shootings in this country, the perpetrators come to the scene with more than one weapon. On the other hand, if we ask about the context of how law-abiding citizens use an AR-15, it is when a homeowner confronts a person who has broken into his or her house. People in these circumstances act as first responders to crimes in their own homes.

In regard to the issue of background checks, most gun sales and transfers in the United States already go through background checks. If one buys a gun from a store, from any sort of brick-and-mortar place, from anyone that the ATF calls "engaged in the business of dealing firearms," your typical gun seller—whether it is at a gun show, a store, or over the internet—federal law already requires a background check.

There is, however, a small number of guns that do not require background checks. These are guns sold within the same state. So if I want to sell my gun in Baltimore to a man in, say, Annapolis, there would be no background check requirement. But if I wished to sell the gun to someone in Richmond, Virginia, then a background check would be required.

In regard to eliminating immunity for gun manufacturers, Mr. Biden's fourth point or area of his proposals, people are usually referring to something known as the Protection of Lawful Commerce in Arms Act. This law is unique because it protects gun manufacturers, sellers, and distributors from lawsuits that try to claim they are responsible and liable for third-party criminal misuses of their guns. In essence, then, if a gun seller sells a gun in compliance with federal law, and for whatever reason, that weapon is employed to harm someone else, the law protects the gun seller, as well as the gun manufacturer, from being sued.

In Mr. Biden's plan, he wishes to eliminate the Protection of Lawful Commerce Arms Act. Interestingly enough, this law is unique to the gun industry. Mr. Biden wishes to make gun manufacturers liable. This is not an attempt to reduce the number of gun crimes in America in any way. It is about choking out the gun industry.

Another question that is important to raise about the Biden gun plan is whether anything we find there makes American culture a safer place. And if not, what should we be doing? The short answer that Amy Swearer gave to that question was this:

> The short answer is no, even if [Mr. Biden's proposals were] 100 percent successful, [and] even if we just ignore any Constitutional problems.[17]

So what may help stop American gun violence?

If we return to the fact that every year, two-thirds of all gun deaths in the United States occur as suicides, then already, two-thirds of all gun deaths in the United States are mental health related.

Add to this fact that relatively little money is spent by the federal government every year on suicide prevention and intervention for people who pose a threat to themselves or others.

There are, in the United States, some proven anti-gang-violence programs that may be helpful.

To cite one example, in the Virginia state legislature, Democrat delegates recently declined to fund "Investing in Education" and "Investing in Communities to Create Stable Families," which were both defeated. Apparently, it did not occur to the Virginian legislators that the destruction of the family structure in the United States may have some relation to gun violence.

Data from the Census Bureau from 2016 indicates that 69 percent of all children under the age of eighteen still live in families with two parents, while 23 percent live with a single parent. From 1960 until 2016, the number of children in America living with a single parent tripled from 8 to 23 percent. By the year 2020, nearly 19 million children in America, about a quarter of all children in the US, lived with a single parent.

None of this discussion we have laid out so far in this sixth essay is related to a number of other fundamental questions that the Democratic New Left Progressives never seem to want to raise, such as "Why is there so much Black-on-Black gun crime in America?" Anyone who raises such a question is, of course, immediately branded a racist. Or how about, "Why is the suicide rate among transgender Americans so high?" A recent survey has shown that 41 percent of all American transgendered people have reported contemplating suicide in their lifetimes.[18]

What role do gangs play in American gun deaths? How do groups like MS-13 and other gangs, like the Crips and the Bloods, contribute to gun violence and other violent crime?

Recently, it was estimated that there are more than one hundred thousand gang members in Chicago, where there are only thirteen thousand police officers.[19] The city of Los Angeles is reported to have more than a thousand separate gangs with tens or hundreds of thousands of members in those gangs.[20] We rarely see anyone from the Left speak of what role gang violence may play in the supposed epidemic of gun violence in America.

How many undocumented migrants are there in the United States? Democrats generally use the eleven million figure often quoted in their remarks about immigration. But some estimates suggest that this number is probably at least twice as high. And more to the present point, how many of the migrants coming to the southern border have firearms with them?

There are no figures available on how many firearms are confiscated from migrants coming to the southern border. There are, however, anecdotal reports of gun confiscation in the local press. On May 7, 2021, for example, in Eagle Pass, Texas, Border Patrol found a bag with eight AK-47-style pistols and ten AK-47-style thirty-round magazines.[21] There is no way of knowing how many other firearms come from south of the southern US border. Research and answers to these questions and many others like them might provide some clues into where the federal government should spend their money in regard to gun deaths in the United States.

One final point needs to be made about the supposed gun violence epidemic, as President Biden has called it. In 1993 and 1994, there were 15,297 and 15,568 homicides by guns in the United States. By 2019, the most recent figures available, there were 14,861 murders by guns in the United States. Gun violence in America is not an epidemic. It is actually decreasing.

Meanwhile, the most recent polls of Americans on stricter gun control indicate that 60 percent are in favor of it and 40 percent are against it. The 2021 positive responses are slightly up from the 57 percent of 2020 and the 52 percent of 2017.[22] This is clearly still an important cultural issue in the United States.

In 2017 in the United States, gun deaths reached their highest level in over forty years, with 39,773 gun deaths that year alone. That included 23,000 suicides, 13,000 homicides, 510 police shootings, 478 unintentional deaths, and 310 gun deaths with indeterminate intent.[23]

About 31 percent of American households report owning firearms, and 22 percent of American adults own "one or more firearms."[24]

This brings us to the sources of this sixth essay, followed by Essay Seven. The central concern of the seventh essay of this critical study on the Progressive New Left's attitudes toward contemporary American issues will be what has come to be called by the New Left Progressives the problems of *hate crimes* and *hate speech.*

ESSAY SEVEN

The New Left and the Problems of Hate Crimes and Hate Speech

I

The main purpose of this seventh essay is to speak about two other issues that have become central since the 1980s among the Progressive New Left politicians, and those are the phenomena of hate crimes and hate speech. We will open the essay with some short comments about the definition of a *hate crime* from the Progressive point of view.

This will be followed by a second section of this essay, in which we will speak of the history of the idea of hate crimes, from ancient times until contemporary American times. These two sections will be followed by a discussion of the phenomenon of hate crimes in the context of the American legal tradition.

In the fourth section of this essay, we will discuss the idea of hate crimes within the context of the views of the American Progressive New Left, including what the Biden-Harris administration has written and promulgated about the phenomenon. And in the fifth and final section of Essay Seven, we will supply a critique of what the Biden administration and the Democratic Party in America in general believe about the idea of hate crimes and hate speech in the United States.

Along the way, we will also speak of a number of examples of supposed hate crimes in America, including the Matthew Shepard case, the James Byrd Jr. case, and the Jussie Smollett case, in which he claimed to be a victim of hate crimes by Donald Trump supporters who told him that where they were in Chicago was "MAGA country"—that is, "Make America Great Again country."

It turns out, however, that Smollett had orchestrated the entire episode in the early morning hours in the city of Chicago, in that he had "hired" two Nigerian friends to commit the supposed hate crime. This brings us to a discussion of the nature, or the definition, of a hate crime.

The Definition of a Hate Crime

The first question in this essay is how we are to define a *hate crime*. One essay on the internet titled "History of Hate Crime" tells us this:

> A hate crime is defined as any wrongdoing perpetrated against a particular group of people. It is a form of prejudice directed at a group of individuals based on their ethnicity, age, sexual orientation, religious preference, or any other defining characteristic.[1]

From this definition, we may garner the following necessary conditions for a hate crime:

1. It is wrongdoing.
2. It is directed at a certain group, against which there is a prejudice.
3. It must be based on (1) ethnicity, (2) age, (3) sexual orientation, (4) religious preference, or (5) any other defining characteristic of that group.

The article on "Hate Crimes" from Wikipedia suggests that a hate crime, also called a *bias-motivated crime* or simply *bias crime*, is a "prejudice-motivated crime which occurs when a perpetrator targets a victim because of his or her membership, or perceived membership, of a certain racial group or racial demographic."[2] This definition of a hate crime puts all the emphasis on race. It says nothing about age, sexual orientation, or religious preference. Thus, it is very different from our first definition.

Another internet entry under the title, "What is a Hate Crime?" tells us this:

> A hate crime is a crime that is motivated by bias or prejudice against someone based upon the person's identity or affiliation with a group.

This definition of a hate crime appears to be in consort with our first definition but at odds with our second definition, for this third definition does not limit a hate crime simply to race. The US Department of Justice defines a hate crime at the federal level as:

> Crimes committed on the basis of the victim's perceived or actual race, color, religion, national origin, sexual orientation, gender, gender identity, or disability.[3]

In regard to hate crimes, the FBI is also involved in a number of activities, including:

- Investigative activities
- Support of state and local law enforcement for the handling and report of hate crimes
- Prosecutorial decisions
- Public outreach and training

On the FBI's website for responses to hate crimes, it reports:

> Hate itself is not a crime—and the FBI is mindful of the necessary protection of freedom of speech, freedom of the press, as well as the protection of other civil liberties, both here and abroad.

The fourth definition of a hate crime, from the FBI, adds *disability* to the mix but otherwise is consistent with the first definition's outline in the previous analysis. In an article called "Hate Crimes That Changed History," Ave Mince-Didier suggested that a hate crime is a "crime committed because of the victim's race, religion, color, gender, ethnicity, or gender expression." [4]This definition adds *gender expression* to the possible groups to whom one may commit a hate crime. How we are to define *gender expression*, however, is another matter entirely.

The government's definition of a hate crime also adds *property* and even *society* as possible objects of a hate crime. One might ask, of course: If this is the proper definition of a *hate crime*, then are all property crimes and invasions in times of war also to be considered hate crimes?

All these definitions of hate crimes say nothing about the difference between *perception* and *reality*. The purported hate crime perpetrated against Matthew Shepard, for example, was supposedly because he was gay, but at the trial of one of his murderers, the perpetrator said his motive was robbery. If that was true, then are all robberies hate crimes?

An episode in which several Asian American women were shot in Atlanta was immediately understood as a hate crime against Asians, but there is no evidence that this was the best explanation for the crimes in that episode. It may only have "appeared" to be hate crimes, but the reality of the event might have been quite different.

The main conclusion we should make about the definition of a hate crime is how difficult it is to establish necessary and sufficient conditions for calling something a hate crime.

Perhaps we will be aided by a look at the idea of hate crimes throughout history, the topic of the next section of this seventh essay.

The History of Hate Crimes

Hate crimes date back to ancient civilizations. One of the earliest examples is from the Roman Empire, which was well known for its persecution of Christians. According to several ancient documents, Christianity was largely tolerated by Emperor Nero until the year AD 64, when a great fire destroyed a large portion of Rome. The emperor was concerned that he was being blamed for the damage to the city, so he, in turn, shifted the blame to the Christians. In fact, he called for anyone who followed the religion of Jesus Christ to be punished.

This led to years of hate crimes in the late first century against Christians, against anyone who professed the Christian faith, and against a number of other Roman religions that were not the traditional Greco-Roman polytheism. The treatment of Jews by Christians in the High Middle Ages up to the Reformation was clearly another example of a hate crime in Western European society.

Some hate crimes have been so great that they have sometimes affected the entire world. Perhaps the most notable in the twentieth century was the Nazi persecution of the Jews. In fact, Adolf Hitler's "Final Solution" called for the total annihilation of the Jewish people, which led to the building of concentration camps and death factories. The Holocaust resulted in the mass murder in these camps and factories of millions of people, including Jews, the disabled, homosexuals, and Gypsies, among other peoples—all apparently hate crimes.

During the 1960s in the American South, civil rights workers and social activists faced violence and threats from members of the Ku Klux Klan (KKK) and other organizations committed to segregation. Local politicians and prosecutors were often unwilling to press charges in regard to these crimes, and in some cases, they were allied with the persecutors. One fine example took place in 1964 in Mississippi, where three civil rights workers—James Early Chaney, Andrew Goodman, and Michael Schwerner—were abducted and murdered by the KKK. All three victims were White men, which angered the Klan members.

Later, in more recent times, the act of genocide—or an attempt to obliterate an entire ethnic, racial, or religious group—has occurred in both Bosnia and Rwanda, Africa. On a somewhat smaller scale, constantly all over the world, Muslims, such as the Palestinians, have a goal of moving the state of Israel from controlling their homeland in the Middle East.

In the United States, the majority of hate crimes before the late twentieth century were racially motivated. Many of these crimes included intimidation, vandalism, and assault of Black people in America. Figures on hate crimes from the FBI have shown that hate crimes are on the rise in this country. In 2006 alone, they reported that there was an 8 percent increase in hate crimes from 2005.

In June of 1998, James Byrd Jr., a Black man, was murdered in Jasper, Texas, by White supremacists who kidnapped, beat, and tied him to the back of a pickup truck and then dragged him for three miles before he was decapitated, followed by his body being dumped at an African American church. Three men were ultimately convicted of the murder of James Byrd Jr.

Just four months later, in October of 1998, university student Matthew Shepard was tortured and murdered by two men in Laramie, Wyoming, simply because he was gay. Both killers received life sentences, but one of them said at his trial that his motive was robbery, so it might not have been a hate crime at all. In 2009, Congress passed the Matthew Shepard and James Byrd Jr. Hate Crimes Prevention Act. This act made it a crime to "cause or attempt to cause injury to any person because of the person's race, color, religion, national origin, gender, sexual orientation, gender identity or disability."

The Jussie Smollett case is perhaps the best known of these contemporary hate crimes. In the early hours of January 29, 2019, Jussie Smollett reported to the police that he had been attacked on a street near his home in Chicago by two men who yelled racist and homophobic slurs at him. But after investigating the incident over the next few weeks, Chicago Police detectives determined that Mr. Smollett had orchestrated the attack himself.

Police detectives working on the case related that Mr. Smollett had hired a pair of Nigerian brothers—Olabinjo and Abimbola Osundairo—to stage the attack. The brothers were reportedly paid $3,500 for their roles in the plot.

Mr. Smollett was originally charged with disorderly conduct. But a month later, on February 20, 2019, Cook County prosecutors dismissed all charges against the actor. A Cook County judge appointed a special prosecutor, Dan K. Webb, to look into the case. Mr. Webb, in his subsequent report, said that the case should not have been dismissed and that he "did develop evidence that establishes substantial abuses of discretion and operational failures by the State's Attorney's Office in prosecuting and resolving the initial Smollett case."[5]

Recent evidence from the National Coalition of Anti-Violence Programs has shown that transgender people, particularly transgender females, are disproportionally targeted for physical violence and even police violence.[6] In 1993, Brandon Teena, a transgender man, was raped and later murdered by two men after they discovered that he was anatomically female. The murder was later dramatized in the film *Boys Don't Cry*.

In 2002, Gwen Araujo, a transgender woman, was murdered in California by four men after two of them had engaged in sexual activity with her, during which they discovered she had a penis. At the subsequent trials of these men, they pleaded what has come to be called "trans-panic," where the defendant claims that the shock of discovery caused them to "panic and attack." The jury ultimately rejected that argument and convicted two of the killers for murder.

As of June 2010, twenty states had laws protecting people who were victimized by hate crimes. By June of 2020, the number of states had increased to forty-seven. The District of Columbia took part as well. Only Arkansas, South Carolina, and Wyoming were without hate crime laws.[7]

As in a national discussion on guns, national discussions on hate crimes usually follow a distinct pattern. Some well-known national event—like Matthew Shepard or James Byrd Jr.—becomes so well known that state or federal legislation follows.

One recent example was the murder of six Asian massage parlor workers in Atlanta, mentioned earlier in this essay, who were killed, it was believed, because they were Asian. This prompted legislation introduced by Representative Grace Meng of New York and Senator Mazie Hirono of Hawaii to introduce a bill that would make the reporting of hate crimes more accessible at the state level.

Thus was born the COVID-19 Hate Crimes Act of 2021. The act came to President Joe Biden's desk on May 20, 2021, and he immediately signed it. At the time, Mr. Biden said, "Hate has no place in America—and I look forward to making it clear this afternoon by signing the COVID-19 Hate Crimes Act into law."

We will say more in this essay about the observations of both Mr. Biden and Vice President Harris about this bill. It is enough now to say that both had visceral reactions to the case in Atlanta. This brings us to a discussion of hate crimes in the context of the American law, the topic of the next section of this essay.

Hate Crimes and American Law

Since the year 1968, federal and state laws on hate crimes have been developed in the United States. Nationally, the Civil Rights Act of 1968 permits federal prosecution of anyone who willfully injures, intimidates, or interferes with any person, or attempts to do so by force or threat of force, because of his race, color, religion, or national origin. Those who violate this statute face a "substantial fine, or up to one year of imprisonment." If bodily injury was involved or a firearm was used in the crime, then the perpetrator is "punishable to up to ten years in prison." The Civil Rights Act of 1968 goes on to say that if the crime involved "kidnapping, sexual assault, or murder, the crime may be punished by life in prison."

In 1990, the United States passed the Hate Crimes Statistics Act, which allows the FBI to gather data on crimes committed because of a victim's race, religion, disability, sexual orientation, or ethnicity. In the act, however, cities and states were not required to send data to the FBI. This bill was later modified in the 2009 Matthew Shepard and James Byrd Jr. Hate Crimes Prevention Act we will speak about in the following analysis.[8] Since 1992, the FBI has released an annual *Hate Crimes Report*. On November 16, 2020, the FBI released its most recent report. It reported 7,317 incidents of hate crimes in 2019. This was an increase from 7,120 in 2018.

In 1994, the United States Congress passed the Violent Crime Control and Law Enforcement Act. This act required the United States Sentencing Commission to increase the penalties for hate crimes committed or the basis of actual or perceived bias based on "race, color, religion, national origin, ethnicity, or gender of any person."

This was followed two years later by the Church Arson Prevention Act of 1996. This made it a federal crime to damage religious property or obstruct "someone from the free exercise of his or her religious beliefs." This 1996 bill provided that the penalty for the offense of this act is ten to twenty years in prison.

Earlier in this essay, we mentioned the Matthew Shepard and James Byrd Jr. Hate Crimes Prevention Act of 2009. The act was signed into law by President Obama on October 28, 2009, and was attached to the National Defense Authorization Act for the fiscal year of 2010.

This 2009 act expanded the existing federal hate crimes law so that crimes motivated by a victim's actual or perceived gender, sexual orientation, gender identity, and disability were added to the list of groups that may be the objects of hate crimes.

In May of 2021, President Joe Biden signed into law the COVID-19 Hate Crimes Act as a response to six women of Asian descent being shot in the city of Atlanta, as mentioned earlier in this essay. An accompanying statement said:

> Documented incidents of harassment and violence against Asian Americans have increased dramatically during the COVID-19 pandemic.[9]

We will say more about this 2021 bill in the next section of Essay Seven. Before we do that, however, we will make some observations about hate crimes in state laws. Forty-six states and the District of Columbia have enacted hate crime penalty-enhancement laws, meaning if someone commits a crime based on the victim's personal characteristics, then the perpetrator faces more severe penalties.

There is not, however, one uniform definition of what a hate crime is in these state bills. Only two-thirds of the states that have these laws consider sexual orientation, gender, or gender identity as "penalty enhancements for crimes." Nearly all states use race, ethnicity, and religion in their hate crime bills. Thirty-one states consider hate crimes on the basis of sexual orientation. The same states also include gender identity in their hate laws. These same states also consider disability to be a reason for designating something a hate crime.

Five states do not have hate crime statutes. These are Arkansas, Indiana, South Carolina, Utah, and Wyoming. All states have vandalism laws, but only nineteen states prohibit cross burning.[10] Data on hate crime statutes is collected by the Anti-Defamation League, while the FBI, as indicated earlier, collects hate crime data and publishes an annual report.

This brings us to the fourth section of Essay Seven, in which we will explore what the New Left Progressives have written and have had to say about hate crimes, followed by a critique of those views.

The Progressive New Left on Hate Crimes

The COVID-19 Hate Crimes Act mentioned earlier in this essay and President Biden's signing of that act provide the most recent Progressive New Left views on hate crimes. Representatives Meng and Hirono's bill instructs that the Department of Justice should designate a point person to expedite the review of COVID-related hate crimes, expand public reporting efforts, and provide guidance on how to make the reporting of hate crimes more accessible at both the local and state levels. The bill ensures that online reporting processes are now available in a number of languages.

On May 21 and May 24, 2021, both President Biden and Vice President Harris have spoken eloquently about hate crime in America. On the former date, they both referred to the supposed increase in "Asian American hate crimes during the COVID-19 pandemic."

On the latter date, both Democratic politicians spoke directly about anti-Semitism. On both dates, these events appear to have been motivated by societal events or incidents.

The events that occasioned the May 21, 2021, addresses were the killing of six Asian massage workers in Atlanta and the Meng-Hirono Act mentioned earlier. The event that appears to be the impetus for the remarks from May 24 was an attack at a Los Angeles sushi restaurant. Indeed, after the LA attack, Hollywood began to use its megaphone to speak out against anti-Semitism with remarks from *Big Bang Theory* star Mayim Bialik, Debra Messing from *Will and Grace*, and political comedian Michael Rapaport.

We have seen this pattern of proposed legislation that follows nationally publicized events in America to be a regular occurrence in public shootings in regard to gun control in the United States as well.

In remarks that President Biden made in Georgia in mid-March 2021, he observed:

> Whatever the motivation, we know this: too many Asian Americans have been walking up and down the streets worrying.

Mr. Biden added:

> It is truly heart-wrenching to listen to Asian American community leaders discuss living in the fear of violence.[11]

Ms. Harris, who was also present at the meeting in Georgia, said after the president's remarks:

> Racism is real in America. And it has always been. Xenophobia is real in America and always has been. Sexism, too.

On April 19, 2021, judiciary Democrats also signaled that they were "committed to addressing anti-Asian hate crimes in America." Indeed, much Democratic support for the COVID-19 bill against Asian American hate crimes was voiced by Dick Durbin of Illinois, Cory Booker of New Jersey, and Chuck Schumer of New York.

Earlier, in 2012, chair Durban held a hearing of the Judiciary Subcommittee on the Constitution, civil rights, and human rights on hate crimes and domestic extremism following the horrific massacre of six worshippers at a Sikh temple in Oak Creek, Wisconsin. After the hearing, what did Mr. Durban do? He led an effort to update the FBI's *Hate Crime Incident Report* to include crimes committed against Sikh Americans, Hindu Americans, and Arab Americans.

One strategy that has clearly been employed by the Democrats is that they have managed to gradually include more and more special-interest groups so that they are covered by hate crime laws, in the same way that they have a more lenient approach to Border Patrol because, among other things, they hope that these migrants will eventually become Democratic voters in this country.[12]

The Democratic view of hate crimes is part of a much larger "cultural civil war," as former secretary of education and drug czar William Bennett spoke of on a recent Fox News program.

He related that we "are in the middle of a new civil war, but this time it is not over a single issue. This new civil war is over a variety of societal issues, including education, immigration, race, and many other questions." Needless to say, two other issues are hate crimes and hate speech as well.

In our analysis in this essay, we so far have said nothing about hate speech and how it may be related to hate crimes as well as what Americans believe about hate speech. This is the subject matter of the next section of this essay.

Hate Speech, Hate Crimes, and Public Opinion

Another aspect of the Progressive New Left's views on hate crimes is what they also have had to say when it comes to what they call *hate speech*. A study that may be found on the YouGov America website reports that the majority of Americans are in support of banning hate speech. Overall, 41 percent are in favor of it, and 37 percent are against it. These numbers are also instructive when we look at the issue in terms of race.[13]

According to the website, 50 percent of Hispanic Americans are in favor of banning hate speech, while 24 percent are against it. Sixty-two percent of African Americans support a ban on hate speech, while only 14 percent are against it. In terms of White Americans, however, 36 percent are in favor, while 43 percent are against the idea of regulating hate speech.

These numbers are interesting when understood in the context of research reported by Emily Ekins in an article for the Cato Institute's *Survey Reports* on October 31, 2017. Ms. Ekins made the claim in her article that is titled "The State of Free Speech and Tolerance in America" that "Nearly three-fourths (71 percent) of Americans believe that political correctness has done more to silence important discussions our society needs to have."

Ms. Ekins added:

> A little more than a quarter (28 percent) instead believe that political correctness has done more to help people avoid offending others.[14]

Ms. Ekins also reports in her article that "58 percent of Americans believe the political climate today prevents them from saying things they believe." She also relates, "Democrats are unique, however, in that a slim majority (53 percent) do not feel the need to self-censor." On the other hand, "strong majorities of

Republicans (73 percent) and Independents (58 percent), say they keep some political beliefs to themselves."

Ms. Ekins's research and her article on it also contain a number of other conclusions about hate speech. Among these are the following:

1. Forty-seven percent of Democrats agree that "the political climate prevents me from saying things I believe because others might find them offensive."
2. Seventy-three percent of Republicans say the same thing.
3. Fifty-eight percent of Independents concur.
4. Fifty-nine percent of Americans think people should be allowed to express unpopular opinions.
5. Forty percent of Americans say that hate speech should be outlawed, while 60 percent believe that hate speech should be allowed.
6. Interesting enough, however, 79 percent of Americans say that it is "morally unacceptable" to engage in hate speech, while 19 percent say that it is morally acceptable.

Despite these findings, Americans are, nevertheless, quite willing to censor, regulate, or punish a wide variety of speech, such as the following:

1. Fifty-one percent of Liberals say that punching a Nazi is morally acceptable.
2. Fifty-three percent of Republicans favor "stripping US citizenship from those who burn the American flag."
3. Fifty-eight percent of Democrats say that employers should be allowed to "punish employees for offensive Facebook posts."
4. Sixty-five percent of Republicans say NFL players should be fired for not standing for the national anthem.

The Progressive New Left's views on hate speech may also be seen in remarks about the matter leading up to the 2020 presidential election. Elizabeth Warren said, "I condemn the speech, and I believe we should be able to hold people accountable for their words."[15]

Democratic candidate Pete Buttigieg, in reference to internet content, related, "Sites that traffic in hate and encourage or fail to moderate abuse and hate should be called out as facilitating socially harmful speech," though he did not provide a definition of that phenomenon.

Andrew Yang, another Democratic candidate for president, observed before the election: "We need to address these issues with tech companies in order to combat the rise of misinformation and hate speech."

Democrats Michael Bennett and Tom Steyer also made comments about hate speech in 2019 and the fall of 2020. Mr. Steyer said that we have to "make sure that hate groups do not find a home on these websites," while Mr. Bennett remarked:

> It is time to revisit the broad immunity provided by Section 230 of the Communications Decency Act, which in many cases has shielded tech companies from accountability for misinformation and hate speech on their platforms.[16]

We will say more about Section 230 and the exemption that Big Tech has been given in that statute in Essay Eleven of this study. It is enough now, however, to point out that social media does have this exemption from liability of their content.

Another American Democrat who is outspoken on the hate crime issue is New York City mayor Bill de Blasio, who said that he wishes to widen the definition of what qualifies as a hate crime. He also said he wants the NYPD to "confront hateful conduct and anything that is not criminal still followed up aggressively, so people feel the presence of law enforcement in the city watching them to make sure this does not happen again."

As indicated earlier in this essay, after the incident in Atlanta, President Biden urged Congress to swiftly pass the COVID-19 Hate Crimes Act proposed by Representatives Meng and Hirono.

Thus, many prominent members of the Progressive New Left have expressed remarks that are perfectly consistent with those made more recently by President Biden and Vice President Harris. The final section of the seventh essay of this study on the views of the New Left will be a critique of what the Progressives have had to say and write about hate crime and hate speech.

A Critique of the Progressive New Left's Views on Hate Speech

Before we get to the critique, I will first make some comments on why I am qualified to speak about ethics and hate speech. During my forty-three-year college teaching career, I taught more than eighty classes on ethics, moral theory, and their applications. I have also, over the years, published six or seven books about ethics and many more articles in peer-reviewed journals.

Both those for and against laws about hate crimes and hate speech in the current debate speak their views in the shadow of English philosopher John Stuart Mill and his book *On Liberty* because that was where the English philosopher set forth his moral principle that he called the *principle of harm*. Essentially, Mill argued that the state is justified in coercing an individual only to prevent "harm" to others and not to condemn that individual for holding objectionable beliefs or for his or her values or personal preferences.

Mill believed that the only way to evaluate whether hate crime bills are morally acceptable is to determine whether the assessment they make of offenders' motives is morally right or wrong.

In other words, do hate crimes, in fact, express valuations that are more reprehensible than those expressed by the perpetrators of other violent crimes?

Using this perspective of John Stuart Mill, my criticisms of the New Left's views on hate crimes are of two types. The first variety has to do specifically with moral matters, while the other kind of criticism has to do with a critique of the FBI's collection of data on hate crimes.

In terms of the philosophical and moral criticisms, the first question that may and should be raised is this: Do hate crime laws inappropriately punish values rather than harms? A second and just as important question is this: Do hate crime laws appropriately punish harms rather than values? In a third philosophical and moral criticism of the New Left's views on hate speech, we will speak of a cluster of Liberal tropes that decision-makers and commentators employ to describe and disguise the hate crime laws' morally judgmental character.

Before we move to my philosophical arguments, however, we must first say a few things about the idea of values as well as more about John Stuart Mill's idea of the principle of harm and the notion of *moral responsibility* in the history of the West.

In the history of Western philosophy, since the time of Aristotle, a distinction has been made between *moral values* and *nonmoral values*. A value, according to Aristotle, is anything we prefer or "value." Thus, the kind of toothpaste I use is a value. But Aristotle also said that certain values are ones that we all should share because they are universal.

Thus, for Aristotle, "Keep your promises," "Don't harm innocent people," and "Tell the truth" are all moral values because we want everyone to hold them.

On the other hand, value statements like "Always use Crest," or "I prefer the one on the left" are both nonmoral values because they don't seem to require a universal consensus, in Aristotle's terms.

John Stuart Mill's principle of harm, which he sketches out in his 1859 book *On Liberty*, tells us this:

> That the only purpose for which power can be rightfully exercised over any member of a civilized community, against his will, is to prevent harm to others.

Mill's idea of the limiting of actions, and perhaps speech as well, depends on whether it causes harm to the person who is the object of the hate crime or hate speech. In philosophical circles in the West, since the time of Mill, philosophers have begun to ask the question, "How is harm to be defined?" Philosopher Joel Feinberg is now widely credited with defining *harm* as "a wrongful setback of one's interests."

The idea of moral responsibility and how to determine it also owes its beginning in the West to Aristotle, who said that an actor is fully morally responsible for his or her actions if he or she meets four conditions. These are:

1. That he or she intended to do the act.
2. That he or she knows right from wrong.
3. That he or she understood the circumstances under which the act was committed.
4. That he or she had the "ability to do otherwise."

By this fourth condition, Aristotle meant that a person was acting freely, "without internal or external constraints." By *internal constraints*, he meant certain kinds of insanity where one's actions could not be different from what they were. By *external constraints*, he meant that no one was holding a gun to the person's head or other ways the actor may be intimidated.[17]

Now, we know that Aristotle is correct about full moral responsibility because of the principal ways we try to avoid responsibility. Consider the four most popular sentences that Americans use in order to avoid responsibility. These are:

1. I did not mean to do it.
2. I did not know it was wrong.
3. I did not understand it was happening.
4. I could not keep from doing it.

It should be clear, of course, that these sentiments are nothing more than Aristotle's ideas of intentions, two kinds of knowledge, and the ability to do otherwise. For Aristotle, one's intentions in a human action are very important, but determining what another's intentions were in an action is not always an easy thing to do.

It should also go without saying that it is not always an easy matter to determine what an individual's motives may have been in his or her action. Those who argue in favor of hate crime legislation must first have decided that the motives of those who commit hate crimes must have been morally bad motives. This would mean, of course, that the locus of a hate crime has shifted from the action itself and the principle of harm to the realm of the human mind and its primary intentions in an action. This says nothing, of course, about dual or multiple motives in a crime or in uttering hate speech.

Additionally, the advocate of hate laws about both actions and hate speech would go on to say that the act itself or the words employed are morally wrong. In other words, hate crimes and hate speech are improper because, at the bottom level, they are morally wrong.

This then raises the question of whether hate crimes and hate speech are for punishing perpetrators or for having inappropriate moral or nonmoral values. In other words, do hate crime laws and punishment for hate speech punish the person's values or his or her actions? Many critics of hate crime legislation say that hate crime laws and punishments for hate speech overly emphasize the bad intentions of the perpetrator while not putting enough emphasis on the application of Mill's principle of harm.

In addition to these philosophical and moral criticisms, other questions can be raised about how we know that hate crimes toward Asian Americans are on the rapid increase during the COVID-19 pandemic. Now, one way to answer that question is simply to say that the FBI says it is on the rise.

But the data on hate crimes in America collected by the FBI comes mostly from the reporting of the police agencies in the United States. All told, the United States has 17,985 police departments. So far, so good. But how many of these nearly eighteen thousand police departments report their hate crimes to the FBI? The answer to that question is illuminating.

Of the slightly less than eighteen thousand police departments in the United States, in the year 2018, the FBI received data from 2,160. If you do math, that comes out to 12 percent. Now, one might obviously ask, if only 12 percent of police departments report their hate crimes to the FBI, how do we know they are on the rise? If we add the fact that a large percentage of reported hate crimes comes from New York and California, then it seems unwise to make any pronouncements about hate crimes in America, if we add the fact that New York and California are among the states with the most restrictive hate crime statutes.

If 88 percent of the police departments in the United States do not report their hate crimes, then how can we arrive at the conclusion that hate crimes directed at Asian Americans are on the rise? It is no surprise, however, that most of the Asian hate crimes in America are in California and New York, if for no other reason than because that is where Asian people reside.

We do know that one in five hate crimes, or 20 percent, in these two states, California and New York, is said to be motivated by homophobia and transphobia. The state of California reported to the FBI that in the year 2020, 1,330 hate crimes occurred in the state. Anti-Black hate crimes were the most plentiful, with 456 cases reported. Crimes against Asian Americans in California more than doubled, from forty-three in 2019 to eighty-nine in 2020.

New York City reported to the FBI in June of 2021 that the city recorded 180 hate crimes from January to May of 2021. This is an increase of 73 percent from the same period in 2020. According to the New York Police Department, eighty NYC hate crimes were reported from January to April of 2021. This is up from sixteen incidents over the same period in 2020. In terms of the New York State numbers, police departments and sheriff offices in New York had an increase of 17.7 percent in 2019, with a total of 619 hate crimes. This means that the total hate crimes in the states of New York and California reached nearly two thousand incidents of the two thousand reported to the FBI for that year. Eighty-five of the New York incidents of hate crimes—two-thirds, or 66 percent—were property crimes, and one-third "targeted people."

Hate crimes against property increased by 32.5 percent, and those against individuals increased by 3.2 percent.

In terms of religious hate crimes, there was a total of 211, with seventy-four of those against Jews and sixty-one against Muslims. The remaining incident was against a Jehovah's Witness. Of the gender hate crimes in the state of New York, fifty-seven were reported to the FBI. Of those, thirty-six were directed at gay men and fourteen at transgender individuals.

One other final aspect of the reporting of hate crimes in the United States over the period from 2016 until 2020 is the number of incidents in those years when it was claimed that the rhetoric of President Donald Trump was cited as a motivation for hate crimes. Just minutes, for example, after a tragic shooting in New Zealand, on the other side of the world, several Democrats mentioned the culpability of Trump's rhetoric in the event.

On March 17, 2019, an article written in *The Hill* reported that "A range of Democrats—including Rashida Tlaib and Senators Tim Kaine and Amy Klobuchar—were critical of Trump."[18]

When was the last time you saw a Republican blame a Democrat for hate crimes or hate speech? You never have, and it is likely you never will.

When, for example, Steve Scalise was shot at a congressional softball game, the Trump administration did not run around Washington, DC, blaming the attack on MSNBC or CNN.

And yet Governor Ralph Northam admitted to wearing blackface while in medical school and dressing as a KKK member, but he was not accused by the Liberal media of a hate crime.

One thing that is clear is there is a double moral standard in this country. Hate crimes against Republicans are dealt with very differently than those directed at Democrats. Speaker Pelosi can go get a haircut when the rest of the state is under a lockdown. The governor of California can go to a fancy French restaurant with his family when there are lockdowns for everyone else and no one in his dinner party wears the mandatory masks. Similarly, the governor of Michigan can conduct a dinner party in her state, without masks, while everyone else in Michigan is forbidden from doing so.

The Democratic Party and the Progressive voices from the New Left need to dial back their speech. In those years from 2016 to 2020, many actions were taken against people wearing Make America Great Again ball caps. They have been kicked out of bars and restaurants for showing support or simply for working for the president of the United States.

And yet when the Progressives speak about hate crimes, it is often in the context of White nationalism or White supremacy, with absolutely no clue that hate crimes were committed by Antifa and Black Lives Matter in the summer of 2020. No politician should ever use a national tragedy as a sign that the other party is wrong. In America today, visibility leads to accountability. The hate crimes against Asian Americans since COVID-19 began were the Democrats' latest example of visibility; with the new COVID-19 Hate Crimes Act, now they want accountability.

The accountability, however, usually comes after some national televised event, often in the form of legislation that follows. Later, the Progressive New Left often attempts to correct the issue by doing what they always do—throw money at it.

A number of other points are in order in terms of the reporting of hate crimes to the FBI. Of the thirty largest cities in the United States, eight of them did not report their hate crimes to the FBI. More than eleven million people live in these eight cities—which include Baltimore, Savannah, Georgia, and Norfolk, Virginia—but not one of these eight cities reported even a single hate crime to the federal authorities.[19]

There are a number of reasons that have been proposed for why there are some gaps in the reporting. For one thing, people are generally reluctant to report hate crimes. The National Crime Victimization Survey, which reports on first-person accounts of people who claim to be victims of crime in the past six months, has suggested that only about half of all hate crimes in the United States are reported.

Many police departments, especially small ones, lack personnel who have the training necessary for gathering proper reporting of hate crimes. In other departments, they lack the political will to properly identity and report hate crimes. Steven Freeman, vice president of the Anti-Defamation League, told us this about the lack of reporting of hate crimes to the FBI:

> It could be in some cases because they would think it would make them look bad so they would rather not do it. There could be others that just don't have adequate training to properly understand exactly what they are looking for.

But this problem of nonreporting of hate crimes needs to be addressed, particularly if the issue remains an important part of the Democratic Party's overall views on crime. Without a comprehensive national standard and reporting practices, then it is left up to the individual states to decide what counts as a hate crime—for not all the states, as we have shown at the beginning of this essay, have exactly the same standards.

In 1942, the US Supreme Court sustained the conviction of a Jehovah's Witness who addressed a police officer as a "God-damned racketeer" and a "damn Fascist" (Chaplinsky v. New Hampshire).[20] The court's opinion in the case stated that there was a category of face-to-face epithets that they called "fighting words" that was wholly outside of the "protections of the First Amendment."

The court added:

> Those ["fighting words"] which by their very utterance inflict injury . . . are no essential part of any exposition of ideas.

Finally, Justice Oliver Wendell Holmes Jr., in a dissenting opinion in the 1929 US Supreme Court decision in the United States v. Schwimmer case, in the context of writing about the US Constitution and the First Amendment, observed that they "are not just about protection."

The justice added:

> Free thought is for those who agree with us, but it is also freedom for the thoughts, words, and actions we hate.[21]

Justice Holmes was quite prescient to include thoughts, words, and deeds when it came to hate crimes and hate speech. But it again raises the philosophical question of whether we are punishing the person for the thought, word, or deed or whether we would be punishing the person's moral values.

With the advent of new technologies and social media, new questions about hate speech and hate crimes will soon arise. France, in July of 2020, passed an anti-hate speech law known as the Avia Law, named after Laetitia Avia, a member of the French Parliament who wrote the first draft of the law. Avia's original version spelled out provisions for regulating hate speech and hate crimes on the internet. We only wonder how long it will take for the Progressive New Left in the United States.

In a recent poll by *The Hill* of five hundred male Americans and five hundred females, 63 percent of those polled said that the speech should be protected even when it is offensive, while 37 percent said it should not be protected. In a Gallup poll of American college students, 78 percent were in favor of their school being allowed to "restrict the use of racial slurs." Interestingly enough, 75 percent said there should be "little government control of free speech."[22]

This brings us to the major sources for Essay Seven, followed by Essay Eight, in which I will speak specifically about the *New York Times* 1619 Project, what the Progressive New Left has said and written about that project, and, finally, a careful and judicious critique of the 1619 Project.

ESSAY EIGHT

The Progressive New Left and the 1619 Project

I

The main purpose of Essay Eight is to introduce the *New York Times* 1619 Project as well as provide a philosophical critique of the same. This essay will unfold in the following five sections, the first of which will be a short introduction to the origins and history of the project.

In the second section, we will explore the ten major claims made by the writers of the project, some staff members of the *Times* as well as a number of academics who had been invited to write essays for the project.

In section three of this essay, we will supply a detailed philosophical critique of the 1619 Project by, among other things, evaluating the ten central claims in Section Two. I shall provide criticisms of each of those ideas.

In the fourth and central section of Essay Eight, we will introduce the views of some members of the Progressive New Left who have written or have made public statements about the 1619 Project, followed by the fifth and final section of Essay Eight, in which we will critique those observations from the Progressive New Left.

The Origins and History of the 1619 Project

What has come to be called the 1619 Project is a long-form journalism project developed by *New York Times* reporter Nikole Hannah-Jones, other writers from the *Times*, and selected scholars invited to write essays for the project. The project was announced in the *New York Times* magazine in order to have the announcement coincide with the four hundredth anniversary of the first "twenty or so Africans" who came to the colony of Virginia in August of 1619.

The project first announced in the magazine included a broadsheet article by Ms. Hannah-Jones, a list of several live events in New York City, and a podcast. In that lead article, Ms. Hannah-Jones related:

> [The 1619 Project] aims to reframe the country's history by placing the consequences of slavery and the contributions of Black Americans at the very center of our national narrative.

The first edition of the 1619 Project appeared in the *New York Times* magazine on August 14, 2019.[1] It consisted of one hundred pages, ten essays, a photo essay, and a collection of poems and fiction by an additional sixteen contributors. The introduction to the one-hundred-page document was written by Jake Silverstein, the editor in chief of the magazine.

The ten essays from August 14, 2019, were the following:

1. "America Wasn't a Democracy, Until Black Americans Made It One," by Nikole Hannah-Jones.
2. "American Capitalism Is Brutal: You Can Trace That to the Plantation," by Matthew Desmond.
3. "How False Beliefs in Physical Racial Difference Still Live in Medicine Today," by Linda Villarosa.

4. "What the Reactionary Politics of 2019 Owe to the Politics of Slavery," by Jamelle Bouie.
5. "Why Is Everyone Always Stealing Black Music?" by Wesley Morris.
6. "How Segregation Caused Your Traffic Jam," by Kevin Kruse.
7. "Why Doesn't America Have Universal Health Care? One Word: Race," by Jeneen Interlandi.
8. "Why American Prisons Owe Their Cruelty to Slavery," by Bryan Stevenson.
9. "The Barbaric History of Sugar in America," by Khalil Gibran Muhammad.
10. "How America's Vast Racial Wealth Gap Grew: By Plunder," by Trymaine Lee.

The one-hundred-page first edition of the 1619 Project also included a "New Literary Timeline of African-American History" as well as a collection of original poems and stories written by contemporary writers. These materials and their authors may be summarized in this way:

1. Clint Smith on the Middle Passage.
2. Yusef Komunyakaa on Crispus Attucks.
3. Eve L. Ewing on Phillis Wheatley.
4. Reginald Dwayne Betts on the Fugitive Slave Act of 1793.
5. Barry Jenkins on Gabriel's rebellion.
6. Jesmyn Ward on the Act Prohibiting Importation of Slaves.
7. Tyehimba Jess on Black Seminoles.
8. Darryl Pinckney on the Emancipation Proclamation of 1863.
9. Z. Z. Packer on the New Orleans Massacre of 1866.
10. Yaa Gyasi on the Tuskegee Syphilis Experiment.
11. Jacqueline Woodson on Sergeant Isaac Woodard.
12. Joshua Bennett on the Black Panther Party.
13. Lynn Nottage on the birth of hip-hop.

14. Kiese Laymon on the Rev. Jesse Jackson's "Rainbow Coalition" speech.
15. Clint Smith on the Superdome after Hurricane Katrina.

If we consider that these fifteen items constitute the "New Literary Timeline of African-American History," then it is instructive of what aspects of Black history in America were left out. There is nothing on Rev. Martin Luther King Jr., nor on George Washington Carver; Frederick Douglass; Thurgood Marshall, the first Black US Supreme Court justice; or Clarence Thomas, the current Black Supreme Court justice.

There are literary pieces on Phillis Wheatley, Crispus Attucks, Isaac Woodard, and Rev. Jesse Jackson, but there is nothing in the "literary timeline" that relates the lives of Abdul-Rahman ibn Ibrahima Sori (1762–1829), Abu Bakr as-Siddiq (1790–1841), Lamine Kebe (1755–1855), or the hundreds of thousands of other African Muslim slaves brought to the US beginning in the seventeenth century.

The magazine issue from August of 2019 was also accompanied by a special section in the Sunday *New York Times* that examined the beginning of the transatlantic slave trade; and on August 20, 2019, a multi-episode audio series titled *1619* began, which was published by the daily morning news podcasts of the *Times*. The Sunday sports section had an essay about slavery's impact on professional sports in the United States that was called "Slavery's Legacy in the Power Dynamics of Sports."

Whenever we see the word *power* in relation to racial issues, one can be sure that the discussion to follow will primarily pertain to Progressive New Left ideas that have to do with the idea of *oppression* being fostered, of course, by the oppressors at the hands of the oppressed. The word *power* is another part of the lexicon of the Marxist-infused creators of the 1619 Project, as we shall see in Essay Nine of this study.

The *Times* also formed a collaborative with the Pulitzer Center, in which project materials were made available to American teachers, free and online. The Pulitzer Center also arranged for guest speakers to visit classes. The school material in the *Times*-Pulitzer Center collaborative developed lesson plans for all levels, from elementary school through college curricula.

One outgrowth of the educational materials produced by the Pulitzer Center is a course taught by Maria Helena Lima at SUNY Geneseo in the spring of 2020. The course, HUMN 222: Black Humanities: The *New York Times* 1619 Project, is based entirely on the *New York Times* essays, with nothing on her required reading list from the many historian critics of the 1619 Project.

Similarly, the Civitas Associates organization, on June 16, 2020, asked its 2020 interns to read the 1619 essays and then to write a short piece of what they thought of what they read. On their website, they feature the responses of twelve of the interns. All of them are tinged with the beliefs of the Progressive New Left. They say things like, "Capitalism is inherently exploitative" and "I hate money. I hate the idea of it. I hate the implications of it" and "I found this article very interesting. I was interested to learn how much of the modern-day method of working was created with the help of slavery."[2] Needless to say, all twelve interns had bought into the "reframing of the American narrative" that was offered about capitalism in the original essays of the 1619 Project.

Regarding the speech that Ms. Hannah-Jones gave at the University of Michigan on January 28, 2020, a graduate student at the university named Justin Woods, who attended the talk, said that her work had "spurred a conversation." He added:

> You really have something here that is going to force you to question what you've been taught, what you have learned, and you have to make grips with the fact that you have been miseducated. It is important to go on that journey.[3]

It is clear that the twenty-nine-year-old graduate student at the University of Michigan, Justin Woods, after hearing Ms. Hannah-Jones's talk, then went on to buy into the 1619 Project Kool-Aid. These three examples I have provided here—the SUNY course, the interns at Civitas, and the comment of the twenty-nine-year-old Michigan grad student—are a good representative sample of how the Pulitzer Center's educational materials are being utilized. It is also no surprise that Nikole Hannah-Jones received a Pulitzer Prize for Commentary for her work on the 1619 Project.

The *New York Times* 1619 Project, however, was not without its critics. Shortly after the August 2019 publication of the project, the *Times* began to receive letters to the editor from a number of prominent American historians who saw many of the claims in the project as either outright wrong or without factual support. We will say more about these critics in the third section of this eighth essay. It is enough now, however, to speak of their existence.

In the second section of this essay, we will turn our attention to the ten most central claims that the writers of the project have made about the history of African Americans in the United States.

The Central Claims of the 1619 Project

In the ten essays of the original publication of the project, the writers of those essays made ten central claims about the history of Black Americans. We will list these claims here and then speak of each one of them individually. These claims from the original ten essays of the project are the following:

1. American history needs to be "reframed" around the year 1619.
2. 1619 is the real founding of the United States, not 1776.

3. America was not a democracy until Black Americans made it so.
4. American capitalism grew out of slavery.
5. America declared independence from Britain because they wished to protect slavery.
6. Black interests and struggles in the United States in America were mostly done on their own.
7. American patriots fought the Revolution mostly to protect slavery.
8. There is no objective history. History is a matter of "interpretation."
9. Equality and freedom are not values to be protected.
10. Abraham Lincoln was a racist.

There are also a host of other claims about African American history to be found in the original essays of the 1619 Project. These other claims to be found there might be labeled "Additional Claims of the 1619 Project." First, however, we will sketch out the ten central claims listed earlier.

In the speech that Ms. Hannah-Jones gave at the University of Michigan on January 28, 2020, the writer remarked:

> One does not create a project in the *New York Times* that says we are going to reframe the American story, that our true founding is 1619 not 1776, that Black people are the perfectors of democracy and that we are as much the founding fathers as the White men you worship in our history and not expect you are going to get a lot of damn pushback.

In the length of this one paragraph, we see the proclaiming of central claims one, two, and three. The third of these claims—about when democracy began in America—is the central question in Ms. Hannah-Jones's lead essay, titled "America Wasn't a

Democracy, Until Black Americans Made It So." This can also be seen in another statement the *Times* writer made in her talk at the University of Michigan, when she said:

> Our Declaration of Independence, approved on July 4, 1776, proclaims that "All men are created equal and endowed by their Creator with certain unalienable rights." But the White men who drafted those words did not believe them to be true for the hundreds of thousands of Black people in their midst.

In the same speech, Ms. Hannah-Jones went on to relate:

> Every American child learns about the *Mayflower*. No American child learns about 1619 and another ship called the *White Lion* that came earlier that is much more important to the American story.

The *Times* writer added:

> This erasure was intentional. The *Mayflower* story glorified the best aspects of our country.[4]

Number four of the central claims—that American capitalism grew out of slavery—was mostly found in the essay that Matthew Desmond wrote for the original August 2019 edition of the project. In his essay, Desmond provided an overview of recent works by historians of capitalism who argued that slavery was foundational to American growth and economic development in the nineteenth century. In Professor Desmond's words, "[Slavery] helped turn a poor fledgling nation into a financial colossus."

Later, in the next section of this essay, we will point out that Dr. Desmond, in his essay for the *Times*, only quoted from a movement known as the New History of Capitalism, or NHC, and that the advocates of that movement are all fully behind Dr. Desmond, who is a professor of sociology at Princeton University and has no training as a historian.

Central claim number five in the aforementioned list—that America declared independence because they wanted to protect slavery—is mostly argued in Ms. Hannah-Jones's essay in the original 1619 Project's publication in August of 2019. This is also true of claim number seven—that Americans fought the Revolution to preserve slavery. Again, we will say much more about these two central claims in the next section of this essay. But as a preview, both of these claims have their serious historical critics as well, mostly because there is no evidence for these two claims.

Central claim number eight—that there is no objective history; there is only "interpretation"—was discussed in the essay by Ms. Hannah-Jones, as well as in a couple of responses written by editor Jake Silverstein to some of the critics of the 1619 Project.[5]

These claims about truth and objectivity are part of a much larger intellectual movement going back to the mid-twentieth century called postmodernism, as we shall see in the next section of this essay. The two foundational principles in the postmodernist movement were "There is no objective truth" and "There is no objective morality." One may ask, of course, if the claim "There is no objective truth" is an objective truth. If one answers yes, then why should we worry about what is real? If the answer is no, then the discussion of truth and objectivity descends into the realm of nonsense. The idea that there is no objective history, only interpretation, was among the original foundational beliefs of the Progressive New Left that we outlined in the first essay of this study.

Claim number nine on our list—that equality and freedom are not central values to be protected in America—is directly related to two items we have seen earlier in this study of the Progressive New Left. The first of these is the claim we saw in Essay One that the idea of *equality* should be replaced by the notion of *equity*. The other thing related to central claim number nine is why, earlier in this essay, we have indicated that Martin Luther King Jr. did not have an essay devoted to his work in the *Times*' literary history of African Americans mentioned earlier.

The Progressive New Left, to which the writers of the 1619 Project for the most part belong, finds fault with Rev. King's claim that "I have a dream that my four little children will one day live in a nation where they will not be judged by the color of their skin but by the content of their character."

Contrary to the beliefs of Dr. King, the writers and editors of the 1619 Project place the color of one's skin as the most central reality about the history of the United States. That is the purpose of the "reframing" of American history. Black Americans should be "at the very center of our nation's narrative," as the writers and editors of the *New York Times* 1619 Project told us. They cannot be in that position if we rely on the thoughts of Martin Luther King Jr.

Finally, Darryl Pinckney's essay, as well as that of lead writer Hannah-Jones, claims that rather than Abraham Lincoln being a symbol of Black independence in America, he should actually be seen as a racist. Ms. Hannah-Jones makes this claim on the basis of a White House meeting that Mr. Lincoln reportedly had with five Black leaders in August of 1862, in which the president asked them what they thought of sending freed Black slaves to an overseas colony.

This episode is the sum total of evidence of Hannah-Jones's claim that Abraham Lincoln was a racist. In the next section of this essay, again we will supply a critical response to this idea as part of the central claims of the *New York Times*' 1619 Project.

In fact, this brings us to the third section of this essay on the 1619 Project, in which we will describe a number of arguments that have been made, mostly by scholarly critics, about the shortcomings of these ten central claims to be found in the original one-hundred-page edition of the *Times*' 1619 Project. Indeed, we will take the central claims one at a time while offering our rebuttals.

Criticisms of the Central Claims of the 1619 Project

Before we comment on our criticisms of the major claims of the 1619 Project, we will make some short and general comments about slavery. Most of these remarks are taken directly from my book *Muslim Slaves in the Chesapeake: 1634 to 1865*, published in 2020 by Calumet Editions in Minneapolis.[6]

First, the 1619 Project portrays slavery as an evil for which the American people bear a unique responsibility and should feel overwhelming guilt, even today. In fact, until recently, slavery and human bondage have been the norm in human history. It was an important part of ancient Egypt, Greece, Rome, and Asia. Focusing just on the US does not provide an adequate picture of the world as a whole.

Slavery was practiced by the Inca and the Aztecs in the New World long before the British American colonies. Today, approximately forty million people are still in enslavement in the world, in places like Pakistan, Bangladesh, India, and China as well as various parts of Africa.

In point of fact, of the twelve million slaves brought to the Americas, less than 4 percent of them were brought to the United States. The other 96 percent were brought to Latin America and the Caribbean, and three or four million were transported to Brazil alone. Of those twelve million slaves, 37 percent went to Brazil, 53 percent to the Caribbean, and 7 percent to Spanish America. Of the twelve million, only about four hundred thousand came to North America, representing 3.8 percent of the total number.

By comparison, there were fourteen times more Africans brought to the Caribbean and ten times more to Brazil than to the United States. There were nearly as many slaves brought to Spanish America between 1511 and 1620 as those who arrived in the United States between 1651 and 1965. In the year 1700, when only twelve thousand slaves arrived in North America, there were already more than a half million captives in the Caribbean and in Spanish America as well.

By the early years of the nineteenth century, the total number of slaves to North America had reached its peak and stabilized between 361,000 and 400,000. For every one slave who arrived in North America, there were more than twenty-six other slaves arriving elsewhere in the Americas—Brazil, Central America, and the Caribbean.

This brings us to one more point before we move to the criticisms of the central claims of the 1619 Project—the date 1619, which was chosen because the editors of the project believed that this was the year when the ship the *White Lion* first brought slaves to North America. This claim is absolutely false. There is sufficient evidence that before 1619, at least two hundred slaves had been brought to the Caribbean, 550 had been brought to Guatemala, and ten thousand slaves had been brought to Cuba before 1619—and many slaves had been brought to Mexico beginning in 1590.

The Spanish Americans and their voyages to Florida, Mexico, and Cuba may have brought slaves to these places before the year 1500, some of them by Christopher Columbus himself. Alex Borucki, David Wheat, and David Eltis's book, *From the Galleons to the Highlands*, gives a clear account of the slave trade routes to Spanish America from far before 1619—indeed, by at least a century before that date.

We have called this study the *1618 Project* to highlight the fact that slavery was going on in North America for at least a century before 1619—and in South America, in places like Peru, for at least three hundred years before that.

The other major function of this section is to point to and assemble the major scholarly responses that have been offered to counteract the project's ten central claims enumerated earlier. As we shall see in this section, the criticisms are wide and deep, and they often involve some of the most gifted and well-respected historians in the United States.[7]

Of the ten central claims made by the 1619 Project are claims two, three, four, and five, which appear in the essays by Hannah-Jones and Professor Desmond. Claims two, three, and five may be found in the former's essay, while claim number four is mostly identified with Dr. Desmond's essay.

One of the arguments that Ms. Hannah-Jones makes is claim number five—that "one of the primary reasons the colonists decided to declare their independence from Britain was because they wanted to protect the institution of slavery" as abolitionists' sentiments began rising in Britain. The major difficulty is that there are no diaries, letters, essays, or the like of American colonists who made this claim. A second difficulty with claim number five is that the abolition movement in Britain was not very active until long after the American Revolution.

Antislavery ideology was a very new thing in the world of the eighteenth century, but there was more antislavery sentiment in the 1770s in America than there ever was in Britain itself.

There is little to no evidence that the colonists declared their independence to preserve slavery. In fact, there was no threat coming from Britain about slavery at all. This is a standard understanding among most historians. The abolitionist movement in Britain did not become a popular movement until the 1780s, long after the years leading up to the Revolution. There were people in England before who were opposed to slavery—like the Quakers and radicals during the English Civil War, who were raising philosophical objections. But there is no evidence for the claim that American revolutionaries worried about English beliefs that slavery should be abolished. To date, there have been no first-person narratives that have made that claim.

Whether "Black Americans had fought for their freedom 'largely alone'"—central claim number six—is certainly subject to vigorous debate. From the antislavery Quakers, who organized the boycotts of goods produced through slave labor, to abolitionists springing fugitive slaves from prison, to union workers massing at a march on Washington, it appears that the struggle for Black freedom was a multiracial endeavor.

This is to say nothing of the hundreds of thousands of White soldiers in the northern army who died to help make Black Americans free. In that regard, Ms. Hannah-Jones, in her lead essay, rarely mentioned the Civil War, probably because the data to be found there did not fit many of her central claims. So Ms. Hannah-Jones only infrequently mentions the Civil War, mostly because it does not fit her narrative.

Nevertheless, Frederick Douglass had William Garrison, the great White leader of abolitionists; W. E. B. Du Bois had Moorfield Storey (1845–1929), the great pacifist and civil rights worker. Even Martin Luther King Jr., who did not appear in Hannah-Jones's essay, had Stanley Levison, White, Jewish adviser and speechwriter for MLK.

The fight for Black freedom was a universal fight. In the end, it also had effects on women's rights in the early twentieth century. Minimizing the contributions of White people to the Black struggles for freedom seems entirely out of place. In response to this criticism, Hannah-Jones related, "It is not saying that Black people only fought alone. It is saying that most of the time we did."[8] This seems to back away from the claim.

Some of the criticisms we have of the central claims of the 1619 Project are purely philosophical, like claim number eight that there is no such thing as objective truth or objective history; there is only interpretation. Editor Jake Silverstein is to be identified with this central claim more than any of his writers on the project.

As suggested earlier, the philosophical movement that lies beneath the central claim that there is no objective truth, nor any objective history, is postmodernism from French philosophical thinkers like Michel Foucault (1926–84), who rejected the very concept of truth and believed that all disputes were nothing more than warring "narratives." But if there is no such thing as truth, then that forces the critic to ask, "Then why should we believe that statement?"

Central claim number eight of the central claims of the writers and editors of the 1619 project can mostly be seen in a letter of response from editor Jake Silverstein, where he wrote, "The complaint [of the historians who complained to the *Times*] goes to a difference of interpretation and intention, not fact."[9]

Whether the United States began in 1619 or 1776, of course, is a matter of fact, not a matter of interpretation, as Mr. Silverstein put the matter. This may be why the editor called 1619 a "metaphor" in one of his writings about the project.[10]

In a tweet, Ms. Hannah-Jones, when asked about objective history, remarked, "Only White historians have produced truly objective history," before then asserting, "There is no such thing as objective history." The shadow of Michel Foucault, who has been dead for thirty-plus years, can be seen in the *Times*' writer's comment. The use of the term *reframed* by the authors and editors of the 1619 Project implies that the old "White" framing is obsolete and needs to be replaced with a new framing, for there is no objective truth.

There is only framing.

This leaves us with two of the project's central claims—that American capitalism grew out of slavery (number four) and that Abraham Lincoln was a racist (number ten). We will move to Desmond's point about capitalism first and then on to Mr. Lincoln, the Great Emancipator.

In Matthew Desmond's essay in the original 1619 Project publication in August of 2019, he provided a review of recent work by historians of capitalism who argue that slavery was foundational to America's growth and economic development in the nineteenth century.

Indeed, Dr. Desmond began his article by quoting Harvard historian Sven Beckert, who suggested, "It was on the back of cotton, and thus on the backs of slaves, that the US economy ascended in the world." Yet at the same time, Professor Desmond neglected to mention, as British writer John Clegg put the matter, that "This claim has been widely rejected by most specialists in the economic history of American slavery."[11]

It is true that cotton was among the world's most widely traded commodities and that it was the Antebellum South's principal export. Contrary to Dr. Desmond's claim, however, the export of cotton in the South was a very small share of the economy, probably less than 5 percent—well less than what Professor Desmond claimed in his 1619 essay.[12]

In his 1619 essay, Professor Desmond also drew on Seth Rockman, Walter Johnson, Edward Baptist, and Caitlin Rosenthal, all to indicate that the southern slave-based economy was a hotbed of dynamic innovation in finance and accounting. Dr. Rosenthal, in her book, *Accounting for Slavery*, is careful to point out that her work "is not an origin story," but that was precisely how Dr. Desmond read it, against the wishes of Dr. Rosenthal herself.

Professor Desmond leaned so much on Beckert, Johnson, Rockman, and Baptist because all four are members of a late twentieth- and early twenty-first-century movement known as the New History of Capitalism, or NHC. One principal thesis shared by all four of these writers is that the production of cotton in the South was inextricably linked to slave labor and that this formed the basis of American economic prosperity in the nineteenth century. This thesis among the NHC members is known as the "cotton is king" theory.[13]

In his essay, Dr. Desmond also contended that slave owners invented new financial instruments or new methods of accounting and that the adoption of these practices on the plantations led them to be widely accepted elsewhere in America. He offered very few examples, however, of cotton growers who employed these new accounting methods.

Dr. Desmond and these other historians whose work he employed have neglected other ways that slavery imposed constraints on economic growth and development.

Gavin Wright, a renowned historian of slavery, recently gave the Tawney lecture to the Economic History Society on these economic techniques and practices. In that lecture, he pointed out that the southern slave owners opposed almost every state and federal economic policy, including investments in education and agricultural improvement. Wright's bottom line conclusion of the lecture was this:

> Slavery most likely reduced the expansion of the American economy, not made it greater.

Dr. Wright's conclusion, of course, is in direct opposition to the thesis of Professor Desmond. Gavin Wright is one of the most respected slavery historians in the country, while Dr. Desmond was not trained as a historian at all.

Other historian critics have also taken up the thesis of Dr. Desmond, including Civil War historian Allen C. Guelzo and Phillip W. Magness, who wrote about the difficulties and shortcomings of the NHC movement for decades before the 1619 Project was published.

In fact, Professor Magness, more than any other economist, has tracked how the 1619 Project follows in spirit and letter the conjuring of the NHC members.

In fact, a week after the publication of the project, Professor Magness published the essay "How the 1619 Project Rehabilitates the 'King Cotton' Thesis" in the *National Review*. This was followed up on in February 2020, when Dr. Magness wrote another essay titled "The Case for Retracting Matthew Desmond's 1619 Project Essay."

In the hubbub that followed Professor Magness's two essays,

he asked Ms. Hannah-Jones about Desmond's article's overreliance on Edward Baptist's mostly debunked claims. She responded by saying, "Economists dispute a few of Baptist's calculations but not the book itself nor its thesis."[14] Keep in mind she was saying this to one of the most respected academic economists in America.

In March of 2021, Dr. Magness published another essay with the title "The 1619 Project: An Epitaph."[15] In that piece, Magness pointed out that the *Times* belatedly changed Hannah-Jones's claim that "the colonists decided to declare their independence from Britain was because they wanted to protect the institution of slavery" to the new claim that only "some of" the colonists did so. She did not, however, say who those *some* were nor what her evidence was. In fact, to date, we still have no first-person comments by early American revolutionary citizens who claimed that the fear of Britain had anything to do with slavery in America.

This leaves us with only the tenth central claim of the 1619 Project—a claim again made by Ms. Hannah-Jones that the sixteenth president of the United States, Abraham Lincoln, was a racist. I might add at this point that part of my background for discussing and evaluating this claim is the research and reading I did for my book *Abraham Lincoln's Religion*, published by Wipf and Stock Press in 2018.[16]

In other words, Hannah-Jones's argument goes something like this: Lincoln gave Black people freedom and equality. But freedom and equality are bad things among the writers of the 1619 Project, so it follows that Abraham Lincoln must be a racist.

In many ways, Ms. Hannah-Jones's observation in her lead essay in the 1619 Project's materials on Abraham Lincoln, that he was "more like a racist than an emancipator," was the most radical of the ten central claims made by the writers of the project. When we understand the *Times* writer's sources for this tenth claim, it begins to be much clearer and more in focus.

One of those sources was the work of a former editor at *Ebony* named Lerone Bennett Jr., whose study *Forced into Glory* offered a biting critique of the nation's sixteenth president. 2020 was the twentieth anniversary of the publication of Bennett's hefty book. Ms. Hannah-Jones's views on Lincoln, her receipt of a Pulitzer Prize, and her renewal of Bennett's treatment of Lincoln all were spoken of, and Bennett was acknowledged, in the acknowledgements of the original August 2019 magazine.

In 1968, in an essay published in *Ebony* that had a headline asking, "Was Abe Lincoln a White Supremacist?" the Black journalist answered this question decidedly in the positive. Mr. Bennett's thesis was later taken up by figures in the Black Power movement, such as Julius Lester, who declared that "Blacks have no reason to feel grateful to Abraham Lincoln."[17]

A number of Black intellectuals in the first half of the twentieth century also took up the same negative view of the sixteenth president, but by the 1970s, views on Lincoln had undergone a complete overhaul in Black American culture. One way to see this change is a 1956 Gallup poll that asked Black respondents to name the three greatest presidents. About 50 percent mentioned Mr. Lincoln. By the year 1999, however, when the same question was asked, only 23 percent mentioned Abraham Lincoln.

When Lincoln scholar Allen Guelzo was asked about this trend recently, he said, "It is a manifestation of a profound nihilism that sees little meaning in American freedom and little hope for real racial progress." Professor Guelzo added:

> If "Lincoln is America," as he appears to be for many of his most public defenders, then the anti-Lincoln enterprise in Black intellectual thought which fed into the 1619 Project is at heart an anti-American enterprise.[18]

When Professor Guelzo made this observation, he may well have had in mind the ninth central claim we have listed of the

1619 Project earlier in this essay—that the ideas of freedom and equality should have little place in the America of the writers of the project.

Perhaps the most bizarre claim made by the writers of the 1619 Project is the essay by Kevin Kruse, in which he says that racism and segregation were responsible for contemporary traffic jams in the United States. Not only is there no real evidence for this claim, but it is also an astounding assertion.

Another odd claim in the 1619 essays can be found in the article by Bryan Stevenson, in which he maintained that the cruel conditions of many prisons in America can also be attributed to slavery and the unhealthy and often violent behavior toward slaves in the United States.

Jamelle Bouie, in his essay for the 1619 Project, also made the claim that Conservative reactionary responses to the Progressive New Left in America can also be attributed to the enslavement of African American slaves.

Another secondary claim by the writers of the 1619 Project was made by Jeneen Interlandi—another 1619 Project author—who even suggested that the major reason that the United States does not have universal health care is principally because of the practice of slavery in America.

A few of the essays in the original 1619 Project made legitimate points about slavery and African American history in the United States, such as Wesley Morris's contribution on Black music comprising much of the foundation of popular American music, or Linda Villarosa's essay, which distinguished race from gender while arguing at the same time that many of the perspectives about race in the United States are actually false beliefs that have been used by the oppressors at the expense of the oppressed. In fact, Dr. Villarosa suggested in her essay that race is an entirely man-made phenomenon and that more than 98 percent of human DNA is the same from race to race.

Trymaine Lee's article on the supposition that slavery was the main cause of the economic gap between the rich and the poor certainly deserves some consideration. But the evidence that he set forth to establish this claim was still short of convincing.

These rare glimpses of clarity in the 1619 essays, however, are few and far between, and none of these moments of enlightenment in the original essays of the 1619 Project do a good job in establishing any of the ten central claims that I have attributed to the *New York Times*' 1619 Project.

This brings us to the fourth section of this essay, in which we will explore what the Progressive New Left has written and said about the 1619 Project. This will be followed by a critique of those New Left observations.

The Progressive New Left on the 1619 Project

There are three principle ways in which remarks from the Progressive New Left on the 1619 Project can be seen: in education, in their founding principles, and in comments from Progressive politicians. We will treat these in reverse order.

In April of 2021, in an article by Andrew Ujifusa for *Education Week*, he gave us the flavor of the Biden administration on the 1619 Project. Mr. Ujifusa wrote:

> The Biden administration wants a grant program for history and civics education to prioritize instruction that accounts for bias, discriminatory policies in America, and the value of diverse student perspectives.[19]

It should be clear that the Biden White House has bought the 1619 Project Kool-Aid as well. This is also confirmed by comments from both Vice President Harris and Mayor Pete Buttigieg, who recently have made glowing and lavish comments praising the project. In fact, Elliot Kaufman, in a 2019 edition of the *New York Times*, wrote, "The project has been celebrated up and down the Liberal establishment, praised by Senator Kamala Harris and Mayor Pete Buttigieg."

Most of the comments in regard to the values of the 1619 Project and the United States have come specifically connected to what was called the 1776 Report, devised by President Donald Trump as a response to the 1619 Project. The 1776 Report was an attempt to recapture the founding values that the Founding Fathers had in mind when they founded this great nation, with freedom and equality being the greatest of those values.[20]

The 1776 Report was compiled by the President's Advisory 1776 Commission, a group of sixteen scholars chaired by the president of Hillsdale College in Michigan, Larry Arnn. The members of the commission were selected by President Donald Trump. Mr. Trump's announcement of his 1776 Report was one of the final things the forty-fifth did in his administration in January of 2021.

What happened next was enlightening. The very next day, on January 21, 2021, the Biden administration canceled any government involvement with the 1776 Report, another sign of the new administration's view of the 1619 Project. It was three months later that the new education secretary, Miguel Cardona, instituted a new scholarship program to reward the teaching of the 1619 Project in schools. This, of course, is another example of how the Progressive New Left always prefers to solve a national problem—throw money at it.

In the literature that accompanied Mr. Cardona's announcement, it relates that until now the founding of the nation was either considered to be the Pilgrim Fathers in 1620—who celebrated on Thanksgiving Day—or the proclamation of independence in 1776. The "1619 Project traces our origin back to the arrival of Black slaves." The materials of the education secretary, however, left out three important facts. First, these "slaves" were imported by Portuguese merchants and not by the British. Second, in legal documents from the Virginia Colony a few years after 1619, the "twenty or so Africans" were listed as "indentured servants" and not as slaves. Third, the British had sent White indentured servants to the North American colonies long before 1619. But in the minds of the Progressive New Left, White people cannot be slaves, so they don't count.

The conclusion we can make about the ongoing discussion is that the doctrine of the current administration, the Biden-Harris administration, is based on a series of historical falsifications. Nevertheless, the teaching of the 1619 Project will be "rewarded" by the administration of the forty-sixth president of the United States by his secretary of education, Miguel Cardona.

This brings us to the final section of this essay, in which we will critique the current administration's views on the 1619 Project, followed by the conclusions and the notes of Essay Eight.

Critique of the Progressive New Left Views of the 1619 Project

Since the publication of the original 1619 Project in 2019, several contradictions about it, and about the current administration's views of it, have arisen. In this critique, we will point to a number of these.

First, both Ms. Hannah-Jones and editor Jake Silverstein seem to contradict themselves about the idea of *literal history*. On the one hand, in the eighth central claim of the 1619 Project mentioned earlier, they both indicated there can be no objective or literal history.

Yet in an article, Mr. Silverstein related that the year 1619 was always meant to be a "metaphor."

In the opening of her essay for the project, Ms. Hannah-Jones indicated that 1619 is "the country's very origin." Needless to say, it is not entirely clear what Hannah-Jones and editor Silverstein believe about literal or objective history. Silverstein seems to think 1619 is a metaphor, while Hannah-Jones sees it as a historical fact.

Second, are the founding principles of the United States, like freedom and equality, principles that the 1619 Project crew believe in or not? The evidence for answering this question is ambivalent at best. Ms. Hannah-Jones has alternately affirmed and denied those principles of the Declaration of Independence and the Constitution to suit whatever the convenience of the moment requires.

In the circles of the Progressive New Left, of which, unfortunately, Joe Biden is now a member, they claim that America is fundamentally a racist country, but then when they are criticized as being anti-American, they insist that the 1619 Project was merely a patriotic testament to the way Black Americans have vindicated, and participated in, the nation's noblest ideals.

Third, the 1619 Project, as well as its writers and editors, leaves out many things that surely have had something to do with the way we have seen the African American experience and the origins of the nation. For one thing, there is next to nothing in the 1619 Project about Rev. Martin Luther King Jr., who referred to the Declaration of Independence as a "promissory note."[21] One might say, of course, that King was only speaking "metaphorically," which the editor of the project tells us is exactly what the 1619 Project does.

The difference, of course, in the uses of metaphor is that the 1619 Project was conceived not in liberty but in slavery, while Rev. King's metaphor is connected to what Hannah Arendt wrote in her book *On Revolution*—that the founding of nations are "fundamentally about binding and promising."[22] Rev. King's comment is also connected to something Abraham Lincoln said at Gettysburg:

that "the nation was conceived in liberty four score and seven years ago"—that is 1776, not 1619.

Fourth, there is nothing in the 1619 Project, or the Progressive New Left's views of it, about the many counterexamples that disprove the ten major claims in it. Take, for example, the state of California, the nation's most productive state. It accounts for 13 percent of the entire agricultural output in the US, 5 percent of its mineral production, and 11 percent of its manufacturing.

If central claim number four discussed earlier is true—that the enslavement of Africans and their descendants accounts for America's economic prosperity—then one might expect California to show that thesis is most evident. And yet Black slavery was never practiced in California, which has always been a free state.

In California, it was instead the cruel experiences of Chinese Americans—forty thousand Chinese immigrants arrived in California in the 1850s to mine gold and later to work on the railroads.[23] When asked about this counterexample, Ms. Hannah-Jones gave an interesting response. She said:

> Most Asian Americans arrived in this country after the end of legal segregation and discrimination, thanks to the Black resistance struggle.[24]

It is nothing but *hubris*, of course, to credit the gains made by Asian Americans in the United States to the result of the "Black resistance struggle." Not only is slavery responsible for the American economy, according to Dr. Desmond, and for the many accomplishments of the African American community, but African Americans are also responsible for any gains made by Asian Americans. This is truly an astounding claim!

Numerous other economic and political counterexamples could be pointed to that fly in the face of the 1619 Project's ten central claims. We have said enough here, however, to suggest that the Biden-Harris administration should be more wary about many of the historical claims made by the project and its contemporary Progressive followers.

Noted historian Gordon S. Wood was asked in a 2019 interview, "What is your initial reaction to the 1619 Project?" His response was instructive. He said at the time:

> Well, I was surprised when I opened my Sunday *New York Times* in August and found the magazine containing the project. I had no warning about this. I read the first essay by Nikole Hannah-Jones, which alleges that the Revolution occurred primarily because of the Americans' desire to save their slaves.

In the same interview, Professor Wood went on to observe:

> She claims the British were on the warpath against the slave trade and slavery and that rebellion was the only hope for the American colonies. This made the American Revolution out to be like the Civil War, where the South seceded to save and protect slavery, and that the Americans seventy years earlier revolted to protect their institution of slavery. I just couldn't believe this.

Dr. Wood went on to speak of his surprise about many other aspects of the 1619 Project, aspects that were riddled with historical inaccuracies and, in some cases, factual errors.[25] As we have seen in this eighth essay on the 1619 Project, I totally agree with the analysis of Professor Wood and other notable American historians as well.

One of the most telling criticisms of the 1619 Project came in an essay by Peter A. Coclanis for the Independent Institute. Mr. Coclanis likened the publication of the 1619 Project to Martin Luther's *Ninety-Five Theses*, Jonathan Swift's *A Modest Proposal*, and Marx and Engel's *Communist Manifesto*.

Mr. Coclanis referred to the 1619 Project as a *polemic* in the same way that these other works have that name as well. In his critique, Coclanis went on to say the following about the 1619 Project polemic:

> The intent of this polemic, on one level, is to dislodge the standard chronology and narrative scaffolding of US history by elevating the importance of racial slavery and what some call racial capitalism in explaining both America's past and our predicament.

Mr. Coclanis then added:

> On another level, somewhat shrouded the project aspires to make the case, if not clinch the deal, for reparations to African Americans, reparations due them not only because of slavery, but also because of Jim Crow and decades of state-sponsored discrimination afterward.[26]

What Mr. Coclanis did not do in his essay, however, was outline a plan of who would provide the reparations and what the rules would be about who would get them. In the remainder of his article, Mr. Coclanis took to task the economic points about capitalism that Matthew Desmond made in his 1619 Project essay.

At any rate, an *Economist* poll from January of 2021 indicated that among those who were aware of the 1619 Project, two-thirds of Americans had "unfavorable opinions," while 34 percent had a "favorable" opinion.* Among Black Americans, only 20 percent

---

* Another web poll about the 1619 Project was conducted on June 13, 2021, with 1,500 American respondents who were asked, "Should critical race theory and the *New York Times*' 1619 Project be banned from public school curriculum?" The results of the poll were much like the January

had a favorable view, while among White Americans surveyed, 50 percent had a favorable view of the 1619 Project, nearly all of those Democrats and Independents.[27]

This brings us to the major sources in this essay, followed by Essay Nine of this study. The subject matter of the ninth essay of this study on the Progressive New Left is what role Marxism has played in the belief system of the Progressive New Left in the United States.

An Addendum to the 1619 Project Essay

Believers in the claims of the 1619 Project also ascribe to a fallacy called *presentism*—that is, the belief that today's ethical views are the final and morally correct points of view. Thus, although Washington and Jefferson owned slaves, which was morally acceptable in their time, we now know that they were on the wrong moral side of that issue. Similarly, we tear down the statues of Confederate leaders across the South because, ultimately, we now know the moral views of the men associated with those statues were morally unacceptable.

The recent scholarship of historian Michael Guasco of Davidson College raises an interesting example of presentism, particularly in regard to the date 1619. Dr. Guasco quotes a book by Theodore W. Allen called *The Invention of the White Race: Racial Oppression and Social Control.* Professor Allen essentially revealed:

2021 poll conducted by the *Economist*. Fifty-nine percent in the web poll answered in the positive. It appears that the American people, by and large, do not want CRT and the "polemic" 1619 Project to be taught to their children.

> When the first Africans arrived in Virginia in 1619, there were no "White" people there. Others living in the colony at that time were English; they had been English when they left England, and naturally they and their Virginia-born children were English, they were not "White."

Professor Allen added, "White identity had to be carefully taught, and it would be only after the passage of some six crucial decades that the word would appear as a synonym for European-American." Dr. Allen also tells us in the same work, "During my study of page after page of Virginia County records, reel after reel of microfilm prepared by the Virginia Colonial Records Project," he could find no reference to *White* as a token of social status before its appearance "in a Virginia law passed in 1691." This law in question referred to "English or other White women."

Historian Winthrop D. Jordan, in his book *White over Black: American Attitudes toward the Negro, 1550-1812*, on page 95 of that work agreed. He wrote, "It was only after about 1680, taking the colonies as a whole, that a new term appeared—White."[28]

Because of the phenomenon of presentism, it is inconceivable that English colonists did not understand themselves as being "White." But if Drs. Guasco, Allen, and Jordan are correct, then there is no evidence that those who established the colony at Jamestown saw themselves that way in 1619.

ESSAY NINE

The Progressive New Left and Marxism

I

The purpose of this essay is to introduce the Marxist movement, its manifestations in America, and how the Progressive New Left appears to be employing Marxist ideas in the twenty-first century United States. Consistent with the other essays of this study, we will also provide a critique of how the Progressive New Left in America has utilized the ideas of Karl Marx and a number of his followers and associates.

Earlier in this work, I spoke of Marxist and postmodernist ideas and thinkers and how they have influenced the Progressive New Left's views, such as in the essay on the 1619 Project. I have also made some allusions to Marxist ideas in the first essay of this study, when speaking of the fundamental beliefs of the Progressive New Left.

This essay will consist of three sections. In the first of these, we will speak of the life of Karl Marx, his principal ideas, and a pattern that seems to have been common since the nineteenth century where Marxism has been tried—Russia, Cuba, Venezuela, and elsewhere in the world in that time period.

In the second section of Essay Nine, we will comment on the phenomenon of Marxist thought in the history of the United States as well as what Marx believed about Marxism in America.

In the third and central section of Essay Nine, we will show where Marxist ideas are sometimes used by the Progressive New Left and the American Democratic Party in their party platforms. We will also offer a critique of the New Left's uses of Marxism in the twenty-first century United States.

Introduction to Marx, His Ideas, and Patterns in Marxist Takeovers

Karl Marx was born in 1818 in the city of Trier, Prussia. He was the oldest surviving son in a family of nine siblings. Both of his parents were Jews who were descended from a long line of rabbi. Marx's father, however, a lawyer, converted to Lutheranism in 1816 because of laws in Prussia at the time that barred Jews from higher society.[1]

Marx was baptized in his father's Lutheran church in 1824 when he was six years old. Later, however, he became an atheist. In fact, he believed that belief in God was the "opiate of the masses," that society used religion to make people docile and not ask questions.

After he'd attended university for a year at the University of Bonn, where he was imprisoned for a while for drunkenness and engaging in a duel with another student, his worried parents enrolled him at the University of Berlin to study law and philosophy. It was there that Marx was introduced to the philosophy of G. W. F. Hegel. Indeed, he joined a club known as the Young Hegelians, which challenged existing institutions and ideas on many fronts, including religion, philosophy, ethics, and politics.

Karl Max moved to Paris in 1843, where he met fellow German émigré Friedrich Engels, who would become Marx's lifetime collaborator. Together, they wrote a criticism of Bruno Bauer's Young Hegelian philosophy titled *The Holy Family*. While the French government was trying to get the two Germans expelled from France, the pair moved to Belgium, where Marx renounced his German citizenship.

By 1847, Karl Marx had moved to London, where he spent his days reading at the British Library. He also founded the Communist League in London and focused more on his economic theories. In 1848, Marx published his *Communist Manifesto* with Engels. In the book, the German pair depicted all of human history as a series of class struggles. He called this *historical materialism*.

Later, Karl Marx wrote as a correspondent for the *New-York Daily Tribune* but never managed to make enough money to survive. After remaining isolated for several years while working on his economic theories, in 1864, he organized the International Workingmen's Association. Three years later, he published the first volume of *Das Kapital*, his masterwork on economic theory. In that work, he purported that he would reveal the economic law of motion of modern society.

In the work, Marx laid out his theory of capitalism as a dynamic system that contained the seeds of its own destruction and subsequent replacement with communism. Karl Marx spent the remainder of his life working on the manuscripts of his additional volume of *Das Kapital*, but the work remained unfinished at the time of his death on March 14, 1883, by a lung disease, probably pleurisy.

In these major works of Karl Marx, we can point to fifteen major ideas. These may be summarized this way:

1. Mankind should look to the future, when mankind will attain an ideal society.
2. This ideal society will be characterized by perfect equality and fraternity.
3. Economic progress in the perfect society will occur through Marx's economic theories.
4. The progress of history will unfold through a dialectical and historical materialism.

5. Progress will be accelerated through conflict.
6. There is only one sin in the new society: the departure from conformity.
7. The individual in the new society must surrender his personal rights in favor of those of the group.
8. Only absolute equality of humans is important. Other forms of equality are not.
9. The new society will deny all property rights.
10. The new society will abolish the institutions of marriage and family.
11. Women will be emancipated in the new society.
12. The new society will have all rights over a child's education.
13. Economics is to be the basis of the new society.
14. The collectivity of the new society controls the individual in every way.
15. Capitalist society needs to be radically changed in order to have the "disappearance of the state."[2]

In addition to our comments on the life of Karl Marx and his fifteen principal ideas, we will also show a pattern that Marxists in the last hundred years have followed when they have attempted to make a takeover of a country or countries. These Marxist takeovers have a pattern of four steps. These are:

1. Demoralizing
2. Destabilizing
3. Crisis
4. Normalization

The steps of this pattern—which we will describe next—were employed after the Russian Revolution, in Castro's Cuba, and in Venezuela, to cite three examples from the past one hundred years.

In the first step, *demoralizing*, the Marxists try to demoralize the people to believe that civilization as we know it has been lost. The goal is to make people begin to wonder about how the past did not really satisfy people. This is tied to the second phase—*destabilization*—which is a "rapid decline in the structure of society" in terms of its economy, military, and international relations.

One might argue that this is already happening in the current American administration, as the Democratic leaders are attempting to tamp down the economy through the shutting down of schools and businesses while using the COVID-19 pandemic as an excuse.

In regard to the third phase, the *crisis* mode can be seen in the Biden administration regarding the January 6, 2021, activities at the Capitol. One might add the pandemic to the crisis mode as well—witness the administration sending people door to door in areas where they have attempted to lower the rate of those who have not been vaccinated for COVID-19.

Recently, when Dr. Anthony Fauci was asked about the many Americans who refuse to be vaccinated from COVID-19, he spoke of the refusals as a "public health crisis," but then he went on to say that the cause of that crisis was what he called *ideology*, without saying anything about what he meant by that term. Perhaps Dr. Fauci's comment is another bit of information implying that we are in the midst of a second civil war in the United States.

We see the phenomenon of *normalization* as well during the pandemic when people have spoken of the "new normal." Mask wearing, social distancing, and avoiding large crowds are other examples of normalization.

Of course, the normalization phase is to be followed by the "revolutionary new government"—that is, the shift from Donald Trump to Joe Biden. And one way to achieve that shift completely is to propose aspects of American society that would be consonant with Progressive New Left principles, the topic of the next section of Essay Nine.

The normalization phase can also be seen in Russia, Cuba, and China in the early to mid-twentieth century. In Russia, after the

1917-to-1921 revolution, the period of normalization began with the many prison camps established there. After 1960, detention camps were also constructed in Cuba to help with the normalization process. Meanwhile, in China, the government built what were known as *laogai* camps, or "hard labor" camps. The Cultural Revolution of 1966 to 1969 in China was also another tool for normalizing the Chinese people.

Any who objected to the process in China came to be known as part of the Anti-Rightist Unification movement.

Before moving to the Progressive New Left's views on the applications of Marxist principles, we first must make some observations about the history of socialism in the United States, the topic of the second section of this ninth essay.

The History of Socialism in America

The history of the socialist movement in the United States spans a variety of collections of people in the country, including Communists, anarchists, Democratic Socialists, Marxists, Marxist-Leninists, Social Democrats, Trotskyists, Utopian Socialists, and many other organizations of Socialists in America.

These movements began in the early nineteenth century with organizations like the Shakers, the missionary movement of Josiah Warren, and international communities inspired by Charles Fourier. Labor activists—mostly from British, German, or Jewish immigrants—founded the Socialist Labor Party of America in 1877. The Socialist Party of America was established in 1901.[3]

An event called the "Haymarket affair" in Chicago on May 4, 1886, was the beginning of International Workers' Day, and it became the most common workers' holiday throughout the world—that is, Labor Day.

The American Socialist Party ran a candidate for president

five times between 1905 and 1920. His name was Eugene V. Debs.[4] In his 1916 campaign, Mr. Debs voiced Socialist opposition to the United States' involvement in World War I, which would come a year later in 1917. In the 1930s, the Communist Party USA took part in many labor and racial struggles in the United States.

The principles of Karl Marx also helped shape W. E. B. Du Bois's 1935 landmark work, *Black Reconstruction in America*, by expanding on Marx's work by more fully accounting for the plunders of slavery. This work, in turn, was employed by Nikole Hannah-Jones in the writing of her lead essay of the 1619 Project.

In *Das Kapital*, Marx observed the following about America:

> The discovery of gold and silver in America, the extirpation, enslavement and entombment in mines of the indigenous population of that continent, and the conversion of Africa into a preserve for the commercial hunting of Black skins, are all things which characterize the dawn of an era of capitalist production.

These idyllic proceedings are the chief moments of primitive accumulation.

Needless to say, Mr. Du Bois read his Karl Marx well. Elsewhere, Marx argued that capitalism would expand its use across the globe and eventually consign slavery, as well as other forms of "primitive accumulation," to the "dustbin of history." Marx believed, as Du Bois did as well, that in the American Civil War, it was the Union side that represented the forces of capitalism, and thus it was also the Union side that was in a position to end slavery. For Marx and Du Bois, slavery was not only morally wrong; it also slowed the expansion of the capitalist labor system and, thus, the development of revolutionary socialist consciousness as well. This, of course, is an idea that flies in the face of Dr. Desmond's 1619 Project essay, where he claimed that American capitalism is a by-product of slavery.

It is of some interest that in his writings about the American Civil War, Marx painted himself as an ally of Abraham Lincoln, which is curious since it is believed that they were ideological opposites. Lincoln championed the free labor system under development across the North. Marx equated free labor with "wage slavery" because laborers had no choice but to sell their labor for survival.

But the perception that the two had opposing views is a product of the Cold War, and in reality, Marx and Lincoln had some important commonalities, especially their hatred for chattel slavery. And Karl Marx saw the attainment of free labor as a fundamental step toward worker emancipation.

In the last fifty years, one of the Progressive New Left's primary missions has been to expand the idea of political freedom to be tied to economic freedom. Without control over our work, our bodies, and our time, human potential becomes stunted, and democracy becomes stillborn. "Freedom" has remained a fixture in the American political lexicon. But Marx and Du Bois had a much better definition of freedom.

At any rate, in the 1950s, socialism was affected by McCarthyism, and in the 1960s, socialism was revived in America by the radicalization of what came to be known as the New Left, a progenitor of the Progressive New Left movement in contemporary America.

Also in the 1960s in the United States, Michael Harrington and other Socialists were recruited to serve in the Kennedy administration and then in the Johnson administration's War on Poverty and the Great Society initiative. At the same time, many Socialists played important roles in the American civil rights movement.

The city of Milwaukee, Wisconsin, has had several Socialist mayors, including Emil Seidel, Daniel Hoan, and Frank Zeidler. Eugene V. Debs garnered more than three million votes in the 1920 presidential election. And Social Democrat Bernie Sanders, in the

2016 presidential contest, won thirteen million votes. In fact, 57 percent of all who voted for Mr. Sanders in 2016 were between the ages of eighteen and forty-four, according to figures in six key states.

Polls of millennials in America have consistently shown that economic issues, such as jobs and college debt, are that generation's chief concerns. Issues like transgender rights and climate change may motivate the media and the denizens of university hothouses like the one from which I retired in 2016. But most young people are far more concerned about the impacts on their lives from more immediate issues.

Relatively few millennials are starting businesses or buying houses. This has led to growing support for rent control and massive housing subsidies from the federal government. This is particularly true in the overpriced markets for young people, such as the West Coast and the Northeast. Even in a place like Orange County, California, polls show that more than 60 percent of citizens favor rent control, at least according to a recent Chapman University poll.

This support for the candidacy of Senator Sanders had many effects in America. Perhaps the most important of these is that his struggle helped to get rid of the stigma of the S-word in the United States. Mr. Sanders's run, as well as his role in the Senate, has also helped to push the socialist agenda in the Democratic Party. The Vermont senator is certainly one of the most important precursors to the Progressive New Left in America.

The democratic socialist movement, unfortunately for the Socialists, did not succeed. But if it had success, it most likely would have been only temporary. When social democratic reforms like the New Deal are implemented, those gains can be—and usually are—rolled back significantly by tenacious forces of capital when they are allowed to continue operating under capitalism and within bourgeois democracy. In short, the reforms themselves are compromises with the ruling class, and therefore, they are watered-down half measures.

Nevertheless, they are subject to the whims of the ruling class, which, of course, has not been overthrown. In addition to our own New Deal legislation being gradually decimated by neoliberalism, things could be even worse, as people living in Chile tragically learned in the year 1973.

These attitudes of millennials toward rent control and other issues raise the question of whether we are facing a new Socialist culture war, as witnessed by the protosocialist city council in the city of Seattle, which is second only to the San Francisco Bay area as the center of the new tech wealth. In fact, San Francisco recently passed a wealth tax to pay for the city's homeless services.[5]

One final point about the philosophical foundations of the American Socialist Party: it was primarily the works of Antonio Gramsci, whose chief legacy arose from his departure from orthodox Marxism. He also affirmed that all societies in human history have been divided into two basic groups: the privileged and the marginalized, the oppressors and the oppressed, the dominant and the subordinate.[6]

Gramsci believed it was necessary first to delegitimize the dominant belief system of the predominant group and then to create a "counterhegemony," or a new system of value for the subordinate group. This has to happen, in his view, before the marginalized group, the subordinate group, can be empowered. Because hegemonic values permeate all aspects of society—schools, churches, the media, voluntary associations—civil society itself is the "great battleground in the struggle for hegemony" (that is, the new system of values for the subordinate, oppressed group).

Antonio Gramsci's ideas were further developed by a group of Jewish Marxists who, during the interwar period, formed a philosophical movement that came to be called the Frankfurt School, whose biggest intellectual addition to the Left was the creation of critical theory, the forerunner of critical race theory.

One of the most influential members of the Frankfurt School was Herbert Marcuse, who immigrated to the United States when the Nazis came to power. This move gave Marcuse the opportunity to spread the ideas of the Frankfurt School in the United States. Before Marcuse could establish his teaching influence, the United States went through the period of the Roaring Twenties, which, among other things, was characterized by drinking and partying as well as sexual promiscuity.

These ideas, which really started to take hold in the 1920s, were beaten back in the postwar 1950s, only to resurge again with a renewed force in the 1960s, when an entire generation of baby boomers became mesmerized with a philosophy that promised them "free love" and an escape from responsibility, followed by the demonstrations against the war in Vietnam.

Many of these baby boomers, like myself, grew up to be college professors and industry leaders of today, who wasted no time in indoctrinating millennials with an even more extreme version of the ideology that then became the Progressive New Left.

For the Biden administration, President Trump's way of doing things was then the dominant point of view, for he got more votes than Hillary Clinton. But the Progressive New Left realized that they had to unseat the legitimacy of the Trump point of view, the oppressor.

Then next, they had to discount or eliminate any traces of his point of view, followed by the establishment of the pristine Progressive New Left with Mr. Biden at the helm of the new Democratic ship.

Some ways to see these Marxist ideas in American culture are in the Progressive New Left's attitudes toward the 1619 Project, as discussed in Essay Eight; the development of affirmative-action programs in America, ostensibly to "right social wrongs"; and the Biden-Harris idea that the rich should be more heavily taxed.

This brings us to the third section of this ninth essay of this study of attitudes toward the Progressive New Left in America. In that section, our major focus shall be on how the Progressive New Left has attempted to apply Marxist and socialist principles to issues in contemporary American politics.

The Progressive New Left's Applications of Marxist Principles

One way to see the current Democratic Party's commitment to Marxist ideas is to look at the Democratic platform on issues like free college tuition, housing reform, bail reform, and Medicare for All. While Joe Biden was running for president, he repeatedly mentioned his view that all high school graduates should get a "free two-year community college" education.

On April 28, 2021, President Biden made good on his promise for free community college when he introduced a plan for $109 billion for two years of free community college "so that every student has the ability to obtain a degree or certificate. Dreamer students would be included."

President Biden's plan includes $39 billion that "provides two years of subsidized tuition for students from families earning less than $125,000 enrolled in a four-year historically Black college." The Biden plan also called for "double scholarships for future teachers from $4,000 to $8,000 per year." The Biden plan also targets $400 million for "teacher preparation at minority-serving institutions and $900 million for the development of special education teachers." Another example of the Left's throw-money-at-it approach.

Mr. Biden's vice-presidential pick, Kamala Harris, while campaigning for president in July of 2019, released a Medicare for All plan. Later, when she learned that Joe Biden was against the idea, she changed her mind about the proposal as well. Mr. Biden related on March 19, 2020, that he would veto the universal health-care legislation known as Medicare for All. While she was in the Senate, Ms. Harris also proposed a bill, as did Social Democrat Senator Bernie Sanders, that called for Medicare for All.

The Senator Sanders version of the bill was cosponsored by four former primary contenders—Senator Harris, Cory Booker, Kirsten Gillibrand, and Elizabeth Warren—all Progressive members of the New Left. The biggest difference between the Harris and Sanders plans is their views on private insurance, about which Harris was ambivalent, while Sanders was decidedly against it. This may be because Senator Sanders has expressed many times that he is enamored with the health-care system of Cuba and believes it may be a good model for the US.[7]

On June 23, 2021, President Joe Biden moved to fire the top US mortgage regulator, and fellow Democrats called on him to use the agency to expand access to loans for lower-income people who have struggled to buy homes since the financial crisis of 2007.

The Supreme Court gave the Biden administration the opportunity to change the direction of the Federal Housing Finance Agency (FHFA) when the court ruled that the agency's leadership structure was unconstitutional and that the president should have more authority to remove the director. Hours later, Mr. Biden fired then-director Mark Calabria, a Libertarian economist nominated by President Donald Trump who had made it his mission to shrink and shore up Fannie and Freddie Mae so they could stand on their own as private companies.

The Biden administration then appointed another senior FHFA official, Sandra Thompson, to serve as acting director. It goes without saying, of course, that Ms. Thompson is a dyed-in-the-wool Democrat.

Perhaps the best way to see the Biden-Harris views on Marxist ideas is in their criminal justice reform plan, which suggests money for bail reform and a host of many other issues that smack of ideas like those of the most famous nineteenth-century German economist.

Joe Biden's new criminal justice reform plan reverses some of the very policies he helped to create when he was in Congress. His plan was actually released long before he became the Democratic candidate for president and before the Minneapolis death of George Floyd, which triggered a national reckoning over race and policing we have discussed in an earlier essay.

Most relevant to the Black Lives Matter protests and police reform was Mr. Biden's suggestion to incentivize police reforms at the state and local levels while also taking steps to make state and local police more accountable for abuses—another case of throwing money at the problem.

This week, President Biden has called for several mayors, governors, and police chiefs to discuss the rise in violent crime since his administration has taken over. He did not, however, invite to the meeting people like Chicago councilman Hardiman, who was dismayed that Biden called Mayor Lightfoot about crime in her city but not Hardiman, who had a plan for dealing with violent crime in the city.

Not surprisingly, when the White House reported on the president's meeting about violent crime, Hardiman told state and local officials to use the Coronavirus Relief Fund for developing strategies for dealing with violent crime. For the Democrats, any solution to a problem is simple—just throw more money at the problem.

Meanwhile, over the Fourth of July 2021 weekend, 108 people were shot in Chicago,[8] and on the following weekend, thirty more were shot, and twelve were murdered. Over that same weekend, nineteen citizens were shot in the Democratic-run New York City; three of them were killed.

Among the things that were not discussed at the White House meeting on violent crime were the following: no mention of the current disrespect for the police in America; no mention of the disempowerment of the police in the contemporary United States; no mention of the morale of police officers in America; no mention of bail reform, which in many places in the United States sends violent criminals back to the streets hours after arrest; and no mention of police officers in the United States leaving the job in droves. In Chicago, for example, in the year 2021, 363 police officers had already left the department—just in the first six months of the year. In the last eighteen months, the city of Seattle has seen the retirements of 270 police officers, and similar numbers can be seen in other American cities. The Defund the Police movement is now reaping what it sowed, and cities across America are not happy about it.

Biden's criminal justice plan also includes a number of other ambitious goals, including decriminalizing marijuana, eliminating mandatory sentences for nonviolent crimes, ending the death penalty, abolishing private prisons, eliminating cash bail, and discouraging the incarceration of children.

His criminal justice plan even calls to end policies that Biden previously backed. The most notable of these was his move to eliminate the sentencing disparity between crack and powder cocaine, which contributed to racial disparities in federal incarcerations. Mr. Biden's new plan is aimed at reducing incarceration and fixing the "racial, gender, and income disparities in the system."

The Biden administration's criminal justice reform plan also provides a new $20 billion that encourages states to reduce incarceration and crime.[9] And he directed the savings from fewer incarcerations at the federal level, along with additional federal money, to boost spending on education, including universal pre-K, another hint that Harris and Biden lean in the direction of Marxist principles.

Mr. Biden introduced his criminal justice plan during the

primary leading up to the general election, mostly in the context of the various Democratic candidates trying to prove their Progressive New Left *bona fides* on criminal justice issues. Mr. Biden's is an incredibly Progressive New Left plan.

For Mr. Biden, his new criminal justice reform plan is of particular interest to him because of his long history in the US Senate, where he went against many of the preferences of today's Progressive New Left Democrats. As a member of the Senate Judiciary Committee, for example, Mr. Biden wrote bills and was key in passing policies that helped develop today's punitive criminal justice system—that escalated mass incarcerations, the war on drugs, and the advent of more aggressive policing.

These previous positions have, at times, made Mr. Biden a target for criminal justice reformers, even going back to Mr. Biden's times as Barack Obama's vice president. As one writer, Naomi Murakawa, related about the president, "There's a tendency now to talk about Joe Biden as the sort of affable, if inappropriate, uncle, as loudmouth and silly. But he's actually done really deeply disturbing, dangerous reforms that have made the criminal justice system more lethal."[10]

Now that Mr. Biden has seen the light and moved more toward the Left and the Progressives of his party, his new criminal justice reform plan is not only a way to mollify criminal justice reformers like Ms. Murakawa, but it is also a way of making up for mistakes he has made.

These mistakes are ones that I am sure the Progressive New Lefters who seem to surround him, including Ms. Harris, have already pointed out to him.

President Joe Biden also has a long record of supporting "tough on crime" policies. Consider these four examples:

1. The Comprehensive Crime Control Act of 1984
2. The 1986 Anti-Drug Abuse Act

3. The 1988 Anti-Drug Abuse Act
4. The 1994 Violent Crime Control and Law Enforcement Act

Item number one on this list was a law spearheaded by Mr. Biden and Senator Strom Thurmond to expand federal drug trafficking penalties and civil asset forfeiture, and it allowed the police to take a citizen's property—whether cash, cars, drugs, or other property—without proving that the person had committed a crime.

Item number two on our list was partially written by Senator Biden. It increased the federal penalties for drug crimes. It also created the sentencing disparity between crack cocaine and powder cocaine mentioned earlier.

The 1988 Anti-Drug Abuse Act was cosponsored by Mr. Biden. This act strengthened prison sentences for drug possession, enhanced penalties for transporting drugs, and established the Office of National Drug Control Policy, which leads and coordinates federal antidrug efforts.

Finally, the 1994 Violent Crime Control and Law Enforcement Act was partially written by Mr. Biden when he was a senator. The act imposed tougher sentences and increased funding for federal prisons. One of the effects of this act was that it was one of the contributing factors in greatly increasing the US prison population from 1990 until 2015. This is a trend that has begun to reverse only since 2016.

Mr. Biden in the 1980s and 1990s was proud of his "tough on crime" record. He even managed to go on national television to criticize a plan from President George H. W. Bush to escalate the war on drugs. "The plan," Mr. Biden said at the time, "did not go far enough."

Now that Mr. Biden appears to be in the Progressive New Left camp, I wonder how long it will take those around him to show the president the way he went wrong?

The next item on the agenda in this essay is to return to the fifteen central beliefs of Karl Marx listed earlier in this essay and to show how some of those beliefs appear to be found in the policies and positions of the Progressive New Left in contemporary America.

It should be clear, for example, that universal health care can be seen in every Western nation throughout the world but the United States. It was particularly true in the Communist Bloc countries of the Cold War. Indeed, Senator Sanders has observed that Cuba's socialist health care system may be a model for the US.

Universal pre-K is another idea that smacks of the Soviet system, as is the idea of who has control, and a say, over how a child gets educated (item number twelve of our list of Marx's principles). In the Cuban system, and in Russia as well, the state maintains control over what children are taught. Given the debate over critical race theory these days, one wonders how long it will be before the United States follows suit.

Marx's idea of absolute equality, in his mind, was the only kind of equality that any society should claim for its citizens. The call for ameliorating the difference in incarceration rates of Black and poor people in the United States seems to be an example of applying Marx's dictum of absolute equality and the move to equity and away from equality.

The notion that the individual citizen's rights should be consumed in the rights of the collective seems to rear its head in the COVID-19 restrictions in states like California and New York, even if Nancy Pelosi could get a haircut while no one else in California could. Mask-wearing rules in Democratic states seemed much more restrictive than Republican-run states—all for the greater good of the collective.

The Progressive New Left's views on abortion, which we have discussed earlier in this study, are very much like the views of abortion in Cuba, "where it is available upon request." The Soviet

Union became the first nation in Europe to make abortion legal and available "for any woman who wants one." One big difference in both Cuba and the USSR, however, is that both countries have much stricter regulations on late-term abortions than the Progressive New Left would like.

Another way the Biden administration's leaning on Marxist ideas can be seen in the administration's "American Rescue Plan," which calls for the Child Tax Credit to be increased from $2,000 a year per child to $3,000.[11] Again, this move is quite a reminder of Soviet-supported childcare practices from the 1950s to the 1980s. At the recent Conservative Political Action Conference meetings in the summer of 2021, Governor Kristi Noem said that the biggest cultural challenge of our lifetime is "defeating anti-American indoctrination."[12]

Marx's idea of what he called the "disappearance of the state," number fifteen on our list of the German economist's core beliefs, can be seen most boldly in the Biden-Harris administration's handling of the many gains from the Trump years. Thus, Mr. Biden has rolled back or canceled the forty-fifth president's views on the border crisis, on cutting taxes, and on federal regulations as well as many key political issues, and all the replacement "solutions" have done little to solve the problems that Mr. Trump sought to fix, such as the southern border crisis, which, according to White House press secretary Jen Psaki, is not a crisis at all.

Perhaps the best way to see how the Biden-Harris administration wishes to solve these problems is to do what the Democratic federal government has always done in the past twenty-five years. That answer is this: "Throw money at it." My guess is that the report that comes from the crime meeting in the White House in mid-July will announce the institution of several "new programs" that will offer incentives for reducing violent crime. Another example, of course, of throwing money at it.

There is a pattern that has developed in the Democratic

Party. If there is a problem at the southern border, send money to the countries of Central America. If there is a precipitous rise in violent crime in Democratic cities in America, throw money at it. If there is still a great disparity in the social conditions of Black and White Americans, between the poor and the rich, throw money at it, but tax the rich more heavily so we can pay for these new programs.

One way to see the "disappearance of the state" idea and the canceling of the Trump administration is to look at the apparent change in regard to nepotism and the idea of family members serving in an administration. The Democrats were very vocal about the issue in regard to Mr. Trump's family.

President Biden's treatment of his son Hunter, on the other hand, is radically different. Hunter Biden has made millions from China, Russia, and Ukraine,[13] not to mention his employment of prostitutes in a Los Angeles hotel for which his father paid the bill.[14] Hunter also failed to apply for a gun permit, when his dad sees gun possession as a major cause in the surge of violent crime since he took office.[15]

Hunter Biden's use of illegal drugs, his failure in the military, and his meeting with Mexican businessmen to discuss "business opportunities," to say nothing of the content of the laptop he left at a Wilmington pawnshop, are all problematic for many people on the Right but not for Joe Biden.[16]

Recently, when White House press secretary Jen Psaki was asked about Hunter Biden's newfound career as an artist—whose paintings have reportedly sold for between $75,000 and half a million dollars—she responded, "Of course, he has the right to pursue an artistic career, just like any child of a president has the right to pursue a career."[17] Meanwhile, the younger Mr. Biden refuses to disclose the identities of the buyers of his artwork.

Even former Democratic ethics chief for the Obama administration, Walter Shaub, recently has related that he finds what

Hunter Biden has done "deeply troubling," and I, who taught ethical theory and its application for forty-three years, wholeheartedly agree with that assessment.[18]

Another way the lean toward the Left in the Biden administration can be seen, as well as the responses to Marxist institutions in the last fifty years, is in the reaction that Vice President Kamala Harris recently gave about what she thought about voter ID in rural areas of America.

Her response gave us another window through which we may observe her administration's policies. She said, "There's no Kinko's, there's no OfficeMax near them [in rural America],"[19] while at the same time obviously not thinking of today's telephone technology that allows us to take photos of nearly everything in contemporary society.

Gone are the days of one-day voting, where one had to prove one's identity to vote. It has been replaced with multiple-day voting and mail-in balloting, even drive-through voting, as well as other provisions that would make it easier to "steal an election" or make it easier to cheat.

Recently, fifty-one of the Texas legislature's Democratic members walked out of a discussion of a Republican proposal for voter reform in their state, where the Republican members are in the majority. Since the Republicans were in the majority, the fifty-one Democrats walked out of the meeting.[20] This, of course, is a reminder of what President Biden said when Republicans in the state of Georgia proposed voter reform in that state. At the time, Mr. Biden called it "Jim Crow on steroids."[21]

About this issue of voter ID in Texas and other states, Mr. Biden, in mid-July 2021, related, "This is the most existential crisis of America since the Civil War." Six hundred and fifty thousand Americans died in the Civil War. In World War II, we defeated Adolf Hitler and his Nazi regime. Today, six hundred thousand Americans and two million people worldwide have died of the

COVID-19 disease. How many Americans have died over the issue of voter ID requirements?

The absurdity of this comment by the president of the United States is among the strangest and most ill-thought-out ideas Mr. Biden has had in his presidency. But then again, it was not really his idea, for once again he read, from his notes and a teleprompter, the words of his Progressive New Left speechwriter. In that regard, we might concede that one of the positive things we can say about the forty-sixth president of the United States is that he clearly knows how to read.

Another repercussion of Georgia's voter rights bill was the movement of the Major League Baseball All-Star game from the city of Atlanta, Georgia, to Coors Field in Denver, Colorado, in the summer of 2021. This is another example of the Democratic Party's clout in the contemporary United States.

The diminishing control of parents over how and what their children are taught is another echo of item number twelve of the most fundamental of Marx's teachings—that Marx's new society will have absolute right over the education of children. If we consider the following facts, then one might well argue that this phenomenon that the state should determine how children are taught already seems to be coming to fruition in America.

First, federal guidelines—like those of the CDC, for example—relate that children should not wear masks if vaccinated. And yet the California Department of Education already has related that all Californian schoolchildren will wear masks in the fall.

Second, the many national teachers' unions and the role they play in American schools show a growing concern on the part of parents about what and by whom their children are being taught. Consider the recent announcement of the largest teachers' union in America, the American Federation of Teachers, by the organization's head, Randi Weingarten, that defends the teaching of critical race theory in American classrooms, despite the many complaints from parents in various jurisdictions about the issue. And what philosophical views are beneath critical race theory? Nothing, of course, but Marxist theory.

Third, the teachers' unions have been among the most consistent backers of the Democratic Party over the past forty years.[22] This is yet another sign of who is in charge of the education of our children. Fourth, and finally, Ms. Weingarten's waffling over who should get vaccinated in schools and when perhaps is another indication of who is in charge in our schools.

It does not take much to get Americans to see that Marx's dictum that the state will have absolute right over the education of its children is beginning to look very familiar in the United States.

None of this, of course, has much to do with the fact that the president rarely speaks extemporaneously in public. He usually reads from a teleprompter or notes, he rarely takes questions, and he seems never to speak or to respond unaccompanied by notes. None of this, of course, is reported in the traditional media. Even Jen Psaki, Biden's press secretary, has taken to bringing prepared responses to questions she is asked and flipping to the right spot in her notebook so she can read her prepared remarks.

And so, the contemporary world we find ourselves living in is a society where the Progressive New Left lobbies for affirmative action programs and employment quotas that mandate race- and gender-based diversity in the workplace. It is the Progressive New Left that shows gay couples kissing on television. It is the Progressive New Left that welcomes massive numbers of hostile and culture-clashing migrants into the United States, most of whom are not tested for COVID-19, although 70 percent of all COVID-19 cases in one Texas town can be identified as coming from the southern border.

It is now the Progressive New Left that defends a woman's right to kill her unborn child under any circumstances from conception until the moment of birth, completely without apology, even if one grew up with a moral value system that strictly forbids the action or if Roe v. Wade strictly limits third-trimester abortions.

The central trust of the Progressive New Left—besides the constant guilt mongering over endless permutations of imagined bigotry—is the idea inherent in its name: that the movement is "progressive." Or that it heralds a new, better way to come in the future. But just a cursory review of the history of political movements in the United States will show that these very same sentiments have ebbed and flowed throughout the course of American history.

The ideas that women should be equal to men in every way, that sexuality should be unrestricted, and that the Judeo-Christian moral family values need to be abolished in order to make room for the new society are, in fact, nearly a century old.

This new society will look more like Marx and Antonio Gramsci than Washington, Jefferson, and Hamilton. And that fact in itself will be a sad fact indeed in this new American society to come.

There are also a number of ways in which contemporary America does not follow the Marxist, Progressive New Left model of the oppressor and oppressed, such as in the example of Asian Americans. Are they to be lumped with the White oppressors or the Black oppressed? Asian Americans have scored better than White Americans on standardized tests for two generations. As a result of this, Harvard and other Ivy League schools have limited the number of Asian Americans in their classes. Economically, Asian Americans do far better than Black Americans—and in some places in America, even better than White Americans. So where are we to put Asian Americans in the Marxist New Left model? With the oppressors or with the oppressed?

One place where we do see the Marxist oppressor/oppressed model in the behavior of US Olympian Gwen Berry, who turned her back to the American flag and hid her face while the national anthem was played at the Olympic trials. Later, she said, "I'll represent the oppressed people."[23] This, of course, is another sign of the influence of Marxist thought in America and another sign that we are in the midst of a second civil war in the United States.

In the early twenty-first century, the United States—and its New Left views on abortion, public health, childcare, Medicare for All, the teaching of children and who is in charge of that teaching, bail reform, free college, and many other aspects of contemporary society—has begun to look more like the Marxist society state of the Soviet Union or Cuba than the land of the free and home of the brave.

Finally, and perhaps most importantly, Elina Kaplan of the Alliance for Constructive Ethnic Studies, a woman who immigrated to the US from the Soviet Union when she was an eleven-year-old girl, has pointed out how similar the language from critical race theory teachers is to the Soviet system in which she was indoctrinated back in the Soviet Union.[24]

When asked specifically about this phenomenon, she commented about how the language about race is nearly identical to the language about class back in the place of her birth: "Both involved intense indoctrination." This is a scary thought indeed.

Polls of American adults over the last decade have indicated that they favor capitalism over Marxism or socialism. Only 6 percent of baby boomers have a favorable opinion of communism, while 22 percent of millennials have that view. A full quarter of Americans, however, favor a gradual elimination of capitalism in America, including 70 percent of millennials.

Perhaps the most interesting figure of this study is the number of millennials who would not vote for a Democratic Socialist, down from 44 percent in 2017 to 29 percent in 2021. Thus, there is clearly a generational divide in America about economic ideologies.

This brings us to the major sources of this essay, followed

by Essay Ten. The subject matter of the tenth essay of this study of attitudes of the Progressive New Left in American culture is the phenomenon that has come to be known as the Green New Deal—or the issue of climate control in America in the twenty-first century.

Meanwhile, as I write this, the most recent approval ratings of the Biden-Harris administration were published on July 29, 2021. Vice President Harris's approval rating is now at 43 percent, only slightly less than her boss's approval rating, 46 percent. The only issue for which the pair got more than 50 percent was their treatment of the COVID-19 pandemic. In a poll a week later, however, even that issue was below 50 percent.

President Joe Biden's administration's Marxist, Progressive New Left agenda seems to be supplying little of the unity and peace that the forty-sixth president promised in his inaugural address. This is a sad state of affairs, indeed.

ESSAY TEN

The Progressive New Left, the Green New Deal, and Climate Control

I

The central focus of this essay is what the Progressive New Left in America has had to say about the Green New Deal and climate control. This essay will unfold in the following parts. First, we will make some fundamental comments on capitalism and its relationship to political life in America.

This will be followed by a second section of this essay on the plan proposed by New York representative Alexandria Ocasio-Cortez and Senator Ed Markey, along with dozens of cosponsors, and called the Green New Deal. These two parts will be followed by a description of the Biden-Harris plan for climate control.

Finally, Essay Ten will close with a philosophical critique of the Progressive New Left's perspectives on the Green New Deal and the Democratic administration's plan for control of the climate in the United States.

Capitalism and Its Relation to American Politics

In his recent book *American Marxism*, Mark R. Levin began his chapter on "Climate Change Fanatics" by quoting several prominent economists in the late twentieth and early twenty-first centuries who spoke of the relation of capitalism to American politics. Among those economists quoted by Mr. Levin were: George Reisman, professor emeritus of economics at Pepperdine University; 1974 Nobel Prize–winning economist, F. A. Hayek; and 1976 Nobel Prize winner in economics, Milton Friedman.

The sole purpose of Mr. Levin quoting these prominent economists was to show, as Milton Friedman put the matter, that "there is an intimate connection between economics and politics, that only certain combinations of political economic arrangements are possible," and that in particular, a society that is based on socialism cannot also be a democratic society. Dr. Friedman, still quoted by Mr. Levin, went on to observe:

> Economic arrangements play a dual role in the promotion of a free society. On the one hand, freedom in economic arrangements is a component of freedom broadly understood, so economic freedom is an end in itself. In the second place, economic freedom is also an indispensable means toward the achievement of political freedom.[1]

In this comment, Dr. Friedman made an important philosophical distinction between those things that are intrinsically good or evil and those things that are instrumentally good or evil—that is, those things that bring about good or evil. In his view, freedom in America is both inherently good and instrumentally good.

If the comments of Mark Levin and, through him, Milton Friedman are economically correct, then there is an intimate connection between economics in the United States—that is, capitalism—and the American political sphere. The pair add, "History suggests that capitalism is a necessary condition of political freedom." It is also possible, however, to have a capitalist system where the people are not free. Look at Cuba and Venezuela as contemporary examples, as we saw in Essay Nine.

Despite this intimate connection between capitalism and freedom in America, there are many voices from the Progressive New Left in the United States who are desirous of ending the capitalist system in America. Among these are Representative Ocasio-Cortez and Vermont senator Bernie Sanders, among others.

It is not at all surprising that both of these Democratic politicians identify themselves as Democratic Socialists, a view that does not profess the intimate connection between economics and politics. And the two Democratic Socialists are not alone. Based on a recent study, 70 percent of all millennials in America claimed that they would have no reservations in voting for a Socialist candidate.[2]

Among the issues on the Progressive New Left's agenda in contemporary America is the idea of climate and its control in this country. Indeed, the subject matter of the second section of this essay is the proposal made to the 116th Congress of a Green New Deal.

The New Left's Green New Deal

The Green New Deal is a congressional resolution that lays out a grand plan for tackling climate change. The resolution was proposed by New York representative Alexandria Ocasio-Cortez and Senator Edward J. Markey of Massachusetts. The proposal calls for the federal government to wean itself from fossil fuels and to curb the planet-warming greenhouse gas emissions across the American economy.

The AOC-Markey proposal also calls for new high-paying jobs in the clean-air and -water industries. The resolution is nonbinding, so even if it is approved by the members of Congress, nothing in it would become law.

Many variations of the AOC-Markey proposal have been around for years from think tanks, the Green Party, and even *New York Times* columnist Thomas L. Friedman, who appears to have been the originator of the name Green New Deal in an article for the newspaper written in January of 2007. At the time, Mr. Friedman wrote:

> If you have put a windmill in your yard or some solar panels on your roof, bless your heart. But we will only green the world when we change the very nature of the electricity grid—moving it away from dirty coal or oil to clean coal and renewables. And that is a huge industrial project—much bigger than anyone has told you. Finally, like the New Deal, if we undertake the green version, it has the potential to create a whole new, clean power industry to spur our economy into the 21st century.[3]

This idea of a Green New Deal was subsequently taken up by Great Britain and its Green New Deal Group, which published a July 21, 2008, report. The concept was further popularized when the United Nations Environment Programme, or UNEP, began to promote the Green New Deal idea. On October 22, 2008, UNEP's executive director, Achim Steiner, unveiled a "Global Green New Deal" initiative with the purpose of creating "jobs in green industries" and thus boosting the world economy as well as curbing climate change.

In the United States, the Green Party was formed in 1996. The party proposed a candidate for president, Jill Stein, who proposed a Green New Deal program in the 2012 presidential election. By 2019, there had been international calls for a Green New Deal in several countries, including the United States in 2018. More recently, there has also been a COVID-19 Recovery Program that proposed all clean energy going forward.

The AOC-Markey Green New Deal proposal was introduced

on February 7, 2019. Republicans have cast the Green New Deal resolution as a "Socialist takeover," and they suggested that the Progressive Democrats are far from the US energy mainstream. Mitch McConnell, the Senate majority leader, brought the AOC-Markey proposal to the floor in February 2019, and it was voted on March 11, 2019. The AOC-Markey Resolution was defeated in the Senate, with fifty-seven votes against the resolution, all Republicans. Forty-three Democratic Senators all voted "Present." Republicans won over Democratic senators Joe Manchin and Kyrsten Sinema as well as one Independent senator, Angus King, who generally votes with the Republicans.

The AOC-Markey proposal had four central goals. These may be summarized this way:

1. The entire world needs to get to **net-zero emissions** by the year 2050.
2. The gradual reduction of **greenhouse gas emissions**. This is to create new jobs and ensure clean air and water and healthy food because those are basic human rights.
3. A ten-year **mobilization plan** to reduce carbon emissions in the United States and to change the country's energy sources to **renewable and zero-emission power**.
4. It is the duty of the government to provide **job training and new economic development**, particularly in regard to those communities that now depend on the **fossil fuel industry**.[4]

On February 6, 2019, in an interview with Steve Inskeep on NPR, Ms. Ocasio-Cortez outlined this four-prong plan. Then she commented, "Even the solutions that we have considered big and bold are nowhere near the scale of the actual problem that climate change presents us." Then AOC added:

> It could be part of a larger solution, but no one has actually scoped out what the larger solutions would entail. And that is what we are really trying to accomplish with the Green New Deal.[5]

Since the time of the NPR interview, Ms. Ocasio-Cortez has begun to make a number of predictions about the climate control crisis. On January 21, 2019, a few days before the Steve Inskeep interview, AOC predicted that "the world will come to an end in twelve years if we don't do something about climate change."[6] Presumably, she was referring to a United Nations report released in December of 2018 that predicted the consequences of man-made climate change would become irreversible in twelve years if global carbon emissions were not immediately and drastically reduced.[7]

On September 12, 2019, while speaking at the National Association for the Advancement of Colored People (NAACP) forum in Florida, she told her audience that "Miami will no longer exist in a few years if the Green New Deal is not passed to combat the effects of climate change."[8]

By November of 2019, AOC repeated her twelve-year prediction. Her spokesman was asked about the twelve-year figure. He said, "We can quibble about the phraseology, about whether its existential or cataclysmic. We are seeing lots of climate change–related problems that are already impacting our lives."[9]

The spokesman for AOC may have been correct, but he did not immediately enumerate what those items that are "impacting our lives" might be. In fact, in the next section of this essay, we will offer a critique of the predictions that AOC made in 2019 and has continued to make after that time.

Another aspect of the AOC-Markey climate bill is that it calls for a plan to establish a 1.5 million strong "Civilian Climate Corps for Jobs and Justice," which is imagined as a modernized version of FDR's "Civilian Conservation Corps." The Civilian Climate

Corps members would act as "ambassadors for climate control and climate change," at least according to the congressional offices of Representative Ocasio-Cortez and Senator Markey. This brings us to a philosophical critique of the AOC-Markey plan, the subject matter of the next section of Essay Ten of this study.

A Critique of AOC's Predictions on Climate Change

Environmental journalists and other advocates of the Green New Deal have also made a number of grim predictions about the environment. Scientist Bill McKibben, for example, has suggested that climate-driven fires in Australia are responsible for making the koala "functionally extinct."

Student activist Greta Thunberg, in her book, wrote, "Around 2030 we will be in a position to set off an irreversible chain reaction beyond human control that will lead to the end of our civilization as we know it." In another section of her book *No One is Too Small to Make a Difference*, Ms. Thunberg wrote:

> If sea levels rise as much as the Intergovernmental Panel on Climate Change has predicted, it will be an unmanageable problem.[10]

Apocalyptic predictions like these can be multiplied many times in the contemporary world. A group of British psychologists, for example, said that children are increasingly suffering from anxiety from the frightening discourse around climate change. In October of 2019, an activist with Extinction Rebellion, or XR—an environmental group founded in 2018—described its purpose as committing acts of civil disobedience to heighten awareness to the threat of climate change. In 2019, one XR spokesman said a genocide like the Holocaust is "happening again on a far greater scale and in plain sight" from climate change.[11]

AOC, then, is not alone in her predictions. But questions must still be raised about what the scientific evidence does say about the issue of climate control. First, no credible scientific figure or body has ever made the claim that climate threatens the collapse of civilization itself, much less the extinction of *Homo sapiens*. "Our children are going to die in the next ten to twenty years," others predict, without providing the scientific basis for the claim.

When BBC reporter Andrew Neil, in October of 2019, asked a visibly uncomfortable XR spokesperson about the scientific evidence that "our children are going to die," the spokesperson related and admitted:

> These claims have been disputed. There are some scientists who agree and some who say it is not true. But the overall issue is that these deaths are going to happen.[12]

Mr. Neil responded to this female spokesperson for XR and said, "But most scientists don't agree with this. I looked through the [Intergovernmental Panel on Climate Change] reports, and I see no reference to the effect that billions of people are going to die, or children are going to die in twenty years. How would these people die?"

The female spokesperson for XR answered this way:

> Mass migration around the world is already taking place due to prolonged drought in countries, particularly in South Asia. There are wildfires in Indonesia, the Amazon rainforest, Siberia, and the Arctic.[13]

In these statements, however, the spokesperson has grossly misrepresented the science. There is robust evidence of disasters displacing human beings worldwide, but there is very little evidence that climate change or sea level rise are the direct causes. Beyond that fact, most mass migration tends to occur within the borders of an affected country, not to other countries.

It must also be pointed out that economic development has made human beings less vulnerable than they have ever been. Since 1931, there has been a 99.7 percent decline in the death toll in the world from natural disasters. In 1931, 3.7 million people died from natural disasters. In the year 2018, only eleven thousand people did. And keep in mind that the world population has increased fourfold since 1931.

What does the science tell us about rising sea levels? Some contemporary Intergovernmental Panel on Climate Change (IPCC) scientists predict that the sea level could rise as much as two feet by 2100.[14] If that figure is true, that hardly seems apocalyptic, or even *unmanageable*, as some put it. Consider the Netherlands, where one-third of the country is below sea level. Now one might object that the Netherlands is rich while Bangladesh is poor. But people in the Netherlands adapted to living below the sea level four hundred years ago, mostly because of the improvements in technology.

What about the predictions of crop failures, famine, and mass death? Worldwide today, human beings produce enough food for ten billion people, or 25 percent more than what we actually need. Most scientists predict increases in food production, not declines.

The Food and Agriculture Organization of the United Nations (FAO) forecasts a crop yield increase of 30 percent by the year 2050, and the poorest parts of the world, like sub-Saharan Africa, are expected to increase their food supplies by 80 to 90 percent.[15]

No one suggests that climate change will not negatively impact crop yields. It certainly may happen. But such declines would need to be put in perspective. Since the 1960s, wheat field production has increased 100 to 300 percent around the world, depending on the location.

Yale University graduate and Nobel Prize–winning economist William Nordhaus predicted that global warming of 2.5 to 4 degrees would reduce the gross domestic product (GDP) by 2 to 5 percent over that same period.

As tragic as animal extinctions are, they do not appear to be affecting human civilization "as we know it," as Greta Thunberg put it.

At any rate, the wildfires in Australia are not making the koala extinct.[16] The main scientific body that tracks the species, the International Union for the Conservation of Nature (IUCN), now labels the koala as *vulnerable*, which is one level less threatening than *endangered*, two levels less than *critically endangered*, and a full three levels below *extinct*.

The survival of the koala has far bigger threats, such as the destruction of habitat, disease, and the invasion of other species. The idea of bushfires as a cause for extinction of the koala is a much more complicated matter than Bill McKibben has made it out to be. This is true of bushfires in the United States as well, as we shall speak about next.

One of Australia's leading scientists related the following about the koala population and bushfires:

> Bushfire losses can be explained by the increasing exposure of dwellings to fire-prone bushlands. No other influence needs to be invoked. So even if climate change has played a role in modulating recent bushfires—and this cannot be ruled out—any such effects on risk to property are clearly swamped by the changes in exposure.[17]

In other words, this great Australian scientist does not ascribe to the wildfire theory as the major cause of the extinction of the koala species. The same scientist also pooh-poohed the idea that the fires are solely due to drought. Richard Thornton of the

Bushfire and Natural Hazards Cooperative Research Center in Australia related, "Climate change is playing its role here but it is not the cause of these fires."

Well, maybe climate control explains the wildfires in the American West. In 2017, American scientists modeled thirty-seven different regions of the United States. Of the ten variables they identified for the causes of the western brush fires, none were as significant as what they called *anthropogenic variables*—that is, factors related to humans, such as house building and wood-full growth within the forests themselves.

Some climate scientists are starting to push back against the exaggerations of activists, journalists, and other scientists. A climate scientist in Australia, Tom Wigley, was asked what he thought of the claim that climate threatens civilization. "It really does bother me because it's wrong," he said. "All these young people have been misinformed. And partly, it is Greta Thunberg's fault. Not deliberately. But she is wrong."[18]

This brings us to the fourth section of this essay, in which we will discuss what Joe Biden and Kamala Harris have written and have had to say about the Green New Deal and climate control.

Biden-Harris on Green New Deal and Climate Control

Both Kamala Harris and Joe Biden have long histories of acting on and commenting upon climate issues. Ms. Harris was one of the cosponsors of the Green New Deal proposal of AOC and Senator Markey. As early as February 7, 2019, Ms. Harris boldly put forward her general view on climate control when she said the following:[19]

> For too long, we have been governed by lawmakers who are beholden to big oil and big coal. They have refused to act on climate change. So it is on us to speak the truth, rooted in science fact, not science fiction.

Ms. Harris went on that day to state what she sees as "the truth":

> Here's the truth. Climate change is real, and it is an existential threat to our country, our planet, and our future. With each passing day, the imminent threat of climate change grows—and we see it in everything from more instances of extreme weather to the rapidly melting glaciers.

The soon-to-be vice president, in the statement from February of 2019, spoke about the timeline of the climate crisis as well as her cosponsoring of the AOC-Markey Green New Deal resolution. She observed:

> We don't have much time to make the urgent changes we need to protect ourselves and our planet. Add your name right now to stand with me in support of the Green New Deal. Bold action takes bold leadership, and I am grateful to Representative Alexandria Ocasio-Cortez and Senator Ed Markey for leading the charge on this critical resolution.

Then Ms. Harris closed her February 7, 2019, statement this way:

> We do not fight this fight for our generation alone—but for generations to come. Thank you for taking direct action today.

Five months later, while running for president of the United States, Ms. Harris, during a presidential debate, was asked by

Chuck Todd to describe her climate change plan. Ms. Harris responded briskly by saying the rapid warming of the planet should be called a climate crisis because it is "an existential threat to us as a species," without alluding to any sense of what she meant by *existential*.[20] Ms. Harris went on to speak of visiting California wildfire sites in 2018 "while the embers were still smoldering." Then she added, "That is why I support the Green New Deal. It is why on day one as president, I will reenter us into the Paris Agreement." Ms. Harris apparently was not aware that similar bushfires in Australia, as we have indicated, have at least ten variable causes that go into the making of climate control perspectives, and only one of those variables is wildfires or bushfires.

Ms. Harris also was referring to an agreement within the framework of the United Nations in which each country "brings its own goals" or a pledge of emissions reduction that it will deliver in the future. This was called a nationally determined contribution (NDC).[21] President Trump pulled the United States out of the Paris Agreement, but the Biden-Harris administration rejoined on their first day in office.

On August 31, 2020, Ms. Harris repeated, "Climate change is an existential threat, and confronting it requires bold action." Again, she gave no indication of what exactly she meant by *existential*. But it is clear that by late 2020, Ms. Harris was totally on board with the Progressive New Left's plan for the environment, global warming, and climate change.

President Biden has also been committed to climate change since at least as early as October 7, 2020, a month before the presidential election. In one of the presidential debates between the two candidates, however, Mr. Biden seemed to be waffling about his views on the Green New Deal. At one point, Biden said, "The Green New Deal is not my plan." Then, just a few minutes later, he said, "The Green New Deal will pay for itself as we move forward."

Then, a few minutes after that, Biden remarked:

> No, I do not support the Green New Deal. I support the Biden Plan, which is different from what Mr. Trump calls the "radical Green New Deal."[22]

A few minutes later, a researcher from the Right introduced language on the Biden website calling the Green New Deal a "crucial framework for meeting the climate challenges we face." In the same debate, and on the same topic, Mr. Biden said:

> The Green New Deal is not a bad deal, but it is not the plan that I have—that's the Biden Green Deal. The Green New Deal is not a bad deal, but it is a damn good start.

This, of course, raises the question of why the president and vice president seem to be at odds on the Green New Deal. And another question might also be raised: How are the Green New Deal and the Biden Green Deal, or the "Biden climate agenda," different? This is the topic of the next section of this essay on the Progressive New Left's views on climate change.

Green New Deal versus Biden's Plan

It goes without saying that there are many more similarities between the two climate plans than differences. Both plans have provisions for or have commented about the following:

1. Both plans say climate is an *existential threat* to our survival.
2. New green jobs.
3. Improved infrastructure.
4. Affordable and safe housing.
5. The reduction of CO_2 emissions.
6. Making transportation more green in America.

7. International participation: rejoining Paris Agreement.
8. Climate change resilience.
9. Eliminating or discouraging fracking.

There are also, however, at least five major differences between the two plans. First, the two plans disagree about a "guaranteed job with a family-sustaining wage and benefits" for every American. The AOC-Markey plan is in favor of this idea, while the Joe Biden plan is against it. The Biden jobs plan is big but not as comprehensive as the Green New Deal's plan. Mr. Biden pledged to create millions of new jobs by retooling the automobile industry into making lower-emission cars.

The Biden plan also proposes a greener future by upgrading and revamping millions of buildings in the United States so that they are more energy efficient. The plan also calls for the construction of 1.5 million new sustainable housing units as well as cleaning up pollution from oil and gas wells and former coal mining sites.

A second issue where the Biden climate plan differs significantly from the Green New Deal is the issue of fracking. The word *fracking* is short for "hydraulic fracturing," a drilling method for extracting natural gas from underground shale formations by injecting liquid at high pressure.[23]

Since the year 2005, the use of fracking in the United States has exponentially grown. Many energy experts say that if it continues, the United States may soon be the number one exporter in the world of natural gas. The Green New Deal does not explicitly mention the fracking process, but in several interviews with Representative Ocasio-Cortez, she has indicated her stance against it.

Mr. Biden's views on fracking, however, seem to be a little more complicated than those of AOC. During the campaign trail in 2020, leading up to the election, some Democratic candidates expressed their views about the banning of fracking. Elizabeth

Warren and Bernie Sanders were two of those candidates. Some Progressives also believe that Joe Biden made a campaign promise that he would ban fracking.

It is true that on January 20, 2021, Mr. Biden's first day in office, he did end "new fracking on any government land" but said they were "not going to ban fracking altogether." It is important to note that only 12 percent of fracking in America occurs on government land; the other 88 percent is on privately owned land, so it is not clear why a complete ban would be appropriate.

Senator Sanders began criticizing Mr. Biden's ambivalent views on fracking in the first presidential debate in 2019. The Vermont senator said at the time to the soon-to-be forty-sixth president, "I know your heart is in the right place, but this requires dramatic bold action. We have got to take on the fossil fuel industry." Senator Sanders went on to observe, "I don't understand why fracking is allowed to continue in the United States. . . . What Joe is saying goes nowhere near enough."

Senator Sanders's criticisms of Biden's views on fracking have not abated since Mr. Biden has become president. And those criticisms have been joined by the other professed Social Democrat, Ms. Ocasio-Cortez. In October of 2020, she dismissed the idea that young Progressives were sitting out the 2020 presidential election to protest Mr. Biden's candidacy over key policy differences like fracking. "But fracking is a bad thing. It really is," she said.[24]

In fact, in February 2020, AOC, along with Rep. Darren Soto, a Democrat from Florida, officially introduced a national fracking ban in the House of Representatives. That bill served as a companion piece to the Senate legislation proposed by Senators Sanders and Jeff Merkley, Democrat from Oregon. Both bills called for the end of fracking in the US by 2025.

Another thing that Joe Biden did on his first day in office was revoke a presidential order to permit the Keystone XL pipeline—that included the elimination of many climate sector jobs. Mr.

Biden, on that same day, also placed a moratorium on planned oil and gas development in the Arctic National Wildlife Refuge.

Katie Pavlich, writing for *Townhall* on January 20, 2021, reported that the Biden administration was following through with its fracking ban. But again, the White House press secretary, when asked about the comment, said it referred to new leases on federal lands, not to a total ban of fracking.[25]

The Biden administration's most recent comment about fracking came on June 23, 2021, when Secretary of the Interior Deb Haaland indicated that the Biden administration would not pursue an oil and gas leasing ban on public lands. Ms. Haaland said at a hearing:

> I do not think there is a plan right now for a permanent ban. The administration is preparing a review of the oil and gas leasing program, which will be released this summer.[26]

Again, Secretary Haaland's comments most likely also referred to new oil and gas leases on federal lands. A third big difference between the AOC-Markey plan and the Biden plan is that the Biden plan is more narrowly focused than the Green New Deal. Fifty percent of the money in the Biden plan is dedicated to the reduction of carbon levels.

The Biden plan would spend $2.2 trillion over a four-year period, which Mr. Biden wants to pay for by increasing corporate taxes. The Green New Deal, on the other hand, proposes to spend $10 trillion over a ten-year period. The proponents of the Green New Deal want to pay for their plan by raising the tax rates of the richest Americans, even calling for rates of 70 percent or higher.

Another big difference between the Green New Deal and the Biden climate plan is the idea of retrofitting existing buildings in the United States. The Biden plan has a goal of upgrading "four million buildings and weatherizing two million homes over four years, or 1.5 million buildings per year." The Green New Deal, on the other hand, has a much more ambitious plan to "upgrade every building in America, about 125 million of them, in a ten-year period." That is 12.5 million buildings a year.[27]

Finally, there is nothing in President Biden's climate plan about incorporating 1.5 million strong national Civilian Climate Corps that would act as "climate change ambassadors," as the AOC-Markey Green New Deal Plan would establish.[28]

Thus, there are major differences between the Green New Deal Proposal introduced by Ocasio-Cortez and Senator Markey and Joe Biden's climate plan. It also appears that Ms. Harris and Mr. Biden may be at odds when it comes to the Green New Deal. Harris many times has said she supports it, while President Biden has indicated many times that he is against the Green New Deal—at other times, he appears to have favored it.

President Biden, as we have suggested earlier in this essay, has said contradictory things about the Green New Deal, some comments supporting the plan and others not supporting the Green New Deal. One time he flip-flopped several times on the issue in the same day, as we have shown earlier in this study.

This brings us to the sixth and final section of this essay, in which we will evaluate and critique the Biden-Harris plan on climate control and environmental studies issues. This will be followed by the major conclusions and notes of this essay. The principal subject matter of Essay Eleven shall be what the Progressive New Left believes about the Big Tech industry and the role as censors in contemporary American culture.

A Critique of the Biden-Harris Climate Plan

One of the major criticisms of the Progressive New Left and the Biden-Harris administration on the Green New Deal and their climate plan—a criticism we have raised in many of the other essays of this collection—is that whenever the Left of whatever stripe perceives a problem, the solution is always to throw lots of money at the problem. If COVID-19 is a major problem for the United States, throw $2.2 trillion at it in the form of a "Coronavirus Relief Fund."

Similarly, if the status of the climate is such that it has become a crisis, or an "existential threat," then there is only one way to solve this problem—the same way the Progressive New Left does anything these days in America—throw another $2.2 trillion at it in the hopes the problem will be solved.

Sometimes the climate issues are put in the context of what is called *environmental justice*. In Western culture, Plato was the first, and perhaps the best, thinker to discuss and define the idea of justice. Plato, in his book *The Republic*, simply related that "justice is nothing more than getting what one is due."

In Plato's thought, however, justice is a solely human enterprise. Thus, it involves human beings giving other human beings what they are due. The environment, in Plato's account, cannot be given what it is due, for the environment has neither moral rights nor moral duties, two necessary conditions for being a moral agent. A moral agent, in Plato's account, must be capable of giving other moral agents what they are due. Thus, the name *environmental justice* appears to be a misnomer and should not be employed in English.

Ms. Ocasio-Cortez, who often attributes moral rights to the environment, has committed the informal fallacy known as the *pathetic fallacy*, which is the attachment of a human emotion or characteristic to nature or an inanimate object, such as the use of expressions like "angry clouds" or "cruel wind."

Many of the other criticisms that we have of the Biden-Harris climate plan are criticisms we have raised earlier in this essay when we critiqued the Green New Deal's perspectives on the environment. Thus, we will repeat some of those in this current analysis. One of those criticisms has to do with the apocalyptic and exaggerated language that often accompanies the speech of those on the Left when they speak of climate issues: "We need to do it now because we only have twelve more years to live" or "The environment is killing our children" or "The very existence of the human race is at stake." Or, as the vice president put the matter: "Don't call it climate change; call it climate crisis."

Even the vice president has contributed regularly to the apocalyptic language about climate control by pointing out, as she did as early as February 7, 2019, and many times as well afterward, that, "climate change is real, and it is an existential threat to our country." In that same forum, Ms. Harris related, "We don't have much time to make urgent changes. We need to protect ourselves and our planet."

The number of statements like these—mostly coming from the Progressive New Left—can be multiplied by many factors of ten in the last thirty years. But in point of fact, no credible scientist or scientific institution has ever made the claim that climate threatens the collapse of civilization or the survival of the human species.

The IPCC is the United Nation's body for assessing the science related to climate change. They have been issuing yearly reports for the past seven years. There is nothing in the first six of their reports that indicates that billions of human beings are going to die—or their children will—in ten to twenty years.

Nowhere, or at least not very often, does anyone indicate how these people will die. One exception to this is the XR, whose spokesperson, as we have indicated earlier, suggested it would be the "product of mass migration."

The science related to this phenomenon of migration has been grossly misrepresented. There is no evidence of large-scale disasters displacing human beings worldwide. Nor is there much evidence in the science of climate control that the sea level rising can be a major contributing factor in mass migration.

In point of fact, deaths by natural disasters across the world have declined by 99.7 percent since the year 1931. In that year, 3.7 million people died from natural disasters, including floods, famines, earthquakes, and other entities that are sometimes called *acts of God*. In the year 2018, nearly a century later, only eleven thousand worldwide died of natural disasters. And we must add to this figure that the world population is now four times greater than in 1931.

So what indeed does the science tell us about rising sea levels? Some IPCC scientists predict that the sea levels could rise as much as two feet by the year 2100. Others say only a foot, or even three feet, by the year 2100. None of those other possibilities, however, seem to indicate that doomsday is just around the corner.

Another boogeyman that the environmentalists point to as a contributing factor in their apocalyptic scenario is crop failures and the inability to feed human beings in the future. Many other crops on earth are in similar circumstances, such as potatoes and bananas. The bottom line on food should be clear. We will not run out of food in nine years (AOC's updated number from 2019).

Well, maybe it will be the increase of the many wildfires in places like Australia and the American West that will be a major factor in the billions of deaths to come and the many endangered species as well. In 2017, a group of American scientists wrote climate models for thirty-seven regions in America and the variables that cause brush fires in those regions. The group's major conclusion was that "anthropogenic variables," or human actions, were the number one cause.

So if we have only twelve years left—or nine now—what will be the causes of the collapse? It will not be crop failure and food shortages. It will not be the oceans and lakes getting higher. It most likely will not be natural disasters, for we have eliminated most deaths by that manner in the last century.

The 1918 influenza pandemic killed fifty million people worldwide and about 675,000 Americans.[29] To date, 650,000 Americans have died of the COVID-19 disease, our most recent pandemic.[30] And this may very well have been what Chinese leaders and scientists had in mind when the disease first appeared in the city of Wuhan.

Finally, the doomsday language about the "climate crisis," as Vice President Harris prefers to call it, and AOC's comment only days after being sworn in as a member of Congress that "we only have twelve years left" have now become part of the lexicon of nearly every Progressive New Left Democrat.

Even Joe Biden, who claims to be a moderate and a "healer of democracy," has joined the fray since his election. Many of the president's remarks about the environment, such as his comments when he introduced his climate plan, have been directly couched in the language of climate and the "dire straits" we find ourselves in.

Ms. Ocasio-Cortez's prediction came from a report by the IPCC, drawn from the work of hundreds of scientists who designated the year 2030 as a prominent benchmark by then. This was mostly based on the signatories to the Paris Agreement who have pledged their emission reductions by then.

But this doomsday prediction leaves out one important final point, a point related to President Biden's April 22, 2021, intention to discuss with China's Xi Jinping the reduction of US greenhouse gas emissions to half of 2005 levels by the year 2030.

This Biden virtual world summit was intended to coax China and other emerging nations to make more aggressive commitments to emission reductions. The United States accounts for about 15 percent of global CO_2 emissions. Mr. Biden told the Chinese president that emissions in the US and Europe have been falling since 2005 as natural gas and renewable energy have replaced coal power.[31]

But why would that be a concern to the People's Republic of China, and why is Mr. Biden so concerned about China and the environment and climate control? The answer to that question is very simple, and this is the final point of this essay.

At the Paris climate summit in 2015, China made no pledge to reduce its carbon emissions until the year 2030, when it will begin to reduce its CO_2.[32] In the meantime, China has continued to build coal plants and expand its industrial production while rapidly expanding its carbon emissions.

In the years between 2015 and 2018, China's carbon emissions increased more than the United Kingdom's total emissions in the year 2018 alone.[33] The rising carbon emissions from China have swamped those declines elsewhere.[34] Why should we worry about CO_2 emissions in the United States if China will not even agree to any plan to reduce its carbon footprint until fifteen years after the Paris climate summit?

During Biden's 2020 presidential campaign, in a town hall event in Iowa City, Iowa, when asked about the Chinese, Mr. Biden replied, "China is going to eat our lunch? Come on, man." Mr. Biden went on to say, "They [the Chinese] are not bad folks, folks."[35] Biden also related at the same event that "the Chinese are not competition to us." One only wonders, more than a year later, if now President Biden still believes those thoughts.

Finally, in a poll conducted by NPR, PBS, and Marist College that surveyed 1,346 Americans over the age of eighteen, 63 percent were in favor of "climate proposals in America, while only 26 percent of Republicans favor the Green New Deal."[36] These 2021 poll results are consistent with similar polls from 2017 and 2020 that suggested that about two-thirds of American citizens were in favor of some climate control regulations by the federal government.

The available evidence of popular opinion is that the American people are in favor of some sort of regulation about dealing with climate control, whether it is the Green New Deal or President Biden's climate plan.

This brings us to the sources of this essay, followed by Essay Eleven. The central subject matter of the eleventh and final essay of this study on the views of the Progressive New Left is their relationship to the Big Tech industry and the question of whether Conservative opinions are silenced or eliminated by social media.

ESSAY ELEVEN

The New Left, Big Tech, and Censorship

I

The purpose of this eleventh essay of this study of attitudes of the Progressive New Left in the United States is to discuss at some length the ever-increasing power of Big Tech in this country and whether organizations and companies like Facebook, Twitter, Google, Instagram, and others actively censor the political opinions of people in America from the Right of the political spectrum in the United States.

We will begin Essay Eleven by citing six cases of purported Big Tech censorship. This will be followed by a second section on research that argues against the notion that Big Tech censors political opinions from the Right of the American political spectrum.

In the third section of Essay Eleven, we will employ a study by the Pew Charitable Trusts that researched public opinion in regard to Big Tech censorship. In the fourth section of Essay Eleven, we will review the Biden-Harris perspectives on Big Tech, and I will provide a critique in the final section of the essay.

Before we do any of these things, however, we will first say something about what is sometimes called "Section 230" in American politics, a part of a 1996 law during the time of President Bill Clinton's administration from 1993 to 2001.

Section 230 is the portion of the 1996 Communications Decency Act that protects third-party publishers, such as

Facebook, in terms of liability for allowing content to stay on their platforms or taking it down.

Section 230, then, provides immunity for website platforms from third-party content. In other words, Section 230 provides immunity from liability or responsibility for providers and users of an "interactive computer service."

Section 230 says this:

> No provider or user of an interactive computer service shall be treated as the publisher or speaker of any information provided by another information content provider.[1]

In other words, large companies like Facebook, Twitter, Google, etc. have been given a pass when it comes to content on their platforms, or what Section 230 expert Jeff Kosseff calls *internet exceptionalism.*

Since 1996, Congress has called the heads of internet companies before them several times, such as on April 10, 2018, and October 5, 2020, for example, often asking them what they believe Section 230 really means. Twitter CEO Jack Dorsey, while testifying before the Senate Judiciary hearing in October of 2020, stated that revoking Section 230 "would collapse how we communicate on the internet." In the United States, of course, the First Amendment prohibits the government from restricting most forms of speech, which would include many proposals to force Big Tech companies to moderate content. A law requiring companies to moderate content based on the political viewpoint it expresses, for example, would likely be struck down as unconstitutional.

Section 230 does allow, however, that private companies can create rules to restrict speech if they so choose. This is why both Twitter and Facebook ban hate speech, for example, even though it is legally permitted in the United States. We have seen in Essay Seven of this study, though, that many Democrats are in favor of legislating hate speech as well.

President Trump believed he was being treated unfairly by Twitter because the forty-fifth president was in favor of Congress repealing Section 230, among other reasons. Interestingly enough, the Media Research Center—a watchdog group on these matters—from a study in October of 2020 reported that Facebook censored Mr. Trump and his campaign sixty-five times, while his political opponent, Joe Biden, was not censored even a single time.[2]

As we shall see later in this essay, President Biden has also expressed a desire to eliminate the protection of Big Tech due to Section 230 of the 1996 Communications Decency Act. This brings us to the first section of Essay Eleven, in which we will address the question of whether Big Tech companies in America censor Conservative opinion.

Does Big Tech Censor Conservative Opinion?

In the history of Western culture, governments have been censoring political opinion going all the way back to 399 BCE, when Greek philosopher Socrates—after fighting off attempts to halt his teaching—was executed by drinking hemlock for having "corrupted the youth of the state." More recently, censorship in the form of book burning was conducted by the military dictatorship in Chile, led by General Augusto Pinochet in the aftermath of the 1973 coup d'état.

In ordering the book burning, Pinochet hoped to prevent the spread of information that conflicted with his campaign to "expurgate the Marxist cancer" of the previous political regime in Chile.

In the United States, the censoring of political opinion does not come from the government. Rather, it comes from Left-leaning Big Tech companies whose leaders often follow many of the basic beliefs of the Progressive New Left in the United States.[3]

This can be seen by looking at six stellar examples of Big Tech censorship, which we will discuss now.

These six examples are the following:

1. Hunter Biden and the *New York Post* (October 2020)
2. President Trump's ban from Twitter (January 8, 2021)
3. The banning of the platform known as Parler in January 2021
4. India and COVID-19 information (May 2020)
5. Banning of information in Colombia (March 2021)
6. Banning of information in Palestine/Israel (March 2021)[4]

On October 14, 2020, the *New York Post* published an article based on what it alleged were emails and photos obtained from Hunter Biden's personal laptop.[5] The story and a follow-up article focused on Hunter Biden's ties to Ukrainian energy company Burisma formed the basis for several earlier political attacks on Joe Biden during his presidential campaign.

Some reports outside the *Post* disputed its allegations as well as its trustworthiness. Then the Big Tech giants stepped in. Facebook reduced the *Post*'s story the morning it was published. Twitter went even further and banned the article altogether from its platform. Later, Twitter said that the story violated its policy on "hacked material." Rather than finding the article, those who attempted to paste the article's URL into a tweet instead saw a message that read:

> We cannot complete this request because this link has been identified by Twitter or our partners as being potentially harmful.

Although Facebook indicates that the *New York Post* piece is "potentially harmful," it said nothing about who it was that might be harmed. One answer to that question might have been that Hunter

Biden's father, who was running for the presidency of the United States, was the one who might be harmed in the coming election in the fall of 2020. Thus, Big Tech squashed the Hunter Biden story.

The blocking of the Hunter Biden article brought accusations from President Trump and his followers, who claimed that the *Post* article was being censored. In a letter to Twitter CEO Jack Dorsey, Senator Ted Cruz wrote about the affair:

> Twitter is not only prohibiting users from sharing the story on their own accounts; it is prohibiting the *New York Post* itself from posting its own content.

A short time later, both Facebook and Twitter gave lame excuses about their content policies, which did not make much sense. What did make sense, however, was that they did not want this sensitive material to be seen by voters too close to the 2020 election for president—just two weeks away.

Policy communication director Andy Stone at Facebook, meanwhile, said that blocking the *Post* story was "part of our standard process to reduce the spread of misinformation." Mr. Stone added:

> I want to be clear that the story is eligible to be fact-checked by Facebook's third-party fact-checking partners. In the meantime, we are reducing its distribution on our platform.

Mr. Stone said nothing, however, about how the *New York Post* article contained "misinformation." He was, nevertheless, using a common ploy that executives of Big Tech often employ: "When you cannot admit the obvious facts, then simply say the post or article in question is 'full of misinformation.'"[6]

On January 8, two days after the riot at the Capitol on January 6, 2021, Twitter suspended the account of President

Trump. At the time, the Big Tech giant said, "We are permanently suspending Mr. Trump's account due to the risk of further incitement of violence." Shortly before that, Twitter had already locked Trump's account over several tweets that it said "contributed to an elevated risk of violence."

On January 8, 2020, the Twitter "safety account" wrote:

> In the context of horrific events this week, we made it clear on Wednesday that additional violations of the Twitter rules would potentially result in this very course of action. . . . We made it clear going back years that these accounts are not above our rules and cannot use Twitter to incite violence. We will continue to be transparent around our policies and their enforcement.

Six months later, in a review of their decision, Twitter announced that the Trump ban was permanent. In May of 2021, Twitter also suspended what some saw as a Trump blog account @DJTdesk. Within hours of the first post on this account, it was suspended. In a statement to NBC News, a Twitter spokesman said:

> As stated in our ban evasion policy, we will take enforcement action on accounts whose apparent intent is to replace or promote content affiliated with a suspended account.[7]

Twitter did not show, however, why they were convinced that the suspended account was actually related to Donald Trump. Facebook also banned President Trump after the riot, but on January 7, 2020, the network's quasi-independent oversight board said that the company was still reassessing how long the ban would remain in effect. Typically, the review process at Facebook takes six months.

A short time later, on January 12, 2021, the platform known as Parler was banned from the Apple Store. Parler was founded in 2018 as a social media site that topped the charts as the most popular free app on the Apple Store in the United States. The Parler platform largely attracted US Conservatives who disagreed with the rules related to content on platforms like Twitter and Facebook.

For Conservatives in America, Parler had become the alternative to using Facebook. Mr. Trump did not have a Parler account, but his "Team Trump" campaign did. Rudy Giuliani and the president's son Eric Trump had Parler accounts, as did some prominent Republicans like Senator Ted Cruz, for example.

The Parler site effectively went dark after Amazon.com suspended its web hosting service. Google also suspended Parler. They said the platform was not doing enough to "prevent the spread of posts inciting violence following the unrest at the US Capitol." Parler, in turn, sued Amazon, accusing the company of an illegal, politically motivated decision to shut it down. Amazon responded by saying the case had no merit, and they cited ninety-eight examples of Parler posts that "clearly encourage and incite violence."

What to make of these developments from early January of 2021 is not entirely clear. But if one is a believer in American Conservative principles, one may well conclude that Big Tech collectively sought to silence the *New York Post*, President Donald Trump, and the Parler platform principally because Big Tech conspired to silence Donald Trump and anyone else who agreed with him.

But these were not the only ways that the tentacles of Big Tech can be seen at work. We will cite three other examples—this time with Instagram. The first of these examples is from India in early May 2020, when it was discovered that many of the posts about the COVID-19 disease were beginning to disappear there.

On May 7, 2020, Instagram said, "This is a widespread global technical issue not related to any particular topic" and that the issue had been "fixed." The following day, however, in both

Colombia and Palestine, Instagram acknowledged that there were posts removed because of unrest in both countries.

When officials at Instagram, which is owned by Facebook, were asked about the removal of materials in Colombia and Palestine, they fell back on the "technical glitch" explanation. One researcher in Bogotá, Carolina Cabrera, who works for a civil rights group in Colombia and who works on technology issues, related:[8]

> We have over 1,000 reports of censorship, and around 90 percent of it was by Instagram and the content was overwhelmingly about the protests.

Ms. Cabrero also reported that the Instagram censorship was related to national unrest and protests, unemployment numbers in Colombia, and the death of a protestor in Bogotá.

Photojournalist Jesús Abad Colorado had his Twitter account suspended after he posted photographs of an armed dispute in Western Colombia. A few days later, when an independent media outlet was doing an interview with Mr. Colorado in a livestream, that media outlet's account was soon blocked as well. In fact, it was removed during the interview, which went dark minutes after it began, while the reporter was on air.

Alison Carmel Ramer, a reporter in Israel who works for a digital rights organization in Haifa, Israel, reported in March of 2021 that she had uncovered one hundred reports of censorship on Instagram. Most of the censored material, Ramer said, was related to the Israeli army storming the Al-Aqsa Mosque in Jerusalem. Other censored material reported by Ms. Ramer was related to the eviction of Palestinians from the Sheikh Jarrah neighborhood in East Jerusalem.

When Ms. Ramer inquired of Facebook why this information was taken down, the response she received was that the majority of the Instagram takedowns were "mistakes" because they did not violate community standards and that the content had "now been restored." But, in point of fact, it was not restored.

Ms. Ramer also reported that Facebook censored the words *Zionism* and *Zionist*. Regarding the censorship by the Israeli government, philosopher Noam Chomsky said, "There have been extensive efforts to block efforts to bring the facts and their significance to the general public. These efforts amount to direct participation [on the part of Israel] in the crimes." Mr. Chomsky, of course, is well known for his philosophical views as well as his Progressive New Left political views against the State of Israel.

Another interpretation of Facebook's response to Ms. Ramer might well be that the censorship in Israel/Palestine was not a "mistake" at all—that it was intentional and not all that different from the censorship of the *New York Post* on Hunter Biden and the Twitter account of Donald Trump or the "taking down" of the Parler platform by social media.

It is likely that the governments of India, Colombia, and Israel also each had a hand in the censorship in their nations. The New Left in Israel has a view not all that different from the Progressive New Left's in America. One way to see that is the response from Alexandria Ocasio-Cortez when she was asked about the recent demonstrations in Havana, Cuba. She said it had nothing to do with the rejection of communism but everything to do with the long-standing embargo of Cuba by the US government.

It is not surprising, of course, that the day after the demonstrations began in Cuba, all internet service in the city of Havana was completely suspended. AOC did not even bother to comment on why so many of the demonstrators in Havana were carrying American flags or holding signs that said, "Señor Biden, help us."

The long tentacles of Big Tech clearly can be seen in the anti-Communist demonstrations in the summer of 2021 by the people of Havana, Cuba, as they could be seen in all the other examples we have discussed in this first section of this essay.

There is, however, a growing body of literature and evidence coming from the Progressive New Left in America that says Big Tech stifles the opinions from the far Right of the spectrum of political opinion in the United States. We will turn to some of that evidence in the second section of Essay Eleven. Before we get there, however, we will provide a list of other Conservatives in the past few years who have also been censored by Big Tech.

1. Candace Owens, Conservative commentator. Online activists claimed that she was suspended from Twitter following a tweet criticizing Michigan governor Gretchen Whitmer's stay-at-home order.
2. GoFundMe shut down Ms. Owens's account for attacking George Floyd's character, saying she "spread falsehoods against the Black community."
3. Candace Owens's Facebook page was demonized and suppressed in 2020.
4. YouTube removed a COVID-19 video that showed Trump's adviser Dr. Scott Atlas because of what was called "misinformation."
5. YouTube removed a video about a man who reversed his transgender surgery.
6. Instagram banned advertisements for Senator Marsha Blackburn's children's book.
7. In January 2021, Project Veritas released a video it received from a Facebook insider when Mark Zuckerberg and other top executives were discussing the company's "wide-ranging powers to censor political speech and to promote partisan objectives."
8. Senator Josh Hawley, in May of 2021, reported that his book *The Tyranny of Big Tech* was banned from many Big Tech platforms.
9. When the House Judiciary Committee announced that it

wanted to eliminate Section 230, the memo about it was taken off Facebook, Twitter, and several other platforms.

10. In January of 2018, *The Hill* reported that Twitter was "shadow banning" Conservative profiles.

Item number seven on this list was added by a disgruntled Facebook employee who taped the comments of Mr. Zuckerberg as he engaged in questioning what strategies the company might employ in censoring political speech from the Right in America. Similar judgments may be made about items eight and nine as well. *Shadow banning* in item ten refers to the disappearance of profiles on Twitter simply because they exhibited heavy Conservative opinions.

These examples, of course, may be multiplied severalfold, and yet Big Tech has repeatedly said that they do not limit the speech of Conservative voices. In fact, there is a growing body of voices from the Progressive New Left who claim that voices like Candace Owens's are not being silenced by the Big Tech companies. This is the subject matter of the next section of Essay Eleven.

New Left Voices Who Say Conservative Voices Are Not Silenced by Big Tech

In the past two years, there has been a growing body of literature that claims Conservative political opinions are not being censored or canceled by Big Tech. We will point to three examples and then evaluate them.

First, Matthew Feeney wrote for *Medium* on May 28, 2020, with a headline that said, "Conservative Big Tech Campaign Based on Myths and Misunderstanding."[9] One does not have to ponder long to determine where Mr. Feeney stands on the issue at hand. In fact, he gave several arguments in the article about why Section 230 is actually a good thing.

Paul M. Barrett joined the fray when he wrote an essay titled, "Big Tech Doesn't Censor Conservatives" in the *New York Daily News* on February 2, 2021. Mr. Barrett's article is filled with sentences like, "But it's not a fact. It is yet one more instance of disinformation to rile up the Republican base" and "The false claim of Conservative censorship . . ." There is that explanation again—"It is all disinformation"—which seems to be anything that disagrees with the Progressive New Left agenda.

Adam Gabbatt, in a *Guardian* article from May 9, 2021, took a different approach to the matter. He titled his article, "Republicans Cry Big Tech Bias on the Very Platforms They Have Dominated." Mr. Gabbatt pointed out that, "Between January 1 and December 15 of 2020, Right-leaning Facebook posts accounted for forty-five percent of all interactions on Facebook."

Republican Josh Hawley, around the same time, also claimed that he had been censored and canceled by social media. Mr. Hawley wrote a book titled *The Tyranny of Big Tech*, in which he argued that Big Tech was silencing Conservative opinion. Ironically, he used Twitter—one of the companies he railed against—to proclaim that his book had been a "bestseller all week" on Amazon, another company he opposed.

Again, the three voices we have described here are a very small percentage of this body of literature that squarely argues that Big Tech does not limit or cancel Conservative views, even though Mark Zuckerberg, at a top executive retreat, said that that is precisely what they do.

This brings us to what the general public believes and has said about the phenomenon of the silencing of Conservative voices by Big Tech companies like Google, Facebook, Twitter, Instagram, and GoFundMe, among many others. This is the focus of the next section of Essay Eleven.

Public Opinion on Big Tech Censorship

Back in Essay One of this study, I indicated that 57 percent of my students I polled in the spring of 2016 believed that the national Liberal media censures the views of the political opinions of Conservatives in the United States. The Pew Research Center also inquired about the same question in August of 2020, not long after the death of George Floyd in Minneapolis, Minnesota.

The Pew Research Center on August 19, 2020, reported on the views of Americans on whether social media sites censor political opinions. The results of their study were striking and somber. Ninety percent of Republicans in their sample agreed that social media sites censor political viewpoints. This is a slight uptick from 85 percent in 2018, when the same question was asked. On the other hand, 59 percent of Democrats polled also agreed that social media sites censor political opinion. This is a slight decrease from the 62 percent in 2018.

Similarly, when Republicans and Democrats were asked in 2018 and 2020 whether large social media companies tend to favor Conservative or Liberal points of view, 70 percent of Republicans said that major Big Tech companies generally support the views of Liberals, while only 25 percent of Democrats said the same thing. The sentiments on this second question in the Pew study have risen slightly over 2018.

A third question asked by the Pew researchers in both 2018 and 2020 was "How much confidence do you have in social media to determine which posts on their platforms should be labeled as 'inaccurate,' 'misinformation,' or 'misleading'?" Twenty-nine percent of all Americans surveyed answered "not at all." That included 50 percent of Republicans and only 11 percent of Democrats.

Democrats and Republicans also have contrasting views about a fourth question asked in 2018 and 2020, which was, "Should social media companies label information as 'inaccurate' or 'misleading'?" Seventy-three percent of the Democrats surveyed said they approved of the process, while just 27 percent of the Republicans in the Pew survey answered this fourth question in the affirmative.

Finally, in the same study, both Republicans and Democrats were asked in 2018 and 2020 if they thought that social media sites censor political views that they (the Big Tech companies) find objectionable. A full 70 percent of Republicans assented to this fifth question in the Pew survey, while 58 percent of the Democrats responded to question five in the affirmative.

The results of the Pew Research studies on attitudes toward social media are not surprising. Democrats and Republicans in America have very different views about social media's place in the United States. The Republicans tend to be wary of Facebook, Twitter, GoFundMe, Instagram, YouTube, and many other large social media companies. Democrats, on the other hand, have much more confidence in the veracity of Big Tech as well as confidence in these large technology companies. One thing the Dems and the GOP have in common, however, is that 70 percent of Americans polled believe that Big Tech silences or censors the views of political opinions on the Right of the political spectrum in the US.

Even if Big Tech says they do not censor or silence Conservatives, the American public certainly believes that they do, as did the students in my 2015 survey. Another way for ascertaining the political beliefs of the heads of social media companies is to examine the contributions they make every year to the Republican and Democratic Parties.[10] The Center for Responsive Politics, an organization that tracks such things, recently reported that employees at the five biggest tech companies, including Alphabet (Google's owner), Amazon, Facebook, Apple, and Microsoft, gave a combined $12.3 million to Biden's campaign and millions more to high-profile Democrats in Senate contests, such as the recently elected Jon Ossoff in Georgia and Raphael Warnock in the run-off in Georgia.[11]

CNBC reported that Netflix's Reed Hastings, alone, gave $5 million to Democrats, most of that to candidates in the closest races like Maine, Texas, and Iowa.[12] Altogether, only 7 percent of the corporate Big Tech political money went to Republicans. Google's parent company, Alphabet; their employees; and their political action committees (PACs) have contributed $21 million to presidential and congressional candidates since 2019. Again, only 7 percent of those political contributions went to Republican candidates.

Amazon contributed $9 million to candidates for the 2020 election. Eight million of that went to Democratic candidates. Amazon gave more money to Joe Biden (1.7 million), Bernie Sanders ($800,000), and the Democratic National Committee (DNC) itself ($790,000), far more than all contributions to Republicans, including Donald Trump.

Facebook gave $6 million to political candidates in 2020. Joe Biden received $2.3 million of that number, followed by Bernie Sanders, whose campaign got $250,000. Apple does not have its own PAC, but the company's employees still managed to contribute nearly $6 million to political candidates. Of that money, only 4.3 percent went to Republicans.

Twitter employees contributed $689,000 to political candidates in 2020. Joe Biden received $157,000, Elizabeth Warren got $30,000, and Bernie Sanders received $46,000.

Only 3 percent of the political contributions from the employees of Twitter went to Republican candidates—most of that to Donald Trump's campaign.

The CTO of Microsoft, Kevin Scott, and the Big Tech company's president, Brad Smith, gave a combined $904,000 to political candidates in 2020. Of that, $106,500 went directly to the

DNC, and $125,000 went to the Senate Majority PAC. Naomi Gleit, vice president of product and social impact of Microsoft, contributed $116,000 to politicians in 2020. The biggest check from that money—that is, $50,000—went to Nancy Pelosi, the speaker of the House.

David Zapolsky, the chief attorney of Amazon, gave $590,000 to political campaigns in 2020. Of that, $250,00 went to Biden's campaign for president. Babak Parviz, one of the vice presidents at Amazon, contributed $59,000 to political candidates in 2020, including $50,000 to the Biden campaign.

The granddaddy of all the Big Tech political contributors is Facebook CEO, Mark Zuckerberg, and his wife, Priscilla Chan. By early October 2020, the pair had donated an additional $100 million to help local Democratic election candidates. This additional $100 million brought their total funding for the 2020 elections to $400 million.

When the Biden campaign and Democratic members of Congress running for election told Zuckerberg and his wife that the party was underfunded in some races, the pair stepped into the fray initially in September of 2020 with $300 million. That is why the Zuckerberg-Chan total donation figure to the Democrats reached $400 million by October 13, 2020, just weeks before the election. No comparable funds, of course, were donated to Republican candidates.

One interesting fact is that Big Tech gave far more money to the Biden-Harris ticket than they did to Hillary Clinton's campaign. This may have been because of the overall desire among the brass of the Big Tech companies, who had a bigger desire to oust Donald Trump in 2020 than they did to elect Mrs. Clinton in 2016.

Kenneth Duda, a software executive of, for example, Arista Network, in an interview with *Vox* just before the 2020 election, said that he "had spent three times as much in 2020 than he did in 2016 to beat Trump."[13] Bay Area tech workers in Silicon Valley gave 22 percent more to Democrats in 2020 than they did in 2016. Those figures include money given to super PACs by Democratic megadonor and San Franciscan Tom Steyer, who is not in the tech field, but he did contribute tens of millions in both 2016 and 2020.

Big Tech employees gave far more to the Biden-Harris campaign than they did to the 2016 Clinton candidacy for president. Donations from these Silicon Valley employees to the Democrats jumped from $8.5 million in 2016 to $14 million in 2020, growing more than 70 percent in the four years.

The figures of small tech companies are no different. In the 2020 election, of the money that went to presidential candidates, more than 90 percent of the total from these companies also went to Joe Biden.

This brings us to what Joe Biden and Kamala Harris themselves have written and said about Big Tech, the subject matter of the next section of Essay Eleven, followed by a critique of their views.

Biden and Harris on Big Tech

The one word that best describes the views of Joe Biden and Kamala Harris on social media and Big Tech companies before the 2020 inaugurations of the Democratic pair is *contradictory*. In an interview with the *New York Times* on January 15, 2020, Mr. Biden called for Section 230 of the Communications Decency Act of 1996 to be "revoked immediately."

A few days before that, in an interview with *The Hill*, Mr. Biden remarked:

> I, for one, think we should be considering taking away Facebook's exemption that they cannot be sued for knowingly engaging in or promoting something that is not true.[14]

Despite these judgments is the fact, as we have indicated earlier in this essay, that many of the largest contributors to the Biden-Harris campaign were Silicon Valley executives and billionaires.

When Vice President Kamala Harris was still involved in California state politics, she raised funds from Facebook and other Big Tech organizations from billionaires, and she participated in a marketing campaign for Facebook COO Sheryl Sandberg's book *Lean In*.

As California's attorney general—the highest-ranking law enforcement official in the state—Harris took a permissive attitude toward Facebook's attempt to absorb its smaller competitors in the tech market, such as Instagram and WhatsApp.

On the other hand, in an interview with CNN in 2019, Ms. Harris took some swings at Big Tech when she raised the idea of "breaking up Facebook." She said at the time, "Facebook has experienced massive growth and has prioritized its growth over the best interests of its consumers." But then Ms. Harris added in the same interview, "We need seriously to take a look at breaking up Facebook. It is essentially a utility that has gone unregulated."

In another interview with the *New York Times* on August 13, 2020, Ms. Harris seems to have indicated that she saw Big Tech as a partner rather than a threat, and consequently, she struck a moderate tone toward the social media industry on several fronts. As a presidential candidate, Ms. Harris did not support the breaking up of Facebook as Senators Elizabeth Warren and Bernie Sanders did, perhaps because Ms. Harris was still intimately connected to Silicon Valley money.

Instead, Senator Harris was open to the idea of strengthening antitrust enforcement. Like President Biden, Ms. Harris also called for an increase in corporate taxes, while she stopped short of supporting a tax on the assets held by the wealthiest Americans, many of whom were the largest contributors to the 2020 Biden-Harris campaign.

In that same August 2020 interview with the *Times*, Ms. Harris remarked at the time:

> I believe that the tech companies have got to be regulated in a way that we can ensure, and the American consumer can be certain, that their privacy is not being compromised.[15]

Ms. Harris was much more evasive, however, when she was asked whether the tech giants should be splintered. This fact may well have been true because of the now–vice president's chumminess with many tech execs when she ran for president, such as Salesforce executive Marc Benioff or cofounder of LinkedIn and former PenPal executive Reid Hoffman.

Even venture capitalist Roger McNamee, a longtime nemesis of Ms. Sandberg's and the author of *Zucked: Waking Up to the Facebook Catastrophe*, was, nevertheless, optimistic about Ms. Harris's prospects as a vice president. Mr. McNamee said at the time:

> She will represent the interests of all Americans because the Biden-Harris ticket will owe its election to the support of voters who were harmed by internet platforms.[16]

It must not be forgotten, of course, that Kamala Harris spent a large part of her early career in San Francisco as the district attorney there before going on to be California's attorney general and then a US senator. Now it is clear that Ms. Harris is expected to fill a vacuum on tech policy, since Mr. Biden has not made Big Tech a priority during his campaign or in his time so far in office. Let us hope that if Ms. Harris is given the job of tech coordinator, she does it better than her performance on the southern border, for which she was also made responsible and took ninety-two days to visit the southern border.

While a vice president candidate, Ms. Harris continued to

have many of her ties to Silicon Valley insiders, as she does now. She is friendly with Laurene Powell Jobs, the billionaire widow of Steve Jobs. Ms. Harris attended the wedding of Sean Parker, the cofounder of Napster and Facebook's first president. She also remains friends with Linked-In cofounder Reid Hoffman as well as venture capitalist John Doerr, both of whom raised money for her presidential bid.

Indeed, Ms. Harris's presidential bid garnered loads of campaign money from the tech industry. Among the top twenty donors to her bid for president were employees from Google's parent company, Alphabet, along with people who worked for Microsoft, Apple, and Amazon, among others. Altogether, Kamala Harris raised $40 million—most of that from Silicon Valley contributors—before dropping out of the race in December of 2019.

Another concern among people on the Right of the American political spectrum is the Biden-Harris administration's tendency, as we saw in the first six months, to stack its federal agencies and appointments with more tech executives than tech critics.[17] Both Biden and Harris also have added to their staffs several officials who formerly were employed at Big Tech companies.

In fact, executives and employees at tech companies are aiming to include the US Commerce Department, the Office of the US Trade Representative, the Office of Information and Regulatory Affairs, and the Department of Defense with former tech executives. The same is true at the Department of Justice and the Federal Trade Commission.

Researcher Max Moran with the Revolving Door Project wrote about appointing top executives from tech companies in the run-up to the 2020 election. He wrote, "In 2020, appointing the CEO or top executives of a tech company directly to your cabinet is bad optics and bad politics."[18]

One prime example of this phenomenon is former chief executive Eric Schmidt, a billionaire and former Silicon Valley titan.

After the Biden-Harris election, he has been making recommendations for appointments to the US Department of Defense—at the same time, Mr. Schmidt has been pursuing military defense contracts.

Mr. Schmidt now chairs the National Security Commission on Artificial Intelligence (NSCAI). His vice chairman is former vice chairman secretary of defense Robert Work, who has also been pegged to give the Biden-Harris administration advice about technology issues.

Reportedly, one of the names that Mr. Schmidt has floated by the new administration is Christopher Kirchhoff, former aide to the chairman of the Joint Chiefs of Staff under the Obama-Biden administration. Mr. Kirchhoff now works for Schmidt Futures.[19]

Mr. Schmidt has also pushed for Jared Cohen—the chief executive of Jigsaw, a tech incubator company that operates as an independent agent under Google—for a role inside the US State Department. When a reporter asked the Biden-Harris crew about this recommendation, they declined to comment on the matter.

Another example that clearly shows the bedfellow relationship between Big Tech companies and the Biden-Harris administration was when two former Amazon executives landed positions in the State Department and the Office of Management and Budget.

Indra Nooyi, former chair of Pepsi, is now on the Amazon board, and her name has been floated as a possibility for head of the US Commerce Department. Former Facebook director Jessica Hertz was the chief counsel to the Biden-Harris transition team. Austin Lin, former program manager at Facebook, now sits on an agency review team for the executive office of the president.

And that is not all. Erskine Bowles, a former Facebook board member, worked with the Biden-Harris transition team, along with his Facebook colleague Jeff Zients, who had been picked to become the new administration's COVID-19 czar. Mr. Biden's secretary of state, Antony Blinken, also has ties to both Amazon and Google. Google was a client of WestExec Advisors, which was founded by Mr. Blinken.

Anthony Blinken also helped Amazon's public policy and communications chief, Jay Carney, get hired into Joe Biden's media team in 2008, while he was President Obama's vice president.

The overall conclusion we can make in regard to these facts we have outlined in this section of this essay is that there seems to be a good bit of nepotism and special favors going on when it comes to the relationships of the Big Tech community with members of the Biden-Harris administration.

This leads us to the final section of the eleventh and final essay of this study of the attitudes of the Progressive New Left toward issues in contemporary American culture, in which we will evaluate the Biden-Harris administration's perspectives on social media and the Big Tech sector of the economy.

A Critique of the Biden-Harris Administration's Big Tech Views

In evaluating the views of the Biden-Harris administration, as well as their personal views, on Big Tech and social media, I will point to six criticisms that may be raised. First, as indicated earlier, Mr. Biden and Ms. Harris have often contradicted themselves and each other in terms of Big Tech issues. Indeed, they have both stated a preference for abolishing Section 230, while at the same time, many of the biggest political contributors to their campaign are executives and employees from social media companies.

We also have shown that while Ms. Harris at times has directly criticized the power that Big Tech companies seem to possess, at the same time, she also appears to remain pals with many Silicon Valley titans, commenting on their books, attending their weddings, and attending sports with tech executives, among other things.

A second criticism of the Progressive New Left and the Biden administration's views on Big Tech involves the many examples that, to me, clearly show that social media and Big Tech companies often hamper or silence voices from the Right of the American political spectrum. In regard to this second criticism of the Left's views on censoring, rather than simply admitting to the process, Big Tech companies have chosen instead to deny the practice, to say it was a "mistake" or attribute it to "misinformation."

One way to justify this practice on the part of Big Tech is to use the ploy that a post contains *disinformation* or *misinformation* or to say "It was a mistake" or "It was a technical glitch." Avoiding responsibility completely.

Third, for the most part among the Progressive New Left and its proponents, such as Kamala Harris and now even Joe Biden, the notion that Big Tech censors Conservative thought is denied not only by tech executives but also by Democratic scholars and politicians.

In fact, a fourth and important criticism of Big Tech and the Biden administration is that they appear to have little concern about public opinion on these matters. As we have shown earlier in this essay, not only do most Republicans believe that Big Tech stifles and censors political opinions on the Right, but most Democratic voters also believe that Conservative voices are canceled or softened.

Fifth, we have shown in this essay that the phenomenon of nepotism has appeared to infiltrate itself into the Biden-Harris administration in terms of the number of federal employees the new administration has hired as part of its operations, many of these people directly from the Big Tech or social media companies themselves.

Ultimately, if these new administration employees have been called into the fray to help regulate Big Tech, then it would appear that they are being asked to regulate the very institutions that taught them the skills needed for that regulation.

Sixth, and finally, Jen Psaki, the White House press secretary, recently has admitted that the Biden administration has consulted with Facebook for the purposes of identifying "misinformation" about COVID-19 vaccinations. Fox News commentator Dan Bongino likens this practice to the government "deputizing Big Tech to suppress free speech." As Mr. Bongino continued in a recent Fox News broadcast:

> President Biden has now admitted that the federal government has a list of individuals on social media who disseminate facts they deem untoward.

Mr. Bongino, who made these remarks on his weekly Fox News show called *Unfiltered*, suggested that Ms. Psaki is "demanding that private companies band together—at the behest of the government—to remove all speech she does not like." Even the surgeon general in the Biden administration, Dr. Vivek Murthy, was brought into the issue when he labeled the behavior on the part of the Biden administration, not surprisingly, as the "product of misinformation and ignorance."[20]

When reporter Peter Doocy asked Jen Psaki about the possibility of Big Brother now spying on American citizens, her response was typical and predictable. Instead of the government spying, she redirected the conversation to say that misinformation about COVID-19 vaccination was really the context for understanding the cooperation of the Biden administration with Facebook.[21]

Ms. Psaki added, "This is an effort to make sure that misinformation about a disease that is killing Americans not be 'misunderstood.'" In France, as we write this in the summer of 2021, a citizen now needs a "vaccine passport" to conduct most activities where French people are gathered, such as shops, restaurants, and most other amenities. Many critics of the Right of the American political spectrum fear that the United States will soon follow this French model.

Big Tech, Americans have concluded, has too much power. Thus, most Americans are also in favor of repealing Section 230 of the United States Communications Decency Act of 1996. And I heartily agree with that assessment.

Most recently, on July 19, 2021, President Biden said Facebook is "killing people."[22] He made this claim because of a report written in March by the Center for Countering Digital Hate (CCDH), which suggested that twelve individuals in America are responsible for most of the "misinformation" on Facebook about the COVID-19 vaccine.[23] Mr. Biden did not mention, however, that the CCDH had been thoroughly debunked by Conservative pundit Ben Domenech.

Also recently, a well-respected physician at the University of Minnesota noted that *masks don't work*, but when the physician and Republican junior senator from Kentucky Rand Paul said the same thing, he was banned from YouTube. It is difficult to believe that the state of affairs was an accident. In fact, CEO of YouTube, Susan Wojcicki, in an interview appeared to be gleeful about censoring Senator Paul.

This, of course, is a woman who was not elected to anything. She should have no authority to control the free speech of members of Congress, or anyone else for that matter. And yet she does—at least for a while—until Section 230 is repealed and Big Tech no longer has the power of censorship.

One final aspect of Big Tech, censorship, and government has to do with US Senator Marco Rubio, Republican from Florida, who introduced the Preserve Online Speech Act. This bill was also sponsored by Senator Roger Wicker of Mississippi, who, in one of his Weekly Reports, made the observation, "My feeling is that if these [Big Tech] companies ever faced the possibility of such lawsuits, they would likely abandon their left-wing bias and start providing more balance in their viewpoints."[24]

All this came after Press Secretary Jen Psaki acknowledged that the White House is "flagging problematic posts" of social media companies.[25] Senator Rubio's act would require social media companies to disclose a US or foreign government's request or recommendation regarding content on their platforms. We may not be free of Section 230 just yet, but Senator Rubio's proposal puts us in the morally correct direction of doing just that.

This brings us to the sources for Essay Eleven.

APPENDIX

On the Principle of Offense

I

In the essay on hate crimes and hate speech of this work, we have introduced John Stuart Mill's notion of the Principle of Harm as a way of the state limiting the liberties of its citizens. In that essay, we have shown that the British philosopher suggested that it is permissible to interfere with an individual's liberty only if in doing so it is "necessary to prevent harm to others."[1]

It should be clear that we may quibble about just what constitutes "harm." And there are additional relevant questions about whether the harm was intentional or not. But we may put those quibbles aside so we can move on to another matter. This matter is the contemporary replacement of the Principle of Harm with what might be called the Principle of Offense in the contemporary English-speaking world.

More specifically, in the past thirty years, as we have shown in the Hate Speech essay, many have called to replace the Principle of Harm with the Principle of Offense. American philosopher, Joel Feinberg, has written extensively on this issue in many essays and in several books, as well.

Professor Feinberg has proposed to narrow the principle of offense as a way of limiting liberties. He does this by narrowing the principle by making six separate points. These may be summarized in the following way:

1. The behavior has to be harmful, that is it has to violate someone's rights.
2. The behavior has to cause universally disliked mental states such as disgust, revulsion, shock, shame, or embarrassment.
3. The behavior has to be serious.
4. Any criminal sanctions have to be both effective and necessary to stop the behavior.
5. Punishment, if any, should be light, along the lines of a parking ticket.
6. Finally, Dr. Feinberg requires that the interests of those who wish to avoid offensive behavior be weighed against the interests must be weighed against those who wish to engage in that behavior.[2]

These factors listed by Feinberg are drawn from similar kinds of weighing in Tort Law. Each party's inconvenience must be taken into account, compared with alternatives, like taking a different bus or getting a room, respectively. The social value of each party's request and each party's motives are taken into account, and so on.

Neither Mill nor Feinberg speaks about the origins of rights, unlike the founding documents of the United States that maintain we are given rights by God and certain of those rights are inalienable. Mill explicitly states that he won't employ any assumptions about the origins of rights.

One might say, however, that Feinberg has raised an objection to the principle of harm, in that he has shown that the regulation of offensive behavior can be legitimate in some cases, whereas Mill appears to eliminate offense as a reason for limiting liberties.

There is no doubt, however, that what counts as "offense" changes very quickly over time. The use of the N-word, for example, or the expression of homophobic and transphobic sentiments.

These kinds of contemporary examples in American culture, as well as many, many others, are all products of what has been called the Fallacy of Presentism. This is a false belief that claims that the moral judgments and values about issues like race and gender from the past have now been replaced by the "proper" moral perspectives. Thus we take down Confederate statues, as well as those of Christopher Columbus because both are to be identified with the oppressors in the Neo-Marxist model.

We have done this in the past thirty years with apparently little understanding that the New Presentism already is on the horizon and many of these "new" moral beliefs of the future will replace the ones that we hold now.

Many new things that we now understand as morally acceptable in the future surely will be seen as offense. Everyone is offended by different things. Professor Feinberg's limits on the Principle of Offense may be helpful in ascertaining what thoughts, words, and actions in the New Presentism should be seen as morally acceptable.

So, stay tuned to the arrival of the New Presentism, for there is absolutely no doubt that it will come in the not too distant future.

ADDENDUM

As I add these remarks to this study of the New Left in America, we must add the following remarks. First, we now know that the Biden administration has not left "about 100" Americans in Afghanistan but in fact closer to somewhere between 500 and 1,000 American citizens. Second, the president's COVID-19 mandates now have put many police and fire department members, along with many nurses and other "first responders" into jeopardy, increasing the danger for Americans as a whole.

Third, Attorney General Garland has now sicked the FBI on American parents who are disgruntled by the teaching of CRT, or Critical Race Theory, in their childrens' schools. Fourth, we are now on a pace to have two million immigrants enter at the Southern Border by the close of 2021.

Fifth, the *Wall Street Journal* reported at the end of October 2021 that the Biden administration plans to settle a thousand suits filed against the United States in which migrant families were separated during the Trump administration. The *Journal* reported that Biden and his crew are ready to pay these migrants, $450,000 a piece, or close to two million dollars for a family of four. That comes out to a whopping two billion dollars for these thousand suits.

Keep in mind, these are migrant families wo have broken the law, for they are "illegal aliens." Nevertheless, the Biden administration appears to be poised to make the payouts, and presumably they think in turn these separated migrants would become Democrats and if they become legal to do so, would then become Democrats.

Sixth, since Joe Biden has become president more Americans have died from fentanyl overdoses than Americans who have died from COVID-19. More people have died of COVID-19 in Biden's first year in office, 2021, than died in President Trump's final year in office.

In regard to the defund the police movement in 2022 several cities such as New Orleans, for example, are now asking for federal funds so they can restore the new well-needed monies taken from their police departments in 2021. In the year of 2022 alone, there have been, according to a Fox News, January 21, 2023 story, 331 shootings of American law enforcement officers and 64 of those shootings were fatal.

Finally, we are left with an important question and what appears to be the motto of the forty-sixth president of the United States, Joe Biden. The question can be put very simply, "Is there intelligent life in the Oval Office?" It seems that the answer to that question is "No!" The new Biden motto is also now very clear, it is simply this:

I have some moral principles and if you do not like them, wait a little while, I have some others.

POSTSCRIPT

Adolf Eichmann had an almost total inability ever to look at anything from the other fellow's point of view.
—Hannah Arendt, *Eichmann in Jerusalem*

The time is coming when people will not endure sound teaching, but having itching ears they will accumulate for themselves teachers to suit their own passions, and will turn away from listening to the truth and wander off into false beliefs.
—2 Timothy 4:3–4

The purpose of this postscript is to add an update on many of the major topics that the essays of this book have dealt with. I am writing this postscript in the autumn of 2022, seven months into the Russian invasion of the sovereignty of Ukraine.

In relation to that war, Vladimir Putin has begun to draft into his army three hundred thousand Russian men between the ages of eighteen and sixty-five, a sign that things are not going well for Mr. Putin. At the same time, twenty percent of the land of Ukraine is now in the possession of the Russian Federation. Not surprisingly, Mr. Putin is also once again posturing about the use of his nuclear arsenal, the largest such collection of deadly weapons on the planet.

On the US domestic front, things appear no less bright for Joe Biden and his New Left handlers. If Mr. Biden could not read, it is clear he would not be able to function as president. Nearly all of his official comments are read directly from a teleprompter or from notes he brought to the podium. Recently, he gave his first one-on-one interview in 208 days with a correspondent from *60 Minutes*, who asked no pointed questions of the 46th president.

Since January 20, 2021, Mr. Biden's inauguration day, he has taken 148 days of vacation, while at the same time he appears to have never been to the southern border of the United States. Mr. Biden referred to what he called "MAGA Republicans" as "domestic terrorists." In fact, his FBI spends more time charging Donald Trump with wrongdoings and prosecuting participants in the events of January 6, 2021, than attending to the more historical concerns of the agency.

Governor DeSantis of Florida has flown fifty migrants to Martha's Vineyard, and they were promptly removed a day later from the mostly New Left island by the National Guard. A few days later, the same migrants filed suit against the Florida governor. The group Citizens for Civil Rights brought the suit, with support from billionaire George Soros.

In regard to the US's southern border, Vice President Harris recently has proclaimed that the border is "secure," while some estimates that include both Border Patrol encounters and runaways for the year 2021 to be much closer to four million people than the two million often predicted for the same year.[1]

Meanwhile, a report from the National Institute on Drug Abuse shows that in 2020 there were 91,799 deaths in America attributed to overdoses, with an increasing number being attribute to the drug fentanyl, a drug that has its origins, not surprisingly, in the People's Republic of China.[2]

On other fronts, in late September of 2022, President Biden announced that the "pandemic is over." Does this mean that some of the COVID-19 relief funds distributed by the government will be returned to the nation's coffers? At the same time, there still has been no national discussion about the origins of the deadly virus, perhaps because that would make doctors Fauci and Francis Collins (former NIH director) uncomfortable.

And Biden and Harris are not alone in discussing the topics of the essays in this book. Stacey Abrams, for example, who is running for the governor of Georgia, recently said in some comments at a southern college that heartbeats recorded at six weeks of gestation are "manufactured sound[s]."[3] In fact, as the Mayo Clinic maintains, bundles of conducting cells are already beginning to form at three weeks in the womb.

In the same talk, Ms. Abrams also indicated that these reports of ultrasounds done in the womb are part of a larger attempt to try to convince people "men have a right to take control of a woman's body." At the same time, a recent AP poll showed that 61 percent of Americans are in favor of abortion in the first trimester, 34 percent are in favor in the second trimester, while 80 percent are against the notion of abortion in the third trimester.[4]

Another New Left advocate, former New York governor Andrew Cuomo, recently expressed that he has been abandoned by top Democratic politicians since he was accused by eleven women of sexual harassment. This, of course, is the same Andrew Cuomo who was responsible for the deaths of 15,000 nursing home residents during his tenure.

On other matters of this book, the Big Tech industry continues to attempt to silence the political speech of Conservative Republicans, often calling it "misinformation." Mr. Biden began a "Misinformation Office," early in his tenure and then promptly shut it down a short while afterward.

And finally—and perhaps most importantly—a forty-one-year-old man in North Dakota murdered an eighteen-year-old man by striking him with his car.[5] The older man admitted his crime and said he did it because the younger man was "part of a Republican extremist group." This, of course, is the same group that Mr. Biden recently told us is a "threat to democracy," without any real understanding that we live in a republic and not a democracy.

The incident in North Dakota is yet another sign that we may well be on the edge of a second civil war, as I have argued earlier in this book. In fact, one recent poll indicated that 43 percent of Americans believe that a second civil war is imminent within the next five years.[6]

A final way in which the ideological divide between Republicans and Democrats gives evidence of a second civil war in America is an October 4, 2021, memo from Attorney General Merrick Garland in which he directed the FBI to investigate vociferous parents at local school board meetings.[7] Protests from parents had led to disruptions at school board meetings. In response, two officials of the National School Board Association asked Mr. Biden for federal assistance in responding to threats made against local school board members.

Mr. Garland's memo takes the wording of the NSBA letter to President Biden so seriously that he incorporated much of the verbiage into the attorney general's October 4 directive to the FBI. And yet, a few op-ed pieces in the *Washington Post*, including one by Salvador Rizzo from October 15, 2021, boldly begins with the heading, "The False GOP Claim that the Justice Department is Spying on Parents at School Board Meetings."

We have gotten to the point where the second American civil war can now be seen in the clash between parents who want a say in their children's education and New Left Progressive school boards, who are one of the most lucrative donors to the Democratic Party in the United States.

Another indication that a second American civil war—this time a cultural war—is at hand is the differing views of the taking down of statues and monuments and the renaming of colleges and universities simply because the names have some former association with racism. Some want Thomas Jefferson's name to no longer be associated with the University of Virginia. The name of Calhoun College was changed at Yale University just for that reason.

The school board members of the city of San Francisco recently voted six to one to remove the names of George Washington, Jefferson, and even Abraham Lincoln from California public schools that bear these names.[8] The board said the figures had "diminished the opportunities of those amongst us to the right of life, liberty, and the pursuit of happiness." Needless to say, the San Francisco school board has been infected with the philosophy of the New Left in America, while most of the seventy-four million MAGA Republicans that President Biden called "extremists who don't believe in freedom" have not. It truly seems like a civil war.

In the early 1960s, philosopher Hannah Arendt, when writing about Adolf Eichmann's trial in Jerusalem, said about the Nazi leader that "Eichmann had an almost total inability ever to look at anything from the other fellow's point of view." Given the political climate in the contemporary United States, one may only wonder, if the philosopher were alive today, whether would she say the same thing about both the Democratic and the Republican parties.

The Nature of a Religion

One final way to see that we are approaching a second civil war in the United States is to ask three fundamental questions about contemporary America. First, what is the nature of a religion? Second, are New Leftism and American Conservatism of the MAGA variety religions?

And third, if the answer to our second question is yes, then who becomes the heretics and apostates in those two religions? I will deal with these three questions one after the other in the following analysis.

What Is a Religion?

Sociologist Émile Durkheim in the mid-nineteenth century defined a *religion* as a "unified system of beliefs and practices relative to sacred or ultimate things." By sacred or ultimate things, he meant "beliefs and practices set apart and forbidden." For Durkheim, a religion was a set of beliefs and practices which unite into a single community, or a church of all those who adhere to them.

In the same work, Durkheim speaks of the Greek word *nomos* and its plural form, *nomai*. For the German thinker, a nomos is a "worldview," a fundamental way of understanding the world and the collection of fundamental beliefs and practices of which that nomos is made. Durkheim also points out that there are many different nomai, or ways of seeing and understanding the world, and that sometimes those ways are consistent and sometimes fundamentally different.

For Durkheim, it is important to understand that it is these sets of beliefs and practices that make something a religion. And those beliefs and practices will provide the individual with a proper understanding of the world and those around him or her. Durkheim firmly believed, like Aristotle did, as well, that a person cannot live without a nomos. It is a fundamental part of being human.

Durkheim also understood that movements like Marxism and Socialism sometimes may take on the character of a nomos, in the same ways that Judaism, Christianity, and Islam also do. Marxism and Socialism had a fundamental belief system, as well as a set of practices that went into the making of that worldview.

Where we find belief in an all-good, all-knowing, and all-powerful God in Judaism, Christianity, and Islam, in Marxism and Socialism we find a belief in a classless society and a dialectical materialism form of history based on Friedrich Hegel's ideas of thesis, antithesis, and synthesis. The practices that go along with the beliefs in Marxism and Socialism are as fundamental as baptism, bar mitzvah, and Ramadan in Judaism, Christianity, and Islam. This leads us to our second question: Are New Left Wokeism and Contemporary Conservatism forms of religion in America.

Are the New Left Woke Movement and MAGA Conservatives Religions?

The simplest answer to this question, I think, is yes. In the beginning of this book, we set out a set of beliefs that I believe the New Left movement in America has come to believe. In that analysis, I suggested ten fundamental beliefs I had in mind. To review, these were:

1. The rejection of absolute or objective truth.
2. All cultures are of equal value.
3. The individual and his or her race, gender, and other characteristics are more important than the collective.
4. Diversity is more important than freedom.
5. Race and gender are not biological but societal constructs.
6. America is a systemically racist nation.
7. Certain races are discussed with much more reverence and attention than others.
8. Individual narratives or storytelling of struggle are often more enlightening than collective expressions.
9. Hate speech and hate crimes in America should be more regulated.
10. America is in the midst of an "existential crisis" regarding the environment and climate control.

I think that if Durkheim were alive today he would say that this collection, along with a few other lesser or minor beliefs, like

"There are more than two genders," or "The individual human has the right to change his or her gender," would be called a nomos. In other words, the belief system of the New Left looks an awful lot like a religion.

It should be just as clear that members of the MAGA Republican group would assent to the idea of objective truth, that some cultures are better than others, that race and gender may not be as important as national identity and other ideas, that freedom is much more important than diversity or inclusion, that America is not systemically racist, that no race should be afforded any more deference than any other, that sometimes national narratives are far more important than individual ones, that hate speech should not be regulated by the government, and that the evidence for the environmental crisis is ambiguous. They would also say that there are only two genders, male and female. This, quite naturally, leads us to our third question, "Given the fundamental sets of beliefs between the Left and the Right in America, who then are the heretics and apostates?"

Who Are the Heretics and Apostates of the Two Contemporary Political Nomoi in America?

The answer to this question, of course, should be obvious. They tend to be members of the other nomos. Heretics and apostates to those on the Left are racists, homophobes, transphobes, those who believe in absolute truth, and people who practice hate speech, etc. In short, they tend to be people who are often cancelled by the Left.

Who are the heretics and apostates of the belief system of those on the Right in the United States? Those who take down the statues of Confederate figures, those who think America is not the greatest nation on Earth, those who are in favor of renaming colleges and schools because the old names smack of racism, or those people who do not believe in the importance of national heroes like Washington, Jefferson, and Lincoln. The Conservative nomos in America would find any belief, or any new set of rights to be found in the US Constitution that the founders did not explicitly mention—such as abortion from conception to birth or an individual has the right to change his or her gender.

In short, perhaps the best evidence that we in the United States are on the verge of a second American civil war is the differing fundamental nomoi of the Progressive New Left and that of the MAGA Republicans.

SJV/9/22/22

ENDNOTES

Introduction

1 "Cori Bush Explains Her Position on "Defund the Police" while Paying for Private Security. Her Full Response," CBS News, August 6, 2021, https://www.cbsnews.com/news/cori-bush-defund-the-police-private-security-response/.

2 Adam Manno, "Democratic mayors in 20 cities that have slashed police budgets or called to defund them also use millions of taxpayers' dollars to fund their own personal security," *Daily Mail*, July 27, 2021, https://www.dailymail.co.uk/news/article-9829861/Mayors-20-cities-call-defund-police-millions-public-funds-private-security.html.

3 The poll alluded to is an opinion poll conducted by Harvard's Center for American Political Studies on July 21, 2021.

4 The quote from Jen Psaki was from July 26, 2021, in a press conference at the White House.

5 Ms. Harris made her remark about the "climate crisis" on June 28, 2019, via Twitter; https://twitter.com/kamalaharris/status/1144742773980975104.

6 "The 1619 Project," *New York Times*, last modified September 4, 2019, https://www.nytimes.com/interactive/2019/08/14/magazine/1619-america-slavery.html.

7 Alex Borucki, David Eltis, and David Wheat, *From the Galleons to the Highlands* (University of New Mexico Press, 2020).

8 Stephen J. Vicchio, *Muslim Slaves in the Chesapeake: 1634 to 1865* (Edina, MN: Calumet Editions, 2019), 11–13.

9 The remarks on the January 6, 2021, committee come from the committee's first public meeting on July 27, 2021.

Essay One

1 Jill Barshay, "What 2018 PISA International Rankings Tell Us About U.S. Schools," *The Hechinger Report*, December 16, 2019, https://hechingerreport.org/what-2018-pisa-international-rankings-tell-us-about-u-s-schools/.

2 Barack Obama, *The Audacity of Hope* (New York: Broadway Books, 2006).

3 Mr. Biden's "No amendment is absolute" statement was made on April 18, 2021.

4 Azam Ahmed and Ron Grossman, "Bellow's remarks on race haunt legacy in Hyde Park," *Chicago Tribune*, April 7, 2007.

5 Hillary Clinton, interview by Tony Dokoupil, *CBS Sunday Morning*, CBS News, October 15, 2018.

6 Andrew Glass, "Clinton settles sexual harassment suit, Nov. 14, 1998," Politico, November 14, 2018, https://www.politico.com/story/2018/11/14/clinton-settles-sexual-harassment-suit-1998-983371.

7 Malia Zimmerman, "Flight logs show Bill Clinton flew on sex offender's jet much more than previously known," *Fox News*, May 13, 2016, https://www.foxnews.com/us/flight-logs-show-bill-clinton-flew-on-sex-offenders-jet-much-more-than-previously-known.

8 Daniel Villarreal, "Bill Clinton Went to Jeffrey Epstein's Island With 2 'Young Girls,' Virginia Giuffre Says," *Newsweek*, July 30, 2020, https://www.newsweek.com/bill-clinton-went-jeffrey-epsteins-island-2-young-girls-virginia-giuffre-says-1521845.

9 The material on Bill Clinton and Jeffrey Epstein was taken from depositions of the latter's trial from June of 2008.

10 Derek M. Griffith et al., "Men and COVID-19: A Biopsychosocial Approach to Understanding Sex Differences in Mortality and Recommendations for Practice and Policy Interventions," Centers for Disease Control, July 16, 2020, https://www.cdc.gov/pcd/issues/2020/20_0247.htm.

11 Arthur P. Arnold et al., "The Brains of Men and Women," *Endocrine Reviews* (March 11, 2021).

12 John Verhovek, "Joe Biden: White America 'Has to Admit There's still

a Systemic Racism,'" *ABC News*, January 21, 2019, https://abcnews.go.com/Politics/joe-biden-white-america-admit-systemic-racism/story?id=60524966.

13 "Vice President Kamala Harris: We Must 'Speak Truth' about History of Racism in America," *Good Morning America*, April 29, 2021, https://www.goodmorningamerica.com/news/story/vice-president-kamala-harris-speak-truth-history-racism-77391730.

14 Biden's comments on racism are from White House speeches from March 21, 2021, and April 29, 2021.

15 The *Washington Post* study on guns began in 2015 and continues today. "The Staggering Scope of U.S. Gun Deaths goes far beyond mass shootings," *Washington Post*, July 8, 2022, https://www.washingtonpost.com/nation/interactive/2022/gun-deaths-per-year-usa/.

16 "Farrakhan: In His Own Words," Anti-Defamation League, January 12, 2013, https://www.adl.org/education/resources/reports/nation-of-islam-farrakhan-in-his-own-words.

17 Shayla Colon, "Yale School of Medicine responds to outcry over guest speaker," *New Haven Register*, June 5, 2021.

18 Brandon Gillespie, "NYC psychiatrist claims White people are 'psychopathic,' lie to themselves with false sense of identity," June 18, 2021, *Fox News*, https://www.foxnews.com/media/new-york-city-psychiatrist-white-people-psychopathic-lie-false-sense-identity.

19 Kamala Harris on Twitter. https://twitter.com/vp/status/1535081670482984961

20 Jack Crowe, "Ted Lieu Admits He Would 'Love to Regulate' Speech But Concedes It's Harmful In the 'Long Run,'" *National Review*, https://www.nationalreview.com/news/ted-lieu-admits-he-would-love-to-regulate-speech-but-concedes-its-harmful-in-the-long-run/.

21 Jeff Stein, "Biden jobs plan seeks $400 billion to expand caretaking services as U.S. faces surge in aging population," *Washington Post*, April 2, 2021, https://www.washingtonpost.com/us-policy/2021/04/02/caregiving-elderly-white-house-infrastructure/.

22 Calvin Woodward and Hope Yen, "Biden seeks a new view of infrastructure, far beyond asphalt," Associated Press, April 9, 2021, https://apnews.com/

article/joe-biden-donald-trump-c73075906838cbdca34a80595b5c1fa5.

23 Grace Segers, "Biden Huddles with Senate Democrats at Capitol on Infrastructure Bills," *CBS News*, July 14, 2021, https://www.cbsnews.com/news/infrastructure-bill-biden-senate-democrats-capitol/.

24 The example of the three boys and the boxes has been used by various sources attempting to explain equity versus equality.

25 "Norton Announces Bill to Require Gender Equality in Crash Test Dummies," Norton.house.gov, June 1, 2021, https://norton.house.gov/media-center/press-releases/norton-announces-bill-to-require-gender-equality-in-crash-test-dummies.

26 Clint Smith, *How the Word Is Passed: A Reckoning with the History of Slavery Across America* (New York: Little Brown, 2011); Kevin Siepel, *Conquistador Voices: The Spanish Conquest of the Americas* (Atlantic Highlands, NJ: Spring Tree Press, 2015); Gwendolyn M. Hall, *Slavery and African Ethnicities* (Chapel Hill, NC: University of North Carolina Press, 2007).

27 "An American Secret: The Untold Story of Native American Enslavement," National Public Radio, November 20, 2017, https://www.npr.org/2017/11/20/565410514/an-american-secret-the-untold-story-of-native-american-enslavement.

28 David Wheat, "Iberian Roots of the Transatlantic Slave Trade, 1440–1640," The Gilder Lehrman Institute of American History, accessed August 5, 2022, http://ap.gilderlehrman.org/history-by-era/origins-slavery/essays/iberian-roots-transatlantic-slave-trade-1440%E2%80%931640.

29 Jim Barrow, *Aztec Mythology* (self-pub, 2021); Hourly History, *Inca Empire: A History from Beginning to End* (self-pub, 2020); Wendy Conklin, *Mayans, Incas, and Aztecs* (Huntington Beach, CA: Teachers Created Materials, 2007).

30 Robert L. Paquette, *The Oxford Handbook of Slavery in the Americas* (Oxford: Oxford University Press, 2016); David Eltis, *The Rise of African Slavery in the Americas* (Cambridge: Cambridge University Press, 1992); Herbert Klein and Ben Vinson, *African Slavery in Latin America and the Caribbean* (Oxford: Oxford University Press, 2007).

31 Linford D. Fisher, *The Indian Great Awakening* (Oxford: Oxford University

Press, 2017).

32 Brett Rushforth, *Bonds of Alliance* (Chapel Hill, NC: North Carolina Press, 2014).

Essay Two

1 John Legend's comments on Defund the Police were made on June 7, 2020. https://twitter.com/johnlegend/status/1269678575617097729.

2 Jessica Chasmar, "Rep. Jerry Nadler says Antifa violence in Portland a 'myth'," *Washington Times*, July 27, 2020, https://www.congress.gov/116/meeting/house/110938/documents/HHRG-116-JU00-20200728-SD037.pdf.

3 "Black people more than three times as likely as white people to be killed during a police encounter," Harvard T. H. Chan School of Public Health, June 24, 2020, https://www.hsph.harvard.edu/news/hsph-in-the-news/blacks-whites-police-deaths-disparity/.

4 Jon Swaine, Oliver Laughland, and Jamiles Lartey, "Black Americans killed by police twice as likely to be unarmed as white people," https://www.theguardian.com/us-news/2015/jun/01/black-americans-killed-by-police-analysis.

5 Dan O'Donnell, "The Truth About Police Shootings in America," MacIver Institute, https://www.maciverinstitute.com/2021/04/the-truth-about-police-shootings-in-america/.

6 Tierney Sneed, "Obama's Policing Task Force Releases Report," *U.S. News & World Report*, March 2, 2015, https://www.usnews.com/news/articles/2015/03/02/obamas-policing-task-force-releases-report.

7 The Obama administration studied the Philadelphia Police Department in 2015.

8 Linley Sanders, "More Support for Redirecting Police Funds to Community Resources than Defunding Police," YouGovAmerica, June 12, 2020, https://today.yougov.com/topics/politics/articles-reports/2020/06/12/redirecting-police-funds-poll.

9 Kendall Karson, "64% of Americans oppose 'defund the police' movement," ABC News, June 12, 2020, https://abcnews.go.com/Politics/64-americans-oppose-defund-police-movement-key-goals/story?id=71202300.

10 I have consulted studies on the Defund the Police movement by YouGov, ABC News, and the Gallup Company, as well as studies by Reuters/Ipsos, the Morning Consult/Politico, *USA Today*, the Pew Research Center, and Sienna College.

11 Lydia Saad, "Black Americans Want Police to Retain Local Presence," *Gallup*, August 5, 2020, https://news.gallup.com/poll/316571/black-americans-police-retain-local-presence.aspx.

12 "Americans supportive of peaceful protests and bipartisan support for police reform," Ipsos, June 12, 2020, https://www.ipsos.com/en-us/news-polls/reuters-ipsos-data-police-reform-george-floyd-2020-06-12.

13 Politico staff, "Poll: Voters oppose 'Defund the Police' but back major reforms," *Politico*, June 17, 2020, https://www.politico.com/news/2020/06/17/poll-voters-defund-police-reforms-324774.

14 Sarah Elbeshbishi and Mabinty Quarshie, "Fewer Than 1 in 5 Support 'Defund the Police' Movement, *USA Today*/Ipsos Poll Finds," *USA Today*, March 7, 2021, https://www.usatoday.com/story/news/politics/2021/03/07/usa-today-ipsos-poll-just-18-support-defund-police-movement/4599232001/.

15 "Majority of Public Favors Giving Civilians the Power to Sue Police Officers for Misconduct," Pew Research Center, July 9, 2020, https://www.pewresearch.org/politics/2020/07/09/majority-of-public-favors-giving-civilians-the-power-to-sue-police-officers-for-misconduct/.

16 Jemima McEvoy, "At Least 13 Cities Are Defunding Their Police Departments," *Forbes*, August 13, 2020, https://www.forbes.com/sites/jemimamcevoy/2020/08/13/at-least-13-cities-are-defunding-their-police-departments/?sh=217e9fe829e3.

17 *Forbes* did a study of cuts in police departments across America in 2020 and 2021.

18 Juliana Battaglia, "Baltimore Will Now No Longer Prosecute Drug

Possession, Prostitution and Other Low-Level Offenses," CNN, March 27, 2021, https://www.cnn.com/2021/03/27/us/baltimore-prosecute-prostitution-drug-possession/index.html#:~:text=CNN%20%E2%80%94%20Baltimore%20City%20State%E2%80%99s%20Attorney%20Marilyn%20Mosby,to%20decrease%20the%20spread%20of%20Covid-19%20behind%20bars.

19 Joshua Rhett Miller, "Murders, Violent Crime Surged in Minnesota Last Year amid Floyd Unrest, Defund the Police," *New York Post*, July 28, 2021, https://nypost.com/2021/07/28/murders-violent-crime-surged-in-minnesota-last-year-amid-floyd-unrest/.

20 Alex Jokich, "Minneapolis 2020 Homicides Surpass Last Year's Total in Just 8 Months," KSTP.com, August 18, 2020, https://kstp.com/kstp-news/top-news/minneapolis-2020-homicides-surpass-last-years-total-in-just-8-months/.

21 "Atlanta Hits 100 Homicides for 2021, Ahead of Last Year's Pace," *Private Officer Magazine*, August 27, 2021, https://privateofficernews.org/atlanta-hits-100-homicides-for-2021-ahead-of-last-years-pace/#:~:text=In%202020%2C%20the%20Atlanta%20Police%20Department%20investigated%20157,reported%20nearly%20a%2060%25%20increase%20in%20homicide%20cases.

22 Sam Charles, "After 3 Years of Progress, Chicago's Murder Tally Skyrockets in 2020," *Chicago Sun-Times*, December 31, 2020, https://chicago.suntimes.com/crime/2020/12/31/22208002/chicago-murders-2020-skyrocket-crime-violence-cpd-homicides#:~:text=As%20of%20Dec.%2031%2C%20the%20city%20recorded%20774,more%20murders%20in%202020%20than%20the%20year%20before.

23 Nathan Diller, "D.C. Has Surpassed 100 Homicides in 2020," WAMU 88.5, July 13, 2020, https://wamu.org/story/20/07/13/d-c-has-surpassed-100-homicides-in-2020/.

24 Nicole Hensley, "Houston Reaches Grim Milestone with 400th Murder of 2020," *Houston Chronicle*, December 28, 2020, https://www.houstonchronicle.com/news/houston-texas/crime/article/Houston-sees-400th-murder-of-2020-15832986.php.

25 Callie Craighead, "2020 Crime Report: Seattle Saw Highest Homicide Number in 26 Years; Overall Violent Crimes Lower," SeattlePI, January 12, 2021, https://www.seattlepi.com/local/seattlenews/article/2020-crime-Seattle-highest-homicide-rate-15864266.php.

26 Jason Rantz, "Rantz: Seattle Police Exodus Worsens, 270 Out Since '20, with 100 More 'Unavailable,'" 770 KTTH, June 1, 2021, https://mynorthwest.com/2942008/rantz-seattle-police-exodus-worsens-270-out-since-20-with-100-more-unavailable/.

27 Paul Jurgens, "Minneapolis Violent Crime Increased by 21% in 2020," KFGO.com, February 8, 2021, https://kfgo.com/2021/02/08/minneapolis-violent-crime-increased-by-21-in-2020/.

28 Callie Craighead, "2020 Crime Report: Seattle Saw Highest Homicide Number in 26 Years; Overall Violent Crimes Lower," SeattlePI, January 12, 2021, https://www.seattlepi.com/local/seattlenews/article/2020-crime-Seattle-highest-homicide-rate-15864266.php.

29 I have employed the National Public Radio account of police retirements and the study by the Police Executive Research Forum that aired on June 24, 2021, on the radio.

30 Jill Leovy in a book called *Ghettoside* coined the term *legal cynicism*.

31 Reis Thebault and Danielle Rindler, "Shootings never stopped during the pandemic: 2020 was the deadliest gun violence year in decades," *Washington Post*, March 23, 2021, https://www.washingtonpost.com/nation/2021/03/23/2020-shootings/.

32 "U.S. Murder/Homicide Rate: 1990–2022," Macrotrends, https://www.macrotrends.net/countries/USA/united-states/murder-homicide-rate.

33 "NEW: Economic Comeback under President Trump Breaks 70-Year Record," Whitehouse.gov, October 29, 2020, https://trumpwhitehouse.archives.gov/articles/new-economic-comeback-president-trump-breaks-70-year-record/.

34 Joel Currier, "No-show St. Louis prosecutors trigger dismissal of 2020 murder case," *St. Louis Post-Dispatch*, July 18, 2021, https://www.stltoday.com/news/local/crime-and-courts/no-show-st-louis-prosecutors-trigger-dismissal-of-2020-murder-case/article_6be57257-6f1a-5640-

a40e-57436c0d3789.html.

35 Joe Biden's comments on bail review and cashless bail were made on July 31, 2020.

36 Horus Alas, "Why L.A. County's District Attorney Has Joined the Movement to End Bail," *U.S. News and World Report*, January 14, 2021, https://www.usnews.com/news/cities/articles/2021-01-14/los-angeles-county-district-attorney-joins-movement-to-end-cash-bail.

37 Brian Naylor, "Kamala Harris Tells Guatemalans Not To Migrate To The United States," NPR, June 7, 2021, https://www.npr.org/2021/06/07/1004074139/harris-tells-guatemalans-not-to-migrate-to-the-united-states.

38 James Gordon, "Rudy Giuliani says Eric Adams 'hasn't done a damn thing' to solve crime and tells the 'playboy' NYT mayor to scale back his social calendar until he gets violence under control," *Daily Mail*, May 9, 2022, https://www.dailymail.co.uk/news/article-10796153/Rudy-Giuliani-says-Eric-Adams-damn-thing-solve-crime-robberies-assaults-soar.html.

10 Staff report, "Chicago's Top Cop Breaks Down Number of Gangs in City, How They're Structured," NBC 5 Chicago, July 22, 2020, https://www.nbcchicago.com/news/local/chicagos-top-cop-breaks-down-number-of-gangs-in-city-how-theyre-structured/2309434/; Alex Hammer, "Chicago Police staffing hits a new low," Daily Mail, April 7, 2022, https://www.dailymail.co.uk/news/article-10696805/Chicago-Police-staffing-lowest-recent-history-department-reels-generation-resignation.html.

39 Lee Zeldin, "With Cashless Bail, New York Is Choosing Criminals Over Its Citizens' Safety, House Passed Bill Would Do the Same," October 12, 2020, https://zeldin.house.gov/media-center/press-releases/cashless-bail-new-york-choosing-criminals-over-its-citizens-safety-house.

40 White House, "Remarks by President Biden and Attorney General Garland on Gun Crime Prevention Strategy," June 23, 2021, https://www.whitehouse.gov/briefing-room/speeches-remarks/2021/06/23/remarks-by-president-biden-and-attorney-general-garland-on-gun-

crime-prevention-strategy/.

41 White House, "FACT SHEET: Biden-Harris Administration Announces Initial Actions to Address the Gun Violence Public Health Epidemic," https://www.whitehouse.gov/briefing-room/statements-releases/2021/04/07/fact-sheet-biden-harris-administration-announces-initial-actions-to-address-the-gun-violence-public-health-epidemic/#:~:text=The%20Justice%20Department%2C%20within%2060%20days%2C%20will%20publish%20model%20%E2%80%9C,danger%20to%20themselves%20or%20others.

42 "What the Data Says About Gun Deaths in the U.S.," Pew Research Center, February 3, 2022, https://www.pewresearch.org/fact-tank/2022/02/03/what-the-data-says-about-gun-deaths-in-the-u-s/.

43 "District of Columbia v. Heller," Oyez, accessed April 26, 2022, https://www.oyez.org/cases/2007/07-290.

44 "McDonald v. Chicago," Oyez, accessed 26, 2022, https://www.oyez.org/cases/2009/08-1521.

45 Sarah Ravani, "Oakland police chief slams council vote on funding as deadly shootings surge," *San Francisco Chronicle*, June 28, 2021, https://www.sfchronicle.com/crime/article/Oakland-police-chief-wades-into-budget-debate-as-16280222.php.

46 Gene Johnson, "Confusion besets Washington's new police reform laws," KNKX Public Radio, July 26, 2021, https://www.knkx.org/news/2021-07-26/confusion-besets-washingtons-new-police-reform-laws.

Essay Three

1 Stephen J. Vicchio, *Ronald Reagan's Religious Beliefs* (Rapid City, SD: Cross-Link Publishing, 2020).

2 Janet Farrell Brodie, *Contraception and Abortion in Nineteenth-Century America* (Ithaca, NY: Cornell University Press, 1992).

3 Marvin Olasky, *Abortion at the Crossroads* (New York: Bombardier Books, 2021); James C. Mohr, *Abortion in America* (Oxford: Oxford University

Press, 1979); Mako Nagasawa, *Abortion Policy in America* (Eugene, OR: Wipf and Stock Publishers, 2021).

4 N. E. H. Hull and Peter Charles Hoffer, *Roe v. Wade: The Abortion Rights Controversy (Updated edition)* (Lawrence, KS: University Press of Kansas, 2021).

5 "Statement of Principles," NARAL Pro-Choice America, accessed April 26, 2022, https://www.prochoiceamerica.org/elections/statement-of-principles/.

6 Sarah Ruiz-Grossman, "Here's Where 2020 Candidates Stand on Repealing the Hyde Amendment," HuffPost, June 6, 2019, https://www.huffpost.com/entry/democratic-candidates-hyde-amendment-abortion_n_5cf964b5e4b06af8b50570bd.

7 Ralph Northam, interview, "Va. Gov. Northam draws outrage from GOP for defending abortion bill", WTOP, January 31, 2019. https://wtop.com/local-politics-elections-news/2019/01/va-gov-northam-draws-outrage-from-gop-for-defending-abortion-bill/.

8 Antonio Olivo, "Del. Kathy Tran was known for nursing her baby on the House floor. Now she's getting death threats over abortion," *Washington Post*, January 31, 2019, https://www.washingtonpost.com/local/virginia-politics/lawmaker-at-center-of-abortion-bill-firestorm-elected-as-part-of-democratic-wave-that-changed-richmond/2019/01/31/d4f76ecc-2565-11e9-90cd-dedb0c92dc17_story.html.

9 Joe Biden, *Promises to Keep* (New York: Random House, 2008).

10 Andrew Kaczynski, "Joe Biden Described Being an 'Odd Man Out' with Democrats on Abortion in 2006 Interview," CNN, June 13, 2019, https://www.cnn.com/2019/06/13/politics/joe-biden-abortion/index.html.

11 Zachary Evans, "Romney Hits Becerra on Partial-Birth Abortion," Yahoo! News, February 23, 2021, https://news.yahoo.com/romney-hits-becerra-partial-birth-175116881.html.

12 "The Biden Plan to Protect & Build on the Affordable Care Act," https://joebiden.com/healthcare/#.

13 Mr. Biden and Communion were discussed in an editorial from the *National Catholic Reporter* on June 3, 2021.

14 "Archbishop Cordileone's Response to Speaker Pelosi's Comments about Pro-Life Voters," Catholic Business Journal Daily, January 21, 2021, https://www.catholicbusinessjournal.com/voices/bishops-corner/archbishop-cordileones-response-to-speaker-pelosis-comments-about-pro-life-voters/.

15 AOC article about being Catholic was published in the *Huffington Post* on June 26, 2021; Alexandria Ocasio-Cortez (@AOC), Twitter, December 10, 2018.

16 Alexandria Ocasio-Cortez, "Alexandria Ocasio-Cortez on Her Catholic Faith and the Urgency of Criminal Justice Reform," *America*, June 27, 2018, https://www.americamagazine.org/politics-society/2018/06/27/alexandria-ocasio-cortez-her-catholic-faith-and-urgency-criminal.

17 The material I have relied on for the Biden/Pelosi/AOC Catholicism, as well as the comments from the various American Catholic bishops, were from internet sources.

18 Wikipedia, s.v. "Canon 915," last modified April 23, 2022, https://en.wikipedia.org/wiki/Canon_915.

19 Dan Zeidler, "Opinion: I Didn't leave the Democrat Party. The Party Left Me on the Abortion Issue," *Milwaukee Journal Sentinel*, October 14, 2020.

20 The Harvard Criteria for redefining death appeared in the *Journal of the American Medical Association* 205, no. 6. (1968): 337–40.

21 Ronald Munson, *Intervention and Reflection: Basic Issues in Bioethics* (Boston: Cengage Learning, 2013).

22 Mayo Clinic website; the BabyCenter staff; and the Cleveland Clinic.

23 Alice Miranda Ollstein, "Supreme Court Puts Biden into an Abortion Fight He Had Not Wanted," *Politico*, May 17, 2021.

24 Ibid.

25 Rick Atkinson and Kathy Sawyer, "Ferraro Defends Her Abortion Stand, But Is Criticized by Scranton Bishop," *Washington Post*, September 13, 1984, https://www.washingtonpost.com/archive/politics/1984/09/13/ferraro-defends-her-abortion-stand-but-is-criticized-by-scranton-bishop/953ea75c-f762-4a2d-9b21-e90c88d9409d/.

26 Lexi Lonas, "Covington Catholic graduate reaches settlement with

NBC," *The Hill*, December 18, 2021, https://thehill.com/homenews/media/586431-former-covington-catholic-student-reaches-settlement-with-nbc/.

Essay Four

1 Josh Rogin, "In 2018, Diplomats Warned of Risky Coronavirus Experiments in a Wuhan Lab. No One Listened," *Politico*, March 8, 2021, https://www.politico.com/news/magazine/2021/03/08/josh-rogin-chaos-under-heaven-wuhan-lab-book-excerpt-474322.

2 In preparing this essay, I have consulted various documents of the World Health Organization in regard to the coronavirus as well as some documents from Republican members of the US Congress, including the passing in the Senate of the March 26, 2020, CARES Act. The Senate also passed the HEALS Act, which provided stimulus checks. I have also employed a study from the journal, *Science Translation Medicine* (June 2020) and another from the *New England Journal Medicine* (May 2020).

3 The Cambridge Working Group produced a report on SARS-CoV-2 on July 14, 2014. It has been helpful in constructing this essay, as has been the 1975 public conference on viruses held at Asilomar; Cambridge Working Group, "Cambridge Working Group Consensus Statement on the Creation of Potential Pandemic Pathogens (PPPs)," July 14, 2014, http://www.cambridgeworkinggroup.org/.

4 Nicholas Wade, "The origin of COVID: Did people or nature open Pandora's box at Wuhan?" *Bulletin of the Atomic Sciences*, May 5, 2021, https://thebulletin.org/2021/05/the-origin-of-covid-did-people-or-nature-open-pandoras-box-at-wuhan/.

5 Kristian G. Andersen's March 17, 2020 letter to *Nature Medicine*; Mr. Daszak's application for "Gain of Function" research; and the March 2020 letter to *Lancet*.

6 Marc Thiessen, "The Case That the Virus Emerged from Nature, Not a Lab, Is Falling Apart," *Washington Post*, June 3, 2021, https://www.wash-

ingtonpost.com/opinions/2021/06/03/case-that-virus-emerged-nature-not-lab-is-falling-apart/.

7 I have also incorporated the observations from several newspaper articles for Essay Four, including pieces in the *Washington Post*, the *New York Times*, *USA Today*, the *Daily Mail* the *Global Times*, and the *Wall Street Journal*.

8 "Letters: 'A Troublesome Inheritance'", *New York Times*, August 8, 2014, https://www.nytimes.com/2014/08/10/books/review/letters-a-troublesome-inheritance.html.

9 The various attempts that China made to blame COVID-19 on the United States were garnered from internet sources, as were the lists of various viral leaks in the essay.

10 Kelsey Piper, "How deadly pathogens have escaped the lab — over and over again," Vox, March 20, 2019, https://www.vox.com/future-perfect/2019/3/20/18260669/deadly-pathogens-escape-lab-smallpox-bird-flu. I have also consulted a number of records on the leaks of viruses held by the CDC.

11 Katherine Eban, "The Lab-Leak Theory: Inside the Fight to Uncover COVID-19's Origins," *Vanity Fair*, June 3, 2021, https://www.vanityfair.com/news/2021/06/the-lab-leak-theory-inside-the-fight-to-uncover-covid-19s-origins.

12 Michael C. Carroll, *Lab 257: The Disturbing Story of the Government's Secret Germ Laboratory* (New York: William Morrow, 2005); Judith Miller, William J. Broad, and Stephen Engelberg, *Germs: Biological Weapons and America's Secret War* (New York: Simon and Schuster, 2002); Tricia White and Ronald W. Davis, *The Puzzle Solver* (New York: Legacy Literature, 2021).

13 Martin Furmanski, "Threatened pandemics and laboratory escapes: Self-fulfilling prophecies," *Bulletin of the Atomic Scientists*, March 31, 2014, https://thebulletin.org/2014/03/threatened-pandemics-and-laboratory-escapes-self-fulfilling-prophecies/.

14 "The 1979 Anthrax Leak in Sverdlovsk," PBS, https://www.pbs.org/wgbh/pages/frontline/shows/plague/sverdlovsk/.

15 Morgan Phillips, "Psaki Says WHO Report on Coronavirus Origin 'Lacks Transparency," Fox News, March 30, 2021, https://www.foxnews.com/politics/psaki-who-report-coronavirus-origin-lacks-transparency.

16 Zbigniew Brzezinski, *The Grand Chessboard: American Primacy and Its Geostrategic Imperatives* (New York: Basic Books, 1998).

17 Felicia Sonmez, "Biden Says China Is 'Not Competition for Us,' Prompting Pushback from Both Parties," *Washington Post*, May 2, 2019, https://www.washingtonpost.com/politics/biden-says-china-is-not-competition-for-us-prompting-pushback-from-republicans/2019/05/01/4ae4e738-6c68-11e9-a66d-a82d3f3d96d5_story.html.

18 Carol E. Lee, "Biden's Tricky China Balancing Act," NBC News, April 27, 2021, https://www.nbcnews.com/politics/white-house/biden-s-tricky-china-balancing-act-n1265429.

19 Nicole Saphier, *Panic Attack: Playing Politics with Science in the Fight Against COVID-19* (New York: Broadside Books, 2021); Alex Berenson, *Unreported Truths about COVID-19 and Lockdowns* (New York: Blue Deep Press, 2021).

20 Josh Boswell, "What WASN'T in Hunter Biden's book," April 8, 2021, Daily Mail, https://www.dailymail.co.uk/news/article-9445105/What-Hunter-Biden-left-tell-memoir-revealed.html.

21 The material on Hunter Biden came from the contents of his laptop and the *New York Post* article on his laptop.

22 Audrey Conklin, "Bobulinski tells Tucker Carlson that Joe Biden lied about son Hunter's business dealings," Fox News, December 11, 2020, https://www.foxnews.com/politics/flashback-bobulinski-tucker-hunter-carlson-biden.

23 Matthew Lee, Aamer Madhani, and Darlene Superville, "Biden Signals that U.S. will refocus on diplomacy abroad," PBS NewsHour, February 4, 2021, https://www.pbs.org/newshour/politics/watch-live-biden-visits-state-department-to-speak-about-multilateral-foreign-policy-approach.

24 Alex Leary and Bob Davis, "Biden's China Policy Is Emerging—and It Looks a Lot Like Trump's, *Wall Street Journal*, June 10, 2021, https://www.wsj.com/articles/bidens-china-policy-is-emergingand-it-looks-a-lot-

like-trumps-11623330000.

25 "Statement by President Joe Biden on the Investigation into the Origins of COVID-19," https://www.whitehouse.gov/briefing-room/statements-releases/2021/05/26/statement-by-president-joe-biden-on-the-investigation-into-the-origins-of-covid-19/.

26 Will Stone, "Unproven Lab Leak Theory Brings Pressure On China To Share Info. But It May Backfire," NPR, June 17, 2021, https://www.npr.org/sections/goatsandsoda/2021/06/17/1006352333/the-mystery-of-the-origins-of-the-pandemic-can-it-be-solved.

27 "Former CDC director believes virus came from lab in China," CNN, March 26, 2021, https://www.cnn.com/videos/health/2021/03/26/sanjay-gupta-exclusive-robert-redfield-coronavirus-opinion-origin-sot-intv-newday-vpx.cnn.

28 "Letters: Investigate the Origins of COVID-19," *Science*, May 14, 2021, https://www.science.org/doi/10.1126/science.abj0016

29 Geoff Brumfiel, All Things Considered, NPR, May 28, 2021.

30 Bruce Goldman, "5 Questions: David Relman on Investigating Origin of Coronavirus," Stanford Health Policy News, June 2, 2021, https://healthpolicy.fsi.stanford.edu/news/5-questions-david-relman-investigating-origin-coronavirus.

31 Jenni Fink, "18 Scientists, Including One Who Worked with Wuhan Lab, Say COVID Lab Leak Theory Needs Study," *Newsweek*, May 14, 2021, https://www.newsweek.com/18-scientists-including-one-who-worked-wuhan-lab-say-covid-lab-leak-theory-needs-study-1591649.

32 Li-Meng Yang, interviews by Tucker Carlson, *Tucker Carlson Tonight*, July 10, 2020 and June 31, 2021.

33 Kelsey Vlamis, "Biden is spending $86 million on hotel rooms for migrants as his administration struggles to handle the surge of families and kids trying to come to the US," Business Insider, March 20, 2021, https://www.businessinsider.com/biden-to-spend-86-million-hotel-rooms-migrants-near-border-2021-3.

34 Lauren Boebert on Twitter, March 21, 2021, https://twitter.com/laurenboebert/status/1373802953652506627?lang=ar-x-fm.

35 "Latest Data on COVID-19 Vaccinations by Race/Ethnicity," Kaiser Family Foundation, https://www.kff.org/coronavirus-covid-19/issue-brief/latest-data-on-covid-19-vaccinations-by-race-ethnicity/.

36 The figures on young African American males and vaccination come directly from the CDC and materials from the New York State Health Department. Joseph Goldstein and Matthew Sedacca, "Why Only 28 Percent of Young Black New Yorkers Are Vaccinated, *New York Times*, August 12, 2021, https://www.nytimes.com/2021/08/12/nyregion/covid-vaccine-black-young-new-yorkers.html.

37 Pradeep Kapoor and Joseph M. Chalil, *Beyond the COVID-19 Pandemic* (New York: The UNN Corporation, 2020); Jeffrey I. Barke. *COVID-19: A Physician's Take* (New York: The American Group, 2020); Jennifer Ashton, *The New Normal* (New York: William Morrow, 2021).

Essay Five

1 John Weber, *From Southern Texas to the Nation: The Exploitation of Mexican Labor in the Twentieth Century* (Chapel Hill, NC: University of North Carolina Press, 2015); Tobin Hansen, *Voices of the Border: Testimonies of Migration, Deportation, and Asylum* (Washington, DC: Georgetown University Press, 2021).

2 Kelly Lytle Hernandez, *Migra! A History of the U.S. Border Patrol* (Berkeley, CA: University of California Press, 2010).

3 Jeff Guinn, *War on the Border: The Texas Rangers, and the American Invasion* (New York City: Simon and Schuster, 2021); Alistair Moffat, *The Borders: A History of the Borders From the Earliest Times* (Edinburgh: Birlinn Limited, 2011); Carmen Boullosa. *Let's Talk About Your Wall: Mexican Writers Respond to the Immigration Crisis* (New York City: New Press, 2020); Megan Carney, *The Unending Hunger: Tracing Women and Food Insecurity Across Borders* (Berkeley, CA: University of California Press, 2015); Sonia Nazario, *Enrique's Journey: The Story of a Boy's Dangerous Odyssey to Reunite with his Mother* (New York City: Random House, 2006).

4 Several interviews with Presidents Obama and Biden were also used in Essay Five, including a 2014 interview with Mr. Obama by George Stephanopoulos; a May 10, 2011, Obama interview with Robert Farley; a Joe Biden interview with NPR on August 5, 2021; and another on February 13, 2021; "Interview with George Stephanopoulos of ABC News 'Good Morning America'," The American Presidency Project, June 27, 2014, https://www.presidency.ucsb.edu/documents/interview-with-george-stephanopoulos-abc-news-good-morning-america.

5 The figures on migrants and unaccompanied minors were taken directly from the U.S. Border Patrol.

6 LuLu Garcia-Navarro via Twitter, August 5, 2020, https://twitter.com/lourdesgnavarro/status/1291000306915057669.

7 White House, "A Letter to the Speaker Of The House And President Of The Senate Regarding the Termination of the National Emergency Concerning the Southern Border," February 10, 2021, https://www.whitehouse.gov/briefing-room/statements-releases/2021/02/11/a-letter-to-the-speaker-of-the-house-and-president-of-the-senate-regarding-the-termination-of-the-national-emergency-concerning-the-southern-border/.

8 Tamara Keith, "Harris Visits The Southern Border After Trying To Keep The Focus Away From It," June 25, 2021, https://www.npr.org/2021/06/25/1009939218/harris-is-visiting-the-southern-border-after-trying-to-keep-the-focus-away-from-.

9 NBC News, "Harris Speaks Out On Why She Hasn't Traveled To Southern Border," https://www.youtube.com/watch?v=omrMRP15q9M.

10 Aviva Chomsky, *Central America's Forgotten History: Revolution, Violence, and the Roots of Migration* (Boston: Beacon Press, 2021).

11 Nicole Narea, "How 'Abolish Ice' Helped Bring About Abolitionist Ideas into the Mainstream," Vox, July 9, 2020.

12 Mohammad Fazel Zarandi, Jonathan S. Feinstein, and John G. Searle, "Yale Study Finds Twice as Many Undocumented Immigrants as Previous Estimates," Yale Insights, http://insights.som.yale.edu/insights/yale-study-finds-twice-as-many-undocumented-immigrants-as-pre-

vious-estimates.

13 Mark Joyella, "President Biden Says He 'Inherited One God-Awful Mess' at the Border," *Forbes*, April 30, 2021, https://www.forbes.com/sites/markjoyella/2021/04/30/president-biden-says-he-inherited-one-god-awful-mess-at-the-border/?sh=41a6a5c02c52.

14 The six claims that the Biden administration has made about the Trump administration's policies on the southern border were garnered from the internet.

15 The comments from Secretary Mayorkas quoted in Essay Five are all from internet sources as well as his May 13, 2021, appearance before the US Senate.

16 Joey Garrison, "White House backpedals after Biden refers to a 'crisis' at the border," *USA Today*, April 19, 2021, https://www.usatoday.com/story/news/politics/2021/04/19/white-house-backtracks-bidens-comment-crisis-border/7288376002/.

17 Claire Hansen, "One-Day Total of Child Migrants Crossing Border Hits Reported High Under Biden," U.S. News and World Report, August 6, 2021, https://www.usnews.com/news/national-news/articles/2021-08-06/one-day-total-of-child-migrants-crossing-border-hits-reported-high-under-biden.

18 Mark Morgan, personal interview with author, July of 2020.

19 Andrew R. Arthur, "Trump Did Not 'Dismantle' or 'Gut' the Asylum System," Center for Immigration Studies, March 24, 2021, https://cis.org/Arthur/Trump-Did-Not-Dismantle-or-Gut-Asylum-System.

20 The many contradictions about the southern border by Secretary Mayorkas of Homeland Security that I have catalogued in this fifth essay were mostly taken from his press conferences and reports on them in national newspapers like *USA Today*, the *Wall Street Journal*, the *New York Times*, and the *Washington Post.*

21 Homeland Security Secretary Alejandro Mayorkas Briefing on Immigration Reform Transcript, Rev, May 7, 2021, https://www.rev.com/blog/transcripts/homeland-security-secretary-alejandro-mayorkas-briefing-on-immigration-reform-transcript.

22 Daina Beth Solomon, “Homeland Security chief says U.S.-Mexico border not open,” June 15, 2021, https://www.reuters.com/world/americas/us-homeland-chief-says-us-mexico-border-not-open-irregular-migration-2021-06-15/.

23 “Oral Testimony of Secretary of Homeland Security Alejandro N. Mayorkas before the U.S. Senate Committee on Homeland Security & Governmental Affairs on ‘DHS Actions to Address Unaccompanied Minors at the Southern Border,’” May 13, 2021, https://www.dhs.gov/news/2021/05/13/oral-testimony-secretary-homeland-security-alejandro-n-mayorkas-us-senate-committee.

24 Paul Gattis, “Tuberville: Are Mexican Immigrants Facing Relaxed COVID Restrictions?,” AL.com, February 16, 2021, https://www.al.com/news/2021/02/tuberville-are-mexican-immigrants-facing-relaxed-covid-restrictions.html.

25 Ken Cuccinelli, “Yes, It’s a Joe Biden-Created “Crisis” at the Southern Border,” The Heritage Foundation, March 22, 2021, https://www.heritage.org/homeland-security/commentary/yes-its-joe-biden-created-crisis-the-southern-border.

26 Rep. Kevin McCarthy website, “The Real State of the Union: A Live Discussion with the American People,” https://www.republicanleader.gov/the-real-state-of-the-union-a-live-discussion-with-the-american-people/.

27 Mike LaChance, “Biden DHS Secretary Caught on Hot Mic Saying Border Crisis Is ‘Unsustainable,’” American Lookout, August 13, 2021, https://americanlookout.com/biden-dhs-secretary-caught-on-hot-mic-saying-border-crisis-is-unsustainable-audio/.

28 The comments and statistics on seizures of drugs and guns at the southern border are from the US Homeland Security Department and Border Patrol, as well as local news stories, particularly in Texas. https://www.cbp.gov/newsroom/stats/cbp-enforcement-statistics-fy2021.

29 I have utilized newspaper articles for Essay Five, including from the *New York Times* (July 8, 2014), the *Washington Post*, the *Baltimore Sun*, and the *Wall Street Journal*.

Essay Six

1 The main sources for the statistics in this essay are reports from the CDC and the Pew Research Center. I have also consulted the FBI's Gun Violence Archive as well as data from the Census Bureau and the University of California at Davis's health statistics on their university website.

2 My remarks on the Second Amendment were mostly gleaned from internet sources, as were my comments on Supreme Court cases on guns.

3 Jan. E. Dizard, *Guns in America: A Historical Reader* (New York City: New York University Press, 1999); Patrick J. Charles, *Armed in America: A History of Gun Rights From Colonial Militias to Concealed Carry* (Buffalo, NY: Prometheus Books, 2019); Thom Hartmann, *The Hidden History of Guns and the Second Amendment* (Oakland, CA: Berrett-Koehler Publishers, 2019); Saul Cornell, *A Well-Regulated Militia: The Founding Fathers and the Origins of Gun Control in America* (Oxford: Oxford University Press, 2008); Carol Anderson, *The Second: Race and Guns in a Fatally Unequal America* (London: Bloomsbury Publishing, 2021); Donald J. Campbell, *America's Gun Wars: A Cultural History of Gun Control in the United States* (Westport, CT: Praeger Publishers, 2019.); Chuck Wills, *The Illustrated History of Guns: From First Firearms to Semiautomatic Weapons* (New York City: Skyhorse Publishing, 2017).

4 WWNYTV7 staff and Associated Press, "Supreme Court to take up right to carry gun for self-defense," WWNYTV7, April 26, 2021, https://www.wwnytv.com/2021/04/26/supreme-court-take-up-right-carry-gun-self-defense-2/.

5 I also have consulted various bills and acts made by Congress, including the Gun Control Act of 1968 and the Protection of Lawful Commerce in Arms Act (2005).

6 Cheyenne Haslett and Samantha Sergi, "Here's where the 2020 Democrats stand on gun control," February 7, 2020, https://abcnews.go.com/Politics/heres-2020-democrats-differ-gun-control/story?id=62970498.

7 The comments on guns and gun control of Democratic candidates for

president were mostly garnered from internet sources. I also have used the NRA's ratings of members of Congress.

8 Jacey Fortin, "Beto O'Rourke Urges Banks to Cut Services for Gun Sales," New York Times, September 12, 2019, https://www.nytimes.com/2019/09/12/us/politics/beto-o-rourke-guns-banks.html.

9 "Protecting Our Communities from Gun Violence," ElizabethWarren.com, August 10, 2019, https://elizabethwarren.com/plans/gun-violence.

10 "VIDEO: On Senate Floor, Klobuchar Highlights Work to Close the Boyfriend Loophole," Klobuchar.senate.gov, June 14, 2022, https://www.klobuchar.senate.gov/public/index.cfm/2022/6/video-on-senate-floor-klobuchar-highlights-work-to-close-the-boyfriend-loophole.

11 Bernie Sanders on Twitter, February 20, 2019, https://twitter.com/BernieSanders/status/1098323885940973569?ref_src=twsrc%5Etfw%7Ctwcamp%5Etweetembed%7Ctwterm%5E1098323885940973569%7Ctwgr%5Eed0426c08125dc29d176e70c3040f46d-7290d7c8%7Ctwcon%5Es1_&ref_url=https%3A%2F%2Fwww.redditmedia.com%2Fmediaembed%2Fastjrg%3Fresponsive%3Dtrueis_nightmode%3Dfalse.

12 Pete Buttigieg on Twitter, October 2, 2017, https://twitter.com/petebuttigieg/status/914863875979345922.

13 "The Biden Plan to End Our Gun Violence Epidemic," JoeBiden.com, June 23, 2021, https://joebiden.com/gunsafety/#.

14 Amy Swearer, "Heritage Explains: Biden's Gun Control Agenda," The Heritage Foundation, March 7, 2021, https://www.heritage.org/firearms/heritage-explains/bidens-gun-control-agenda.

15 Alana Abramson and Brian Bennett, "Biden Administration Unveils Plan to Combat Uptick in Gun Violence," *Time*, June 23, 2021.

16 Glenn Kessler, "Biden's false claim that the 2nd Amendment bans cannon ownership," Washington Post, June 28, 2021, https://www.washingtonpost.com/politics/2021/06/28/bidens-false-claim-that-2nd-amendment-bans-cannon-ownership/.

17 I also have again utilized a document titled, "The Biden Plan to End Our Gun Violence Epidemic."

18 I also have employed a twenty-two minute presentation and questioning of Amy Swearer of the Heritage Foundation, "Biden's Gun Control Agenda." It was given on March 7, 2021, and included participation by Michelle Cordero, also of the Heritage Foundation and comments from the White House press secretary, Jen Psaki, about gun issues and President Biden. https://www.heritage.org/firearms/heritage-explains/bidens-gun-control-agenda.

19 Justin Tanis, "The Power of 41%: A Glimpse into the Life of a Statistic," *Am J Orthopsychiatry* 86, no. 4 (2016): 373–377.

20 Bradford Betz and Andrew Murray, "Chicago gang members outnumber cops 10 to 1 as crime spike reaches fever pitch," Fox32, July 13, 2021, https://www.fox32chicago.com/news/chicago-gang-members-outnumber-cops-10-to-1-as-crime-spike-reaches-fever-pitch.

21 Jill Serjeant, "Little glamour in L.A., "gang capital of America," Reuters, February 8, 2007, https://www.reuters.com/article/us-gangs-losangeles-culture/little-glamour-in-l-a-gang-capital-of-america-idUSN0846153020070209.

22 "Border Patrol Agents Seize Abandoned Weapons," U.S. Customs and Border Protection, May 7, 2021, https://www.cbp.gov/newsroom/local-media-release/border-patrol-agents-seize-abandoned-weapons.

23 The poll of attitudes toward gun control was a study conducted on January 25, 2021, by Alison Durkee and *Forbes*.

24 The statistics on gun deaths in the United States and their history come mostly from the Centers for Disease Control and the Federal Bureau of Investigation's "Gun Violence" archive.

25 Finally, the sources for gun ownership in the United States that I have consulted for Essay Six came from a study by the Rand Corporation of Gun Ownership from 2007 to 2016 and the Pew Research Center in a study from 2010 to 2020.

Essay Seven

1 "History of Hate Crime," The Crime Museum, https://www.crimemuseum.org/crime-library/hate-crime/history-of-hate-crime/. The various definitions of a *hate crime* were taken from the internet, as were the facts of the Matthew Shepard, James Byrd, and Jussie Smollett cases. The US Department of Justice and the FBI also have defined a *hate crime*. Newspaper articles about hate crimes and hate speech from the *New York Times*, the *Washington Post*, *The Hill*, and a number of others have been incorporated in Essay Seven.

2 "Hate Crime," Wikipedia, March 2017, https://en.wikipedia.org/wiki/Hate_crime.

3 "Learn About Hate Crimes," The United States Department of Justice, accessed September 2022, https://www.justice.gov/hatecrimes/learn-about-hate-crimes.

4 Ave Mince-Didier, "Hate Crimes That Changed History," CriminalDefenseLawyer, https://www.criminaldefenselawyer.com/resources/hate-crimes-changed-history.html.

5 Peter Szekely, "Independent Counsel Faults Chicago Prosecutor's Dismissal of Jussie Smollett Case," *Reuters*, August 17, 2020, https://www.reuters.com/article/us-people-jussie-smollett-idCAKCN25D2CV.

6 I have found data from the National Coalition of Anti-Violence Programs to also have been valuable, particularly about violence against transgender people.

7 Jake Levin, *Hate Crimes Revisited* (New York City: Basic Books, 2002).

8 I have also employed the recent COVID-19 Hate Crimes Act of 2021, the Civil Rights Act of 1968, the 2009 Matthew Shepard and James Byrd Jr. Hate Crimes Prevention Act, and many reports from the FBI on hate crimes—most recently from 2016 and 2017. I also have consulted the 1994 Violent Crime Control and Law Enforcement Act and the Judiciary Subcommittee on the Constitution, Civil Rights, and Human Rights on Hate Crimes, chaired by Dick Durban. Finally, I have employed what is known as the Avia Law in France from June of 2020.

9 "Statement of Administration Policy: S. 937 – COVID-19 Hate Crimes Act of 2021," The American Presidency Project, April 14, 2021, https://www.presidency.ucsb.edu/documents/statement-administration-policy-s-937-covid-19-hate-crimes-act-2021.

10 William B. Fisch, "Hate Speech in the Constitutional Law of the United States," *The American Journal of Comparative Law* 50, no. 1 (Fall 2002): 463–92.

11 The remarks of various Democrats on the speech and hate crimes mostly came from internet sources.

12 Jeremy Waldron, *The Harm in Hate Speech* (Cambridge: Harvard University Press, 2014); Stanley Fish, *The First: How to Think About Hate Speech* (New York: Atria/One Signal Publications, 2020); Henry Louis Gates, *Speaking of Race, Speaking of Sex: Hate Speech, Civil Rights, and Civil Liberties* (New York City: New York University Press, 1996); Judith Butler, *Excitable Speech: A Politics of the Performative* (Oxford: Routledge, 1997); Ben Shapiro, *Facts Don't Care About Your Feelings* (New York: Creators Publishing, 2019); Samuel Walker, *Hate Speech: The History of an American Controversy* (Omaha: University of Nebraska Press, 1994).

13 For hate crimes and public opinion, I have used materials from YouGov America. Peter Moore, "Half of Democrats Support a Ban on Hate Speech," YouGov America, May 20, 2015, https://today.yougov.com/topics/politics/articles-reports/2015/05/20/hate-speech.

14 Emily Ekins, "The State of Free Speech and Tolerance in America," *Survey Reports*, Cato Institute, October 31, 2017.

15 "Free Speech Q&A: Elizabeth Warren," Pen America, February 3, 2020, https://pen.org/elizabeth-warren-on-free-expression-in-america/.

16 Rani Molla and Emily Stewart, "Should Social Media Companies Be Legally Responsible for Misinformation and Hate Speech? 2020 Democrats Weigh In," Vox, December 5, 2019, https://www.vox.com/policy-and-politics/2019/12/3/20965459/tech-2020-candidate-policies-section230-facebook-misinformation-hate-speech.

17 I also have consulted the works of various philosophers in the history of the West, including Plato, Aristotle, and John Stuart Mill and his principle of harm.

18 Michael Burke, "Officials dismiss criticism that Trump rhetoric to blame for New Zealand attack," *The Hill*, March 17, 2019, https://thehill.com/homenews/sunday-talk-shows/434450-administration-officials-dismiss-criticism-that-trump-rhetoric-to/.

19 Beatrice Jin, "Biden signed a new hate crimes law — but there's a big flaw", Politico, May 20, 2021, https://www.politico.com/interactives/2021/state-hate-crime-laws/.

20 The 1942 Supreme Court case New Hampshire v. Chaplinsky was also a source for Essay Seven, as were Oliver Wendell Holmes's 1926 comments in the United States v. Schwimmer case.

21 Tom Head, "Six Major U.S. Supreme Court Hate Speech Cases," ThoughtCo, July 19, 2019; Michael Herz and Peter Molnar, *The Content and Context of Hate Speech* (Cambridge: Cambridge University Press, 2012); Geoffrey Stone, "Hate Speech and the U.S. Constitution," *East European Constitutional Review* 78, no. 3 (1994); David van Mill, "Freedom of Speech," in *The Stanford Encyclopedia of Philosophy* (Spring 2021 Edition), ed. Edward N. Zalta, Stanford University; Victoria Munro, *Hate Crime in the Media: A History* (Westport, CT: Praeger, 2014); Lily Wu, "Attorneys: First Amendment Protects Hate Speech, Not Hate Crimes," KWCH, April 16, 2021; Cailin Ring Carlson, *Hate Speech* (Boston: MIT Press, 2021).

22 "Hill.TV poll: Majority says Constitution should protect hate speech," *The Hill*, August 13, 2018, https://thehill.com/hilltv/what-americas-thinking/401581-hilltv-poll-majority-say-they-think-the-constitution-should/.; "College Students See Free Speech, Inclusivity as Equally Important," Philanthropy News Digest, May 6, 2020, https://philanthropynewsdigest.org/news/college-students-see-free-speech-inclusivity-as-equally-important.

Essay Eight

1 "1619 Project," *New York Times*, August 14, 2019.

2 Civitas Associates, "Student thoughts on 1619 essay, Capitalism," June

16, 2020, https://www.civitas-stl.com/student-thoughts-on-1619-essay-capitalism/.

3 Jennifer Chambers, "1619 Project reframing history of slavery draws crowd to Ann Arbor," January 28, 2020, https://www.detroitnews.com/story/news/education/2020/01/28/1619-history-slavery-ann-arbor-university-michigan-new-york-times/4588817002/.

4 Ibid.

5 Jake Silverstein, "We Respond to the Historians Who Critiqued the 1619 Project," *New York Times*, December 20, 2019, https://www.nytimes.com/2019/12/20/magazine/we-respond-to-the-historians-who-critiqued-the-1619-project.html.

6 Stephen J. Vicchio, *Muslim Slaves in the Chesapeake: 1634 to 1865* (Edina, MN: Calumet Editions, 2020).

7 Peter W. Wood, *1620: A Critical Response to the 1619 Project* (New York City: Encounter Books, 2020); David North and Thomas Mackaman, eds., *The New York Times 1619 Project and the Racialist Falsification of History* (Royal Oak, MI: Mehring Books, 2021).

8 Carlos Lozada, "The 1619 Project started as history. Now it's also a political program." *Washington Post*, December 19, 2021, https://www.washingtonpost.com/outlook/2021/11/19/1619-project-book-history/.

9 Another source for Essay Eight is the writings of Editor Jake Silverstein of the *Times* magazine, particularly in his beliefs about objective history.

10 Jake Silverstein, "On Recent Criticism of The 1619 Project," *New York Times*, October 16,2020, https://www.nytimes.com/2020/10/16/magazine/criticism-1619-project.html.

11 John Clegg, "How Slavery Shaped American Capitalism" Bunk History, August 28, 2019, https://www.bunkhistory.org/resources/4836.

12 Phillip W. Magness, "The 1619 Project Resurrects King-Cotton Ideology of the Old South," American Institute for Economic Research, September 11, 2019, https://www.aier.org/article/the-1619-project-resurrects-king-cotton-ideology-of-the-old-south/.

13 I have relied on Peter Wood's book on the New History of Capitalism movement. I also have employed some criticisms of that movement by

historian Gavin Wright, Allen Guelzo, and Phillip W. Magness, among other scholars, many of whom are in the North/Mackaman volume.

14 Magness, "The 1619 Project Resurrects King-Cotton Ideology of the Old South."

15 Magness, "The 1619 Project Resurrects King-Cotton Ideology of the Old South."

16 Stephen J. Vicchio, *Abraham Lincoln's Religion* (Eugene, OR: Wipf and Stock, 2018).

17 E. James West, "The 1619 Project and the 'Anti-Lincoln Tradition'," Black Perspectives, August 11, 2020, https://www.aaihs.org/the-1619-project-and-the-anti-lincoln-tradition/.

18 Ibid.

19 Andrew Ujifusa, "Biden Administration Cites 1619 Project as Inspiration in History Grant Proposal," EducationWeek, April, 19, 2021, https://www.edweek.org/teaching-learning/biden-administration-cites-1619-project-as-inspiration-in-history-grant-proposal/2021/04.

20 For Donald Trump's views on the 1619 Project I have relied on his forming of the *1776 Report*, as well as various comments he made in 2018 and 2019 that I have garnered from internet sources; "The 1776 Report," The President's Advisory 1776 Commission, January 2021, Trump White House Archives, https://trumpwhitehouse.archives.gov/wp-content/uploads/2021/01/The-Presidents-Advisory-1776-Commission-Final-Report.pdf.

21 David Pendered, "How Georgia Received What MLK Later Called a 'Promissory Note of Freedom,'" Saporta Report, February 10, 2020.

22 I also have utilized the thoughts of a number of Western philosophers in Essay Eight, including Plato, Aristotle, Hannah Arendt, and Frenchman Michel Foucault.

23 Iris Chang, *The Chinese in America* (New York City: Penguin, 2004); Pawan Dhingra, *Asian America* (Cambridge: Polity Books, 2021); Charles Park, *An Inconvenient History* (self-pub, 2021).

24 Nikole Hannah-Jones on Twitter, August 13, 2020, https://web.archive.org/web/20200823132227/https:/twitter.com/nhannahjones/status/1294011155636199431.

25 Tom Mackaman, "An interview with historian Gordon Wood on the New York Times' 1619 Project," World Socialist Web Site, November 27, 2019, https://www.wsws.org/en/articles/2019/11/28/wood-n28.html.

26 My comments on Peter Coclanis's article on the shortcomings of the Matthew Desmond's 1619 Project article and the "hidden" agenda of Reparations come from his essay for Independent Institute published on August 12, 2021.

27 The poll on the 1619 Project alluded to in this essay was conducted by the *Economist* on January 24–26, 2021. Several other polls since then have emerged on the same topic with mostly similar results on the 1619 Project among American citizens. "Americans who have heard of critical race theory don't like it," *Economist*, June 17, 2021, https://www.economist.com/graphic-detail/2021/06/17/americans-who-have-heard-of-critical-race-theory-dont-like-it.

28 Winthrop Jordan, *White Over Black: American Attitudes toward the Negro, 1550-1812* (Omohundro Institute and University of North Carolina Press, 2012).

Essay Nine

1 Hourly History, *Karl Marx: A Life From Beginning to End* (self-pub, 2017); Jonathan Sperber, *Life of Karl Marx* (New York City: Liveright Publishing, 2014).

2 The main sources for Essay Nine are some of the works of Karl Marx, including *The Holy Father*, *The Communist Manifesto*, and *Das Kapital*, as well as essays he wrote for the *New York Daily Tribune*.

3 Dinesh D'Souza, *United States of Socialism* (New York City: All Points Books, 2020); Mark R. Levin, *American Marxism* (New York City: Threshold Books, 2021); Marsh Miller, *Paul M. Sweezy and the History of American Marxism* (self-pub, 2021); Seth David Radwell, *American Schism: How the Two Enlightenments in America are the Key to healing Our Nation* (Austin, TX: Greenleaf Books, 2021).

4 Eugene V. Debs, *Eugene V. Debs Speaks* (New York City: Pathfinder Press, 1980); Eugene V. Debs, *Labor and Freedom*, ed. Chris Chundanaya (New York City: Pathfinder Press, 1980).

5 Monica Nickelsburg, "Why San Francisco's big business tax for homeless relief succeeded after Seattle's crumbled," GeekWire, November 7, 2018, https://www.geekwire.com/2018/san-franciscos-big-business-tax-homeless-relief-succeeded-seattles-crumbled/.

6 Walter Adamson, *Hegemony and Revolution* (Brattleboro, VT: Echo Point Books, 2014); David Forgacs and Eric Hobsbawm, eds., *Antonio Gramsci Reader: Selected Writings, 1912 to 1935* (New York City: New York University Press, 2000); Kevin Mitanidis, *Looking Through Gramsci's Eyes* (self-pub, 2018).

7 Bernie Sanders, *Bernie Sanders Guide to Practical Revolution* (New York City: Henry Holt and Co., 2017); Bernie Sanders, *Our Revolution: A Future to Believe In* (New York City: Thomas Dunne Books, 2016); Bernie Sanders, *The Speech: On Corporate Greed and the Decline of Our Middle Class* (New York City: Bold Tape Books, 2015).

8 Megan Crepeau and Katherine Rosenberg-Douglas, "Chicago's Independence Day weekend marred by violence, with at least 108 people shot, 17 fatally," Chicago Tribune, July 6, 2021, https://www.chicagotribune.com/news/criminal-justice/ct-independence-day-weekend-shootings-violence-20210705-krc6q7g705grzit3qpoavxlr3e-story.html.

9 "Criminal Justice Reform," JoeBiden.net, http://www.joe-biden.net/justice.html#:~:text=The%20Biden%20Plan%20will%20shift%20our%20country%27s%20focus,inspired%20by%20a%20proposal%20by%20the%20Brennan%20Center.

10 Alex Shephard, "Joe Biden's Half-Baked Political Gimmicks," *New Republic*, March 22, 2019, https://newrepublic.com/article/153378/joe-bidens-half-baked-political-gimmicks.

11 For the Biden-Harris plan I have relied on the "American Rescue Plan," as well as comments made by Jen Psaki in many of her press conferences art the White House; "American Rescue Plan: President Biden's Plan to Provide Direct Relief to Americans, Contain COVID-19, and

Rescue the Economy," WhiteHouse.gov, accessed September 2022, https://www.whitehouse.gov/american-rescue-plan/.

12 Morgan Matzen, "Gov. Noem: Biggest cultural challenge is 'defeating anti-American indoctrination,'" *USA Today*, May 3, 2021, https://news.yahoo.com/gov-noem-biggest-cultural-challenge-234428814.html.

13 "Hunter Biden: What was he doing in China and Ukraine?," BBC News, April 6, 2021, https://www.bbc.com/news/world-54553132.

14 Josh Boswell, "Hunter Biden could face prostitution charges for transporting hookers across state lines and disguising checks to them as payments for 'medical services,'" *Daily Mail*, July 11, 2022, https://www.dailymail.co.uk/news/article-10966153/Hunter-Biden-spent-30k-prostitutes-FIVE-MONTHS-documents-reveal.html.

15 Jacob Sullum, "The Consequences That Hunter Biden Could Face for Violating Arbitrary Gun Laws Should Give His Father Pause," Reason, October 12, 2022, https://reason.com/2022/10/12/the-consequences-that-hunter-biden-could-face-for-violating-arbitrary-gun-laws-should-give-his-father-pause/.

16 Sam Cabral, "Hunter Biden: The struggles and scandals of the US president's son," BBC News, October 6, 2022, https://www.bbc.com/news/world-us-canada-55805698; Miranda Devine, "Hunter Biden used Joe's VP perks to pursue deal with Carlos Slim," New York Post, July 1, 2021, https://nypost.com/2021/07/01/hunter-biden-used-joes-vp-perks-to-pursue-deal-with-carlos-slim/.

17 Kipp Jones, "White House Jumps to Defense of Hunter Biden: 'He Has the Right to Pursue an Artistic Career,'" *Western Journal*, July 10, 2021, https://www.westernjournal.com/white-house-jumps-defense-hunter-biden-right-pursue-artistic-career/.

18 David Smith, "Is Hunter Biden's art project painting the president into an ethical corner?" *Guardian*, October 2021, https://www.theguardian.com/us-news/2021/oct/16/hunter-biden-joe-art-ethics-paintings.

19 Khaleda Rahman, "Kamala Harris Slammed for 'Insulting' Claim Rural Communities Can't Photocopy IDs," *Newsweek*, July 11, 2021, https://www.newsweek.com/kamala-harris-slammed-insulting-claim-ru-

ral-communities-cant-photocopy-ids-1608603.

20 For my comments on the fifty-one Democrats who walked out of the Texas state legislature in the summer of 2021, I have mostly relied on internet sources, and for my comments on teachers' unions as well. This story is still unfolding.

21 Colleen Deguzman, "Texans, Where's Your Democratic Lawmaker?," *Texas Tribune*, July 14, 2021, https://www.texastribune.org/2021/07/14/texas-democats-walkout/.

22 Andrew Stiles, "Jim Crow on Steroids: Georgia Turnout Hits Record High after Democrats, Woke Corporations Blasted State's 'Voter Suppression' Law," *Free Beacon*, October 18, 2022, https://freebeacon.com/democrats/georgia-turnout-voter-supression-scandal/.

23 Luke Rosiak, *Race to the Bottom* (New York City: Broadside Books, 2021); Peter Brimiloe, *The Worm in the Apple: How the Teachers Unions are Destroying American Education* (New York City: Harper, 2004).

24 Harriet Alexander, "Hammer thrower Gwen Berry, who turned back on US flag, says she's 'earned right to wear the uniform' after making it through qualifying round in Tokyo and says she'll 'continue to do what she's doing," Daily Mail, August 1, 2021, https://www.dailymail.co.uk/news/article-9849773/Gwen-Berry-says-shes-earned-right-wear-uniform-appearance-Tokyo-Games.html.

25 Angelica Stabile, "Soviet immigrant, registered Democrat warns critical race theory resembles Marxist curriculum," Fox News, July 30, 2021, https://www.foxnews.com/media/soviet-immigrant-democrat-critical-race-theory-resembles-marxist-curriculum.

Essay Ten

1 Mark R. Levin, *American Marxism* (New York: Threshold Editions, 2021).

2 Stef W. Kight, "70% of millennials say they'd vote for a socialist," Axios, October 28, 2019, https://www.axios.com/2019/10/28/millennials-vote-socialism-capitalism-decline.

3 The Thomas Friedman article in the *New York Times*, in which he coined the name "Green New Deal" was published on January 19, 2007.

4 Lisa Friedman, "What Is the Green New Deal? A Climate Proposal, Explained," *New York Times*, February 21, 2019, https://www.nytimes.com/2019/02/21/climate/green-new-deal-questions-answers.html.

5 I have utilized a number of interviews and talks of Alexandria Ocasio-Cortez on the Green New Deal such as on February 6, 2019, with NPR; another on January 23, 2019, in the same venue; and many others. On September 12, 2019, at a talk for the NAACP Forum in Florida, she also spoke of the GND. AOC made her first prediction of the twelve-year limit on September 12, 2019, and has repeated it many times since then. This prediction was based on the United Nations' Intergovernmental Panel on Climate Change.

6 Danielle Kurtzleben, "Rep. Alexandria Ocasio-Cortez Releases Green New Deal Outline," NPR, February 7, 2019, https://www.npr.org/2019/02/07/691997301/rep-alexandria-ocasio-cortez-releases-green-new-deal-outline.

7 Jack Crowe, "Ocasio Cortez: The World Is Going to End in Twelve Years If We Don't Address Climate Change," Yahoo! News, https://news.yahoo.com/ocasio-cortez-world-going-end-150517060.html.

8 Nearly all of the grim predictions that the "world will come to an end by the year 2030" come from a United Nations report from 2019.

9 Cliff Saunders, "WATCH: AOC Says Miami Will Stop Existing If Her Green New Deal Isn't Passed," KRTH Radio, September 16, 2019, https://ktrh.iheart.com/featured/houstons-morning-news/content/2019-09-16-watch-aoc-says-miami-will-stop-existing-if-her-green-new-deal-isnt-passed/.

10 Andrew Freedman, "Climate Scientists Refute 12-Year Deadline to Curb Global Warming," Axios, January 22, 2019, https://www.axios.com/2019/01/22/climate-change-scientists-comment-ocasio-cortez-12-year-deadline.

11 Greta Thunberg, *No One is Too Small To Make a Difference* (London: Penguin Books, 2019).

12 Michael Shellenberger, "Why Apocalyptic Claims About Climate Change Are Wrong," *Forbes*, November 25, 2019, https://www.forbes.com/sites/michaelshellenberger/2019/11/25/why-everything-they-say-about-climate-change-is-wrong/?sh=2c69229f12d6.

13 Andrew Neil's reporting on the environment was done for the BBC in October of 2019. Naomi Adedokun, "Andrew Neil Dismantles Extinction Rebellion's Claim That 'Billions of Children Will Die,'" Express, October 10, 2019, https://www.express.co.uk/news/uk/1188717/extinction-rebellion-andrew-neil-climate-change-protest-london-emergency-bbc.

14 Michael Shellenberger, "Why Apocalyptic Claims About Climate Change Are Wrong," *Forbes*, November 25, 2019, https://www.forbes.com/sites/michaelshellenberger/2019/11/25/why-everything-they-say-about-climate-change-is-wrong/?sh=2c69229f12d6.

15 My comments on the IPCC come mostly from internet sources, as well as articles in the *Washington Post*, the *New York Times*, and the *Wall Street Journal*, from November 2020 until the present.

16 I have also employed statistics from the United Nations' Food and Agriculture Association, as well as predictions from Yale scholar William Nordhaus.

17 Natasha Daly, "No, Koalas Aren't 'Functionally Extinct' Yet," *National Geographic*, November 25, 2019; "Is There a Koala in Danger Near You?" *National Geographic*, April 2012; "Stopping Koala Extinction is agonizingly Simple, But Here's Why I Am Not Optimistic," *National Geographic*, May 1, 2020; "Koala," WWF-Australia, accessed April 29, 2022.

18 John McAneney, "Climate change and bushfires - you're missing the point!", The Conversation, October 31, 2013, https://theconversation.com/climate-change-and-bushfires-youre-missing-the-point-19649.

19 Shellenberger, "Why Apocalyptic Claims About Climate Change Are Wrong"

20 Kamala Harris, "Green New Deal," Medium, February 7, 2019, https://kamalaharris.medium.com/green-new-deal-2699b33ba666.

21 Robinson Meyer, "The Green New Deal Finally Makes a Debate Appearance," *Atlantic*, June 27, 2019, https://www.theatlantic.com/

science/archive/2019/06/kamala-harris-first-mention-green-new-deal/592915/.

22 Samantha Gross, "Barriers to achieving US climate goals are more political than technical," Brookings Institute, May 10, 2021, https://www.brookings.edu/blog/planetpolicy/2021/05/10/barriers-to-achieving-us-climate-goals-are-more-political-than-technical/.

23 David Roberts, "What Joe Biden was trying to say about the Green New Deal," Vox, October 7, 2020, https://www.vox.com/energy-and-environment/21498236/joe-biden-green-new-deal-debate.

24 Coin Jerolwick, *Up to Heaven and Down to Hell: Fracking, Freedom, and Community in One American Town* (Princeton: Princeton University Press, 2021); Bethany Mclean, *Saudi America: The Truth About Fracking and How it Changed the World* (New York City: Columbia Global Reports, 2018); Jessica Alcorn, John Rupp, and John D. Graham, "Attitudes Toward Fracking: Perceived and Actual Geographic Proximity," *Review of Policy Research* 34, no. 4 (March 23, 2017): 504–36; Eric de Place, "Public Opinion is Moving Against Natural Gas and Fracking," Ohio River Valley Institute, August 9, 2020; Hilary Boudet, "Survey Finds Ignorance of 'Fracking' Despite Emerging Importance," Oregon State University, December 23, 2013.

25 Senator Sanders's and Representative Ocasio-Cortez's comments on fracking were made, among other times, in February of 2020.

26 Katie Pavlich, "Biden Administration: Yes, We Are Following Through with a Fracking Ban, Townhall, January 20, 2021, https://townhall.com/tipsheet/katiepavlich/2021/01/20/biden-administration-yes-we-are-following-through-with-a-fracking-ban-n2583476.

27 Rachel Frazin, "Haaland: No plan 'right now' for permanent drill leasing ban," *The Hill*, June 23, 2021, https://thehill.com/policy/energy-environment/559857-haaland-no-plan-right-now-for-permanent-drill-leasing-ban/.

28 Michael Thomas, "Biden's Climate Plan is Definitely Not The Green New Deal", Medium, October 22, 2020, https://medium.com/@curious_founder/bidens-climate-plan-is-definitely-not-the-green-new-deal-

88e19555bad7.

29 Joe Biden, "The Biden Plan for a Clean Energy Revolution and Environmental Justice," joebiden.com, accessed April 29, 2022.

30 Arthur Franklin, *The Spanish Flu: A History of the Deadliest Plague of 1918* (self-pub, 2020); Salvador Macip and Julie Wark, *Modern Epidemics* (New York City: Polity Books, 2021).

31 The figures I have relied on for COVID-19 deaths worldwide and in the United States are those provided by the School of Public Health at the Johns Hopkins University, who, in the first ten months of the epidemic, gave daily updates.

32 Editorial Board, "Biden's 10-Year Climate Plan," *Wall Street Journal*, https://www.wsj.com/articles/bidens-10-year-climate-plan-11619132440?mod=flipboard.

33 Barbara Finamore, "Paris Climate Agreement Explained: Next Steps for China," NRDC, December 12, 2015, https://www.nrdc.org/experts/barbara-finamore/paris-climate-agreement-explained-next-steps-china.

34 The figures on British carbon emissions and their comparison to what is going on in China have mostly been taken from internet sources or from the *USA Today*, the *New York Times*, the *Baltimore Sun*, the *Wall Street Journal*, as well as other American newspapers.

35 Jingzheng Ren, *Renewable Energy-Proven Future* (Cambridge: Academic Press, 2020); Eva Sternfeld, ed., *The Routledge Handbook of Environmental Policy in China* (Routledge, 2017).

36 Adam Edelman, "Biden's Comments Downplaying China Threat to U.S. Fire Up Pols on Both Sides," NBC News, May, 2, 2019, https://www.nbcnews.com/politics/2020-election/biden-s-comments-downplaying-china-threat-u-s-fires-pols-n1001236.

37 The Marist College-NPR-PBS poll on climate change was conducted in January of 2021.

Essay Eleven

1 "CDA 230: The Most Important Law Protecting Internet Speech," Electronic Frontier Foundation, accessed September 2022, https://www.eff.org/issues/cda230.

2 The Media Research Center in October of 2020 published a report on Facebook and censorship.

3 Philip Bennett and Moises Naim, "21st-Century Censorship," *Columbia Journalism Review*.

4 The materials on banning content in the nations of Colombia, Israel and India were garnered from internet reports.

5 The *New York Post* article on Hunter Biden was published on October 14, 2020, and taken down that same morning.

6 Mike Murphy, "After Uproar, Twitter Explains Why New York Post Story on Hunter Biden Was Blocked," October 14, 2020, MarketWatch, https://www.marketwatch.com/story/after-uproar-twitter-explains-why-n-y-post-article-on-hunter-biden-was-blocked-11602723220?mod=article_inline.

7 NBC News did a story on Trump's banning from Twitter on January 7, 2021.

8 Rishika Pardikar, "Cyber Censorship Hits Colombia, India and Palestine," Toward Freedom, June 3, 2021, https://towardfreedom.org/story/archives/asia-archives/cyber-censorship-hits-colombia-india-and-palestine/.

9 The other examples of banning by Big Tech were also taken directly from the internet sources, as were the reports from Paul Barrett, Adam Gabbatt, and Matthew Feeney.

10 The contributions reported to Democrat causes and candidates are all matters of public record.

11 Krystal Hur, Big tech employees rally behind Biden campaign," Open Secrets, January 12, 2021, https://www.opensecrets.org/news/2021/01/big-tech-employees-rally-biden/.

12 Ari Levy, "Here's the Final Talley of Where Tech Billionaires Donated

for the 2020 Election," CNBC, November 2, 2020, https://www.cnbc.com/2020/11/02/tech-billionaire-2020-election-donations-final-tally.html#:~:text=Of%20current%20CEOs%20at%20large-cap%20tech%20companies%2C%20Netflix%E2%80%99s,closest%20races%2C%20like%20in%20Maine%2C%20Texas%20and%20Iowa.

13 The interview of Ken Duda with *Vox* was on July 11, 2021.

14 Eli Blumenthal and Queenie Wong, "Joe Biden slams Facebook, calls Zuckerberg a 'real problem'," CNET, January 17, 2020, https://www.cnet.com/news/politics/joe-biden-slams-facebook-calls-zuckerberg-a-real-problem-in-new-york-times-interview/.

15 I have also utilized articles from the *New York Times* from August 13, 2020, in determining Ms. Harris views on the environment.

16 Roger McNamee, *Zucked: Waking Up to the Facebook Catastrophe* (London: Penguin, 2020).

17 Most of the materials on Big Tech personnel hired by the Biden-Harris administration were also gleaned directly from the internet.

18 I have also utilized the observations of Max Moran of the Revolving Door Project. Nandita Bose, "INSIGHT Big Tech's Stealth Push to Influence the Biden Administration," Reuters, December 21, 2020, https://www.reuters.com/business/insight-big-techs-stealth-push-influence-biden-administration-2020-12-21/#:~:text=%22In%202020%2C%20appointing%20the%20CEO%20or%20top%20executives,begun%20to%20emerge%20as%20candidates%20for%20Biden%20jobs.

19 Nandita Bose, "Big Tech's stealth push to influence the Biden administration," Reuters, December 21, 2020, https://www.reuters.com/business/insight-big-techs-stealth-push-influence-biden-administration-2020-12-21/.

20 The comment from Dr. Vivek Murthy comes from May 4 and May 7, 2021 at two different White House announcements, as well as comments made to Judy Woodruff in an interview on May 4, 2021.

21 The comments from Dan Bongino and Peter Doocy were taken directly from FoxNews broadcasts.

22 "Covid Misinformation on Facebook is Killing People – Biden," BBC.com,

July 17, 2021, https://www.bbc.com/news/world-us-canada-57870778.

23 "The Disinformation Dozen," Center for Countering Digital Hate, https://counterhate.com/research/the-disinformation-dozen/.

24 The quotation from Senator Wicker in Essay Twelve was taken from his Weekly Report from January 1, 2016.

25 A number of Jen Psaki's news conferences also have been referred to in Essay Eleven.

Appendix

1 John Stuart Mill. 1859. *On Liberty*, p. 267.

2 Ibid., pp. 283-284.

Postscript

1 Todd Bensman, "Of course the border is secure—since Kamala Harris changed the definition of 'secure,'" *New York Post*, September 12, 2022, https://nypost.com/2022/09/12/kamala-harris-said-border-is-secure-despite-record-breaking-migration/.

2 "Overdose Death Rates," National Institute on Drug Abuse, https://nida.nih.gov/research-topics/trends-statistics/overdose-death-rates#:~:text=Overall%2C%20drug%20overdose%20deaths%20rose,overdose%20deaths%20reported%20in%202020.

3 Ronny Reyes, "Stacey Abrams Stuns Panel as She Says Fetal Heartbeats Are "A Manufactured Sound," *Daily Mail*, September 22, 2022, https://www.dailymail.co.uk/news/article-11239717/Stacey-Abrams-stuns-panel-says-fetal-heartbeats-manufactured-sound.html.

4 David Crary and Hannah Fingerhut, "AP-NORC poll: Most say restrict abortion after 1st trimester," Associated Press, June 25, 2021, https://apnorc.org/ap-norc-poll-most-say-restrict-abortion-after-1st-tri-

mester/#:~:text=The%20new%20poll%20from%20The%20Associated%20Press-NORC%20Center,and%2080%25%20said%20that%20about%20the%20third%20trimester.

5 Stephanie Pagones, "North Dakota Man Free after Admitting He Mowed Down 'Republican' Teen over Politics, Records Show," Fox News, September 21, 2022, https://www.foxnews.com/us/north-dakota-man-freed-50k-bond-fatally-striking-republican-extremist-car-records-show.

6 Matthew Loh, "Poll Finds 43% of Americans Believe It's Likely Civil War Will Break Out within the Next 10 Years," Insider, August 31, 2022, https://www.businessinsider.com/poll-43-percent-americans-expect-civil-war-within-10-years-2022-8#:~:text=A%20new%20poll%20of%201%2C500%20American%20citizens%20found,of%20the%20-growing%20concern%20about%20America%27s%20political%20divide.

7 Melissa Quinn, "Garland Defends Memo on Violent Threats to School Boards," CBS News, October 27m 2021, https://www.cbsnews.com/news/merrick-garland-school-board-violence-memo-attorney-general/.

8 Divina Ramirez, "San Francisco Votes to Remove Washington, Lincoln from School Names," PoliticalCorrectness.News, February 10, 2021, https://www.politicalcorrectness.news/2021-02-10-san-francisco-school-board-cancels-historical-figures.html#:~:text=Historical%20figures%20like%20George%20Washington%2C%20Thomas%20Jefferson%20and,26%2C%20after%20months%20of%20review%20and%20national%20attention.

ACKNOWLEDGMENTS

Over the course of writing these essays, I have been aided greatly by several conversations with the following family members and friends: my son, John "Jack" Vicchio; my student and friend, Tina Gioioso; my cousins, John Appel, Nick Caprio, and Peter Celli, Sr.; my college friend, Linda Canestraro; and my cleaning lady and friend, Irene Burell, who keeps my life in order. I am also indebted to my attorney, Amar Weisman; *mio fratello*, Mario Villa Santa; and CEO and Publisher of Amplify Publishing Group Naren Aryal, as well as the Amplify team.

ABOUT THE AUTHOR

Stephen Vicchio is the author of more than forty books, including in-depth studies of the religious beliefs of Ronald Reagan, George Washington, Alexander Hamilton, and Thomas Jefferson. Other previous books include *Evil in World Religions*; *The Idea of the Demonic*; and *Muslim Slaves in the Chesapeake: 1634 to 1865*.

Known to many as "Baltimore's philosopher laureate," he is the recipient of numerous writing awards in various genres, including first prize at the Young American Playwrights Conference; the A. D. Emmart Award for Outstanding Writing in the Humanities; the Frank Muir Prize for fiction; the Thomas Gray Prize for most distinguished doctoral thesis in a British university; and Professor of the Year in the state of Maryland.

Before his retirement from academia in 2016, he taught for more than forty years at the University of Maryland, Johns Hopkins, St. Mary's Seminary in Baltimore, and various other institutions across the United States and Great Britain.

Visit Stephen online
StephenJVicchio.com